PORTFOLIOS

CLARIFYING, CONSTRUCTING, AND ENHANCING

NANCY JEAN JOHNSON, Ph.D.
UNIVERSITY OF SIOUX FALLS

LEONIE MARIE ROSE, Ph.D.
CENTRAL MICHIGAN UNIVERSITY

TECHNOMIC
PUBLISHING CO., INC.
LANCASTER · BASEL

Portfolios
a **TECHNOMIC**®publication

Published in the Western Hemisphere by
Technomic Publishing Company, Inc.
851 New Holland Avenue, Box 3535
Lancaster, Pennsylvania 17604 U.S.A.

Distributed in the Rest of the World by
Technomic Publishing AG
Missionsstrasse 44
CH-4055 Basel, Switzerland

Printed in the United States of America
10 9 8 7 6 5 4 3 2

Main entry under title:
  Portfolios: Clarifying, Constructing, and Enhancing

A Technomic Publishing Company book
Bibliography: p. 335
Includes index p. 347

Library of Congress Catalog Card No. 96-61634
ISBN No. 1-56676-476-9

To our children and spouses

Chapter 3: Getting Started   49

PART TWO: CONSTRUCTING

Chapter 4: Clarifying the Role of Self-Assessment   73

Chapter 5: Choosing from Multiple Sources for
Data Collection   105

PORTFOLIO assessment has numerous benefits for elementary, middle, and secondary schools. Unless the school leader understands this promising practice, it will not receive the promotion, sustained resources, and continued staff development necessary to fulfill its potential. And so, this book is written to assist principals as they lead schools to implement portfolios. Every technique, figure, and suggestion has been tested in schools.

The book is divided into three parts: Clarifying, Constructing, and Enhancing. The first section consists of background work for you to prepare for a major change in your school's assessment practices. The largest part of the book, Constructing, is the actual implementation of portfolios. Teachers want practical advice and ideas they can use. For this reason, we included examples of inservices, assessment tools, self-reflection activities, and types of portfolios. Finally, when portfolios become commonly used in your school, you will want to sustain the change, avoid serious problems, and build on portfolios' potential to enhance the school climate to one of a community of learners.

Each chapter begins with a true scenario that we have experienced from working with school districts. The names and details have been altered to respect confidentially of the principals, teachers, parents, students, and superintendents. At the end of each chapter, we included a section on troubleshooting. The problems are ones we have dealt with over the last few years in our roles as a principal, consultant, or professor.

Chapter 1 opens with a statement from a principal who is frustrated by the perceived importance of standardized tests. The rest of the chapter clarifies ways in which portfolios can be a solution to his dilemma.

Wanting to implement portfolios and actually doing it requires more than desire. Skills to implement widespread change are required. In Chapter 2, we discuss obtaining the necessary background information, building a vision of assessment, locating resources, scheduling time for teachers to learn about portfolios, developing a schoolwide problem-solving system, and forming collegial support teams. Without this foundation, when teachers go into their classrooms and close the doors, portfolios may not be used.

Part Two, Constructing, provides examples of portfolio assessment tools. We explain procedures, uses, benefits, and concerns for each tool. You may reproduce many of the forms and distribute them to your staff.

Chapter 3 provides three staff development sessions that are designed to allow teachers to define and adapt portfolios for the uniqueness of your school. After completing the inservices, teachers will be ready to begin using portfolios in their classrooms.

Self-assessment is a powerful way to document and reflect on one's own learning. Chapter 4 explores the benefits, problems, issues, and concerns that may arise when educators and students begin to assess themselves as learners. Chapter 5 provides numerous sources for collecting data and suggests ways to limit selections. The practical, nuts and bolts logistics such as types of containers, storage of portfolios, ownership of different types of portfolios, accessibility versus the right to privacy, and curriculum decisions are discussed in Chapter 6. The chapter ends with a problem that principals hear frequently from teachers, "There's no space in my room for storage cabinets!"

The final section, Enhancing, goes beyond implementation to solving problems that arise and to expanding the uses of portfolio assessment. This section will be useful after your staff begins using portfolios.

Chapter 7 suggests solutions to common problems that surface during this stage, such as philosophical differences, data overload, resistance, legal concerns, mandated high-stakes portfolios, and grading issues. With sustained staff development, Chapter 8 describes ways to extend portfolios to include peer coaching, peer evaluation, and community involvement. The final chapter examines the issues of accountability. Data from portfolios can provide feedback for assessing student progress and educational changes, evaluating results of educational programs and their effects on students, and reporting school progress to specific stakeholders.

The book was designed for principals with various degrees of experiences with portfolios. Those who have less background with portfolios will need the first two parts of the book, while those who are looking for techniques to expand portfolio assessment will find the last part most helpful. Like any innovation, the secret to success is to tailor it to fit your needs and those of your community.

THIS book reflects ideas, tools, and problems we have gained and dealt with from our work with administrators and teachers.

We are especially indebted to the work of Dean Cooledge for his editorial assistance, for offering advice, and for improving the quality of the work.

Teachers from Mary McGuire School in the Mt. Pleasant Public Schools, a professional development school associated with Central Michigan University, generously shared their work on portfolios for other teachers to adapt and use. We would like to thank especially Nancy Cantrell, Jan Eversole, Sue Horgan, Jan Shippee, and Harriet White for sharing their reflections, assessment forms, and students' work.

We would also like to thank Sara Shriver from the Lakewood Public Schools for sharing forms that she used in her portfolios for her Title 1 students.

Administrators from Midland Public Schools, Kentwood Public Schools, Traverse City Public Schools, Sioux Valley Schools, and others have shared their joys and frustrations as they have gone through this process. Many of their experiences are incorporated in the examples we used.

We want to thank Diane Zehder for sharing her view of her daughter's student-led conference. Her perceptions as a parent reflect comments that many teachers have shared with us after conducting these conferences around portfolios.

Our graduate students and colleagues have contributed ideas and suggestions that we have applied. Their comments provided valuable information.

Michael Rose contributed to our efforts by sharing some of his portfolio work as a student and by creating some of the forms in assessment figures and appendices.

We also want to thank Joseph Eckenrode, Ph.D., Director, Editorial Development, Technomic Publishing Company, who encouraged us to share our portfolio experiences with administrators. Without his suggestions and insights, this book would not have been written.

CLARIFYING

Clarifying the latest buzzword with an unclear meaning consists of back-ground work that will prepare you and your staff for a major change in your school's assessment practices. After completing Part One, teachers will be ready to begin using portfolios.

CHAPTER 1

Defining a Portfolio

One Principal's View of Traditional Assessment

A parent just called me about the article *The Sun* printed about our low test scores this week. I tried to explain that school performance is based on more than simply test scores, which are only one measure of accountability, but the media and public, in general, have come to equate standardized test scores with school success and quality education. Real estate agents even quote school test scores to prospective buyers.

Yet my teachers complain about the time taken away from classroom instruction while they prepare students to take the tests, as well as the actual time it takes to administer them. The tests narrow our curriculum to basic skills because teachers are worried about how the scores reflect on their teaching competence. The tests don't measure important school goals such as higher level thinking skills, responsibility, and cooperation. In addition, there is such a time lag in getting the results back that they are often irrelevant to daily classroom instruction and student needs.

Central office, the school board, and policymakers at the state level want proof that our school is accountable, yet test scores don't provide an accurate total picture of student learning in many areas. There has to be a better way!

EXPANDING ASSESSMENT

MANY principals feel exactly as Mr. Woods does. In this chapter, we will examine the limitations of traditional testing, introduce authentic assessments, and define portfolios as one assessment alternative to traditional testing. After we have described what is involved in portfolio assessment, we will explore the potential that portfolios can provide for a dynamic school climate and educational change. The chapter concludes with some misconceptions that we have heard about portfolios.

In past generations, mastery of basic math and reading skills would be considered sufficient knowledge for a successful life. Traditional assessments such as standardized tests, state mandated examinations, and textbook chapter tests were considered an adequate measure of basic skills. Traditional evaluation reflects time-honored practices such as memorization of facts, learning as a product, desirability of objectivity, early tracking of students, and scientific measurement (Bertrand, 1991).

As society has changed, the workforce now faces increasing demands for complex tasks that require higher level thinking and decision making. We are now discovering additional ways to assess the kinds of learning people need in today's world. As learning theory and practice have undergone change through research, assessment needs to change to adequately reflect the instruction that is taking place in today's classrooms (Caine & Caine, 1991; Valencia et al., 1994; Herman et al., 1992; Walberg, 1990). Teaching, learning, assessment, and evaluation must be congruent. Educators cannot claim and practice one set of beliefs about learning and evaluate from a completely different perspective (Anthony et al., 1991).

Limitations of Traditional Tests

While numerical scores from norm-reference and criterion-referenced tests can yield useful information about how well students, schools, and districts do in comparison to others, they do not provide useful information for daily instruction. A numerical test scores cannot tell us

- what students think about material they are learning
- how students feel about learning
- what strategies students use
- how students use information to make meaning of their world
- if students verify and revise their own thinking
- whether students have accepted ownership for learning (Church, 1991)

For years, educators have noted limitations of traditional standardized tests. Criterion-referenced tests, norm-referenced tests, textbook tests, weekly spelling tests, and many other published tests narrow the curriculum to basic skills, rather than multifaceted thinking. From such test, students learn that, for every question, there is a single correct answer and, for every problem, a single correct solution. The correct solution is known to the test maker, and the student's task is to converge upon this (Eisner, 1991). The California Achievement Test, Iowa Test of Basic Skills, SAT, ACT, and most state tests require one correct answer to items. In classrooms where teachers are applying current research and practices, there is a mismatch between what is measured on these tests and what is taught (Valencia et al., 1994; Harp, 1991). In states where rewards and sanctions are attached to test scores, students listen to the teacher, read short sections in textbooks, respond with brief answers, and take multiple-choice quizzes. Rarely do they plan or initiate learning, create their own products, read or write complete stories, or engage in analytical discussions (Goodlad, 1984).

Standardized tests are not generally intended to be used to make decisions about daily instruction of students. Teachers need additional assessments that meet the instructional needs of their students (Vacca & Vacca, 1993; Herman et al., 1992). While standardized tests separate teaching, learning, and testing, more naturalistic assessments such as portfolios merge the three.

Authentic Assessment

Sound assessment is anchored in tasks, materials, and contexts involving students and teachers through classroom instruction. Grant Wiggins (1993) coined the phrase *authentic assessment* to describe assessments that are performance-based, realistic, and instructionally appropriate. Measures are taken on tasks we want kids to be able to do within a range of categories. These activities are integratged into ongoing classroom life and instruction. They are not something we do during a specified week in April. During daily classroom experiences, students apply information, relate to others, and solve problems. Examples of informal work grounded in classroom events give us insights into the problems, abilities, learning styles, and potentials of students (Wolf, 1988).

Authentic assessments, alternative assessments, and performance tests share many common characteristics. In each, students are required to perform something or produce a product. Students are encouraged to demonstrate use of higher level thinking skills and problem-solving abilities. Required tasks represent meaningful instructional activities, rather than contrived, special test situations. These tasks involve applications that resemble those used by society at large, rather than just those needed for success in an educational setting. Subjective judgements based on teacher knowledge and experience are used, rather than machine scoring. Finally, all three require teachers to assume new roles in both instruction and assessment (Herman et al., 1992).

Multiple sources of information provide a clearer view of learning. Standardized tests tell us how well students attained bits of information compared to other students. Portfolios offer additional information.

WHAT IS A PORTFOLIO?

From Vermont to Alaska, from kindergarten through graduate school, portfolios are becoming a popular alternative form of assessment. Misconceptions and partial answers are common when asked the question, "What exactly is a portfolio?" Responses we have heard lead us to believe that this latest buzzword seems to have an unclear meaning. The definition, form, and content vary, depending on its specific purpose. In the simplest form, a portfolio is a container of examples of students' accomplishments and skills. When used to the fullest, portfolios span across all curriculum areas and throughout all grade levels. They are a way for students to demonstrate a broad variety of achievements and skills. Instead of simply having students select an answer, this type of alternative assessment requires students to generate responses while accomplishing complex and significant tasks, activating relevant prior knowledge, and applying recent learning and relevant skills to solve realistic problems (Herman et al., 1992; Wiggins, 1993).

A working definition for a portfolio developed at the Northwest Regional Educational Laboratory in Portland, Oregon, takes into account the purposes and uses in numerous school districts across the nation (Arter, 1990). According to their definition, "A portfolio is a collection of student work gathered for a particular purpose that exhibits to the student and others the student's efforts, progress or achievement in one or more areas." Tierney et al. (1991) define portfolios as "vehicles for ongoing assessment that are composed of purposeful collections which examine achievement, effort, improvement, and processes such as selecting, comparing, sharing, self-evaluation, and goal setting." Herman et al. (1992) maintain that portfolios are collections of student work that are reviewed against criteria in order to judge an individual student or program.

Most educators agree that portfolios are not a collection of a student's work haphazardly thrown together, a writing folder into which a student's compositions for the school year are placed, or a replication of a student's permanent record of test scores with samples of classroom work (Cooledge, 1992; DeFina, 1992). Rather, a portfolio is a purposeful, systematic anthology of a student's work over time that includes

- student participation in selection of content
- evidence of student self-reflection
- criteria for selection
- criteria for judging merit

STUDENT PARTICIPATION

Student participation in selection of information[1] that is placed into the portfolio is one of the key features of an accurate representation of achievement and ability (DeFina, 1992; Anthony et al., 1991). Learning involves all the important stakeholders in education. As one of those stakeholders, students must be involved in gathering data for portfolios because they are the ones who ultimately own their learning. Teachers and students collaborate in deciding what goes into portfolios to demonstrate growth and accoplishments. Some items will be the teacher's choice, some the student's, and some will be evidence they both believe to be important.

SELF-EVALUATION

Another component includes students' involvement in self-evaluation[2] of both their progress in learning and the contents of their portfolio (Harp, 1991; Tierney et al., 1991). Portfolios may include students' self-evaluations in the form of checklists, book lists, essays, drafts, goal setting, and statements of what they believe they have learned. Students also need to reflect upon and state why they placed each item in their portfolios. When this component is utilized to its fullest potential, students become more willing to accept responsibility for their learning and are more likely to recognize the relationship between classroom instruction and how it relates to their world. They also begin to understand how to assess and evaluate their own learning, which is a lifelong skill that is necessary for future success.

CRITERIA FOR SELECTION

Decisions need to be made for determining what is placed into a portfolio (Baskwill & Whitman, 1988; Goodman, 1986). The criteria used for selection clarifies to everyone why items are included in this collection. Criteria are best developed at the building level by a team of teachers, students, parents, community representatives, and administrators. While general policies may be determined at the district or state level, principals are crucial in guiding and supporting teachers and students in determining specific criteria for inclusion of materials in each building. Principals provide valuable information concerning district policies, legal aspects, and curricular considerations.

JUDGING MERIT

Evaluation standards are the final essential component of a portfolio (Tierney et al., 1991; Herman et al., 1992). Before implementing a portfolio system, there must be aggrement on the criteria that will be used to determine what constitutes excellence of entries, mastery of subject matter, evidence of social growth, and other required contents. The principal's role includes guiding, assisting, and supporting teachers along with their students in setting benchmarks for success. Another key role for the principal is to assist with the dissemination of this information to central administration, parents, and other important stakeholders.

HOW DOES A PORTFOLIO LOOK?

The actual form and content depend on the school district's purpose of portfolios. Portfolios used to obtain employment[3] will look quite different from portfolios used to communicate with parents and other teachers. In some districts, each student has a shoe box containing examples of writing, photographs of projects and awards, audiotapes of readings or interviews, and videotapes of performances. The contents of this type of portfolio tracks growth in a variety of ways for parents, students, and teachers to observe. Other districts might provide each child with an expandable folder to hold charts of literature studied; artistic media such as illustrations, maps, and paintings; narratives or a journal of opinions, feelings, and problems encountered during collaborative work; attitude surveys; lists of extracurricular activities; and goals for the future. This type of portfolio is valuable for future use for employability or college admission. Still another form of portfolio might consist of a computer disk for each student to record information concerning progress and goals. Figure 1.1 illustrates several examples of the many possible forms, contents, and purposes of portfolios. In Chapters 4, 5, and 6, more examples are provided.

Much of the confusion surrounding portfolios stems from the wide variety of their purposes and uses. Some schools use them to demonstrate accountability for North Central Accreditation, while others might develop them to meet national standards in subject areas such as math, science, and language arts. A few go through the motions to fulfill a mandate for obtaining state aid. In successful districts, portfolios are a tool for developing student ownership,[4] increasing responsibility, and attaining goals.

When we only focus on portfolios as a product, we've missed their potential power, which comes from the process of creating them. It is the decision-making process concerning what entries are placed in the collection and why each was selected that actually builds the power of the portfolio by personalizing education for the student (DeFina, 1992; Glazer & Brown, 1993; Herman et al., 1992).

Differences between standardized tests and portfolios are delineated in Figure 1.2. When used in combination with standardized tests, portfolios give a better measure of the full range of multiple educational perfor-

Purpose	Form	Contents
Employment	Three-ring notebook, Report form	Grades, attendance record, Extra curricular activities, Community service, Honors, Collaborative work
Communicate to parents and teachers	Folder, Shoe box, Expandable folder	Work in progress, Attitude survey, Goals, Self-evaluation, Narratives or logs
Progress and goals	Expandable folder, Computer disk	Charts of literature studied, Artistic media, narratives or logs, Attitude surveys, Lists of extracurricular activities, Goals, Grades

Figure 1.1. Examples of Portfolio Possibilities.

9

Traditional Tests	Portfolios
• Separate learning, testing, and teaching	• Link assessment and teaching to learning
• Fail to assess the impact of prior knowledge on learning by using short passages that are often isolated and unfamiliar	• Address the importance of student's prior knowledge as a critical determinant to learning by using authentic assessment activities
• Rely on materials requesting only literal information	• Provide opportunities to demonstrate inferential and critical thinking that are essential for constructing meaning
• Prohibit collaboration during the assessment process	• Represent a collaborative approach to assessment involving both students and teachers
• Often treat skills in isolated contexts to determine achievement for reporting purposes	• Use multi-faceted activities while recognizing that learning requires integration and coordination of communication skills
• Assess students across a limited range of assignments that may not match what students do in classrooms	• Represent the full range of instructional activities that students are engaging in their classrooms
• Assess students in a predetermined situation where the content is fixed	• Can measure the student's ability to perform appropriately in unanticipated situations
• Assess all students on the same dimensions	• Measure each student's achievements while allowing individual differences
• Only address achievement	• Address improvement, effort, and achievement
• Seldom provide vehicles for assessing students' abilities to monitor their own learning	• Have student self-assessment as a goal by asking students to monitor their learning
• Are mechanically scored or scored by teachers who have little input into the assessment	• Engage students in assessing their progress and/or accomplishments and establishing on-going learning goals
• Rarely include items that assess emotional responses to learning	• Provide opportunities to reflect upon feelings about learning

Sources: Adapted from Tierney et al., 1991; Glazer and Brown, 1993; and Caine and Caine, 1991.

Figure 1.2. Differences between Traditional Tests and Portfolios.

mances and observations of students' abilities and talents. Learning is not reduced to a single score. The combination of standardized test scores and portfolios communicates a more complete depiction of learning.

POTENTIAL POWER

Portfolios offer benefits for all participants. They empower students to accept responsibility for their learning, shift the role of teachers to "kid watchers," require collaboration among stakeholders, merge assessment and instruction into the same tasks, assess local curricular goals and objectives, hold schools accountable for complex learning, and create dynamic school climates.

Student Responsibility for Learning

Portfolios empower students to accept responsibility for their learning. When students are required to reflect on what information they need, how they will learn it, and what they have learned, they begin to view learning as a process within their control. Responsibility emanates from setting learning goals, developing plans to accomplish them, using the information, and documenting attainment of those goals. For example, second-grade students might set a goal to learn how to regroup double-digit numbers. They might then decide to use math manipulatives, computer games, and several textbook problems to accomplish this goal. The textbook chapter test could be chosen to prove growth. Throughout this cycle, students are focused on their goals, engaged in the activities to promote growth, and proud of their accomplishments (Cooledge, 1992). Portfolios provide the vehicle for writing the goals, making plans, and reflecting upon how well these goals have been met.

Empowering students to be responsible for their learning can improve the quality of their work. If students have a say in the kinds of activities they're pursuing, they will be working from their own interests towards goals that are understandable to them. Ownership, choices, and self-evaluation give students a stake in the learning accomplishments they are producing. When they select what they're doing, they are more likely to want it to be good (Tierney et al., 1991; Kohn, 1993).

Motivation

For years, exemplary educators have recognized that a relationship exists between emotions and learning. Different fields of research agree that humans have an innate need for self-determination (Caine & Caine, 1991; Kohn, 1993). We are intrinsically motivated to engage in tasks that are personally meaningful, while we tend to ignore those that make no sense to us. When students care enough about an experience or problem to think about it, deeper meaning occurs. Cognitive processes work to address affectively driven issues. When students make a connection that matters to them, it is meaningful learning. Many of us waited to learn how to program a VCR until something particular was on television that we wanted to see. Programming the VCR was purposeful and personal. We had to learn a new skill if we were to satisfy our need to watch the show. Learning was relevant because it was personal to us.

Similarly, when students are allowed to set goals and develop plans to achieve these goals, cognition and emotions meet. Questions such as the following foster learning that is purposeful and relevant:

- What do I want to know about this topic?
- How can I learn this information?
- What activities do I need to do?
- How will I know when I have learned this information?

Students can record their plans for answering these and other questions in logs that can be included in their portfolios. By participating in this process, students are empowered to accept responsibility for their own learning.

Practice Responsibility

Responsibility is a value that must be taught and practiced. It doesn't matter whether teachers directly instruct or model how to set goals, select activities, and evaluate learning as long as students are given numerous opportunities in multiple ways to practice responsibility. By participating in selecting the contents of portfolios and by evaluating the entries, students are provided with a means for beginning the process of increasing their responsibility for their own lifelong learning.

To facilitate this growth, principals and teachers must trust students as decision makers. Two fundamental beliefs must be present before students can function as decision makers:

- Students can and will learn when given the opportunity.
- Students are capable of planning experiences that encourage process, progress, and achievement (Valencia, 1990).

Practicing these beliefs creates a fundamental shift in the teacher–learner relationship. It changes the role of students to decision makers and goal setters, thus placing children at the center of the educational process (DeFina, 1992; Goodman, 1992). The teacher's role becomes one of demonstrator, collaborator, and facilitator. Principals are the key by encouraging and supporting teachers in making the necessary curriculum changes to obtain these prerequisites for successful portfolio implementation.

THE SHIFTING ROLE OF TEACHERS

As students become decision makers, a corresponding shift occurs in the role of teachers. To facilitate the changing teachers' role, a good leader finds ways to communicate the message of change with gentle support that encourages risk taking. Helping teachers become comfortable with change can be accomplished with a combination of readings, discussions, workshops, presentations, peer support groups, and mentoring (Clingman, 1992).

Select and Create Assessment Tasks

Too often, teachers believe the curriculum is absolute, and they are reluctant to tamper with it, even when students are having difficulty understanding it. Many blindly follow district curriculum guides or teacher manuals. Principals must communicate trust in teacher intuition by empowering teachers to select and create measures of students' talents and needs so that appropriate instructional opportunities can be provided to meet curricular goals for all students. The ambiguity of not having a formula for assessing and planning student learning activities is bewildering for many teachers. The principal must provide encouragement to teachers to become more confident as decision makers who know what's best for their students. In time, teachers will begin to trust their own abilities (DeFina, 1992; Valencia et al., 1994).

Shared Decision Making

In many classrooms, teachers select what predetermined topics will be covered next, how the information will be delivered, what is meaningful learning, and what are good or poor examples of student work. Cooperative students comply with teachers' directions, memorize information, and recite it at test time. Less cooperative students often question if the goal is meaningful, second-guess what happens next, or ignore what teachers determine to be important. Too often, learning becomes lost in a power struggle for control. When teachers give students responsibility for setting goals and developing plans to attain those goals, teachers team with students in decision making. The teacher–student relationship becomes a collaborative partnership with a focus on students' needs, as well as learning accomplishments (DeFina, 1992; Tierney et al., 1991; Goodman, 1992).

This reallocation of roles does not relinquish the teacher from responsibility for classroom management and learning. Sharing decision-making responsibilities and offering students choices do not dilute the teacher's power. The opposite is true. Collaboration precipitates the bond between students and teachers (Valencia et al., 1994). Frequent cooperation in goal setting and student involvement in classroom decision making have a positive influence on learning (Walberg, 1990; Goodman, 1992).

Kid Watchers

Rather than simply being the sage on the stage[5] teachers become "kid watchers" as students take on more responsibility for their own learning (Y. M. Goodman, 1978). In this role, teachers must develop keen observational skills to determine progress, benchmarks of learning, and areas that need further attention. At the same time, they must facilitate learners in their quest for knowledge that will prepare them to become productive citizens in tomorrow's world. Teachers will need encouragement and assistance in managing this role (Pappas et al., 1990; Routman, 1991; Heald-Taylor, 1989).

When teachers become more responsible for both curriculum and assessment in their classrooms, they also become risk takers. With no manual for teachers to follow, teachers must become confident in their own knowledge of learning theory, research, and best practices to enhance learning. Risk taking is scary for most teachers because there is always the worry of failure and unfavorable evaluations by administrators (Goodman, 1986; Weaver, 1994; Routman, 1990; Pappas et al., 1995). Principals play an important role by encouraging teachers to try new assessment techniques and allowing them to learn from their failures as well as their successes (Hutchinson, 1991; Heald-Taylor, 1989).

Teacher-Learners

Teachers are also retaining the role of learner, rather than that of expert. In classrooms where teachers are collaborating with students, they are all learning together. Teachers are becoming lifelong learners throughout their careers. They are continually expanding their knowledge of best teaching practices, current learning theories, classroom inquiry[6] as teacher researchers,[7] ways of addressing student needs, and matching assessment with daily instruction (Glazer & Brown, 1993; Harp, 1991; Tierney et al., 1991).

Shared Expertise

In the past, teaching has been a field of professional isolation. Teachers remained in their own classrooms with students and rarely had contact with their peers beyond meetings and informal breaks during the school day. Now, in many schools, teachers are beginning to share expertise through collaborative work in areas such as portfolios, curriculum development, and site-based management. Teachers who are more comfortable with experimenting with portfolios can share their successes and failures with others. More experienced teachers can serve as mentors for those who are just beginning to use portfolios in their classrooms (Valencia et al., 1994).

COLLABORATION AND REFORM

School reform emphasizes a broad base of collaboration among administrators, teachers, students, noncertified staff, parents, and community members. Principals have a pivotal role in facilitating, cultivating, and inspiring a participative climate. Portfolio planning, implementation, and evaluation are topics readily suited for collaboration. Effective principals involve teachers, staff, and parents in defining objectives, sharing ideas, and developing a process for implementation (Valencia et al., 1994; Hutchison, 1991; Heald-Taylor, 1989; Wells & Chang-Wells, 1992).

Collaboration with Parents and Community

One reason many states are requiring parent and community input into school decision making is to spread ownership and responsibility for those decisions. Another is to infuse new views into the educational process. Each group will bring a different perspective with diverse ideas. Parents may find portfolios to be a worthwhile history of children's learning. Paraprofessionals may value the process of assisting students to organize the contents. Teachers may use them as a means to develop student responsibility for learning. Administrators may see portfolios as a means of establishing accountability. Employers may find them helpful in selecting candidates for positions. These varying points of view are reasons for collaboration in designing the school's portfolio system. Through the process of planning, the needs of all stakeholders can be met.

Portfolios are not a panacea to our educational woes, however; they are a means by which teachers, parents, and students can cooperatively plan to improve learning. Careful consideration and articulation need to go into deciding the purpose of the portfolio, what goes into it, who will select items, how entries will be evaluated, and the role of each participant.

Collaboration among Teachers

In addition to being a vehicle for conferencing with students and parents, portfolios offer an opportunity to improve communication among teachers. Teachers need time with one another to learn about portfolios and to reflect on successes and necessary modifications. By discussing portfolios with teachers in the grade before theirs and the one succeeding them, teachers can acquire a sense of curricular continuity (Wolf, 1994). Principals are a key in arranging this time through a variety of strategies such as school restructuring, inservice days, and redistribution of staff development funds.

Collaboration across Subject Areas

Teachers in different disciplines also need time to plan together. Rich, complex learning opportunities cross subject areas. Artificially established boundaries between reading, mathematics, social studies, science, writing, computers, art, and other subjects disappear in the search for knowledge. Communication among teachers becomes necessary to break down subject area barriers. This becomes increasingly important at the middle school and high school levels.

If a group of students decided to write and perform a play about Columbus's voyage to America, they would use skills from several subject areas. They might use computers to create the play, the library to locate resources, language arts to write the script, history for the facts and views of the period, geography to map out the voyage, art to create their props, and drama to perform the play. The various teachers could use this project as a rich source for both instruction and evaluation of student skills in each of these areas.

MERGE ASSESSMENT AND INSTRUCTION

When used to their fullest, portfolios can be an integrating component of curriculum and assessment. Instruction and assessment become one and the same activity. Learning is not interrupted to take a test.

Assess the Curricular Goals

Effective portfolio assessment can begin only after district learning goals are defined. Authentic assessment measures what has been defined as valuable. Without a clear focus, portfolios will lack the cohesiveness necessary to provide comprehensible information about learning (Valencia, 1991). The process of creating criteria for what goes into portfolios and criteria for standards necessitates the examination of curricular goals and objectives. Through this process, portfolios become linked to classroom instruction.

Gathering measurements without knowing what to measure is akin to beginning a trip without a map. There will be no way to determine where you are, how far you've come, and how you should proceed. To observe a student in a science lab or to examine a piece of writing without a clear sense of how the behavior or skill fits into the total curriculum is likely to lead to piecemeal instruction, and it is even more likely to lead to unreliability (Valencia, 1990). Entries into portfolios should be evidence of student work in the areas of the school's goals and objectives.

Coordinate Goals with Daily Classroom Activities

The burden is on the principal to facilitate coordination of goals with daily classroom activities. Teachers usually need assistance in translating goals to specific student behaviors. For example, if the goal is to be "a responsible, contributing citizen," what types of classroom and schoolwide activities will teach fourth-grade students to be responsible, contributing citizens? What can be put into the fourth grader's portfolio to illustrate this behavior? What constitutes attainment of this goal? Questions such as these have to be discussed by the staff, clarified by the principal, and communicated to parents.

Student learning goals such as "a responsible, contributing citizen" are not easily determined by standardized tests. We can test student knowledge of government, laws, and history, but we have more trouble measuring the student's ability to prepare for and master various "roles" that will be encountered.

The process of creating contents of portfolios is part of curriculum, instruction, and assessment. Daily classroom activities are the assessments. A portfolio approach to assessment captures the best each student has to offer, encourages the use of many different ways to evaluate learning, and has an integrity and validity that no other type of assessment offers (Valencia, 1990; Wiggins, 1993). Teachers and students do not take time away from instruction to take tests. Instructional activities are also the assessment activities. Evaluation of this type is a continuous, ongoing process. Thus, instruction and assessment are simultaneous.

SCHOOL ACCOUNTABILITY

Accountability is a term heard with increasing frequency. Administrators are pressured to prove that students are learning, taxpayers are getting their money's worth, and employers will have a supply of competent employees. State funding, national accreditation, and administrative jobs are often dependent upon district and individual school verification of student improvement.

Inadequate School Assessment

Most often, a single, standardized state or national, multiple-choice test is used as the measure of student learning. In many communities, standardized test scores are published in newspapers by district, school, grade, and even classroom. Standardized tests have been widely misinterpreted as measures of program success (Madaus, 1991). For example, the Scholastic Aptitude Test is a self-described measure of potential for success in college, rather than a measure of high school performance. It has been inappropriately used by the press and accepted by the general public as an assessment of school competence. As the stakes get higher and higher, many educators are questioning the authenticity[8] of a single measure of student knowledge. Learning is too complex and assessment too imperfect to rely on any single index of achievement (Glazer & Brown, 1993; Wiggins, 1993; Darling-Hammond, 1991).

Standardized tests ignore a great many kinds of knowledge and types of performance that we want from students, such as structuring tasks, generating ideas, and solving problems (Darling-Hammond, 1991; Shepard, 1991). Historically, policymakers have attempted to improve public education by setting standardes and measuring attainment of the standards. The push for minimum-competency testing in the 1970s and reform movements of the 1980s were motivated by legislators' efforts to raise education standards (Shepard, 1991). Results have been increased scores on tests of basic skills and lowered scores on assessments of higher-level thinking and problem solving (Jaeger, 1991).

Considering the publicity and decisions based on the results of the tests, the old adage of "What gets tested, gets taught" is often true. Standardized tests have influenced what teachers teach, how it is taught, what pupils study, how they study, and what they learn. Thus, test makers shape the curriculum into memorization of bits of information. In fact, several national councils on education and research attribute the decline in higher-level thinking skills to the overemphasis on tests of basic skills. They maintain that this imbalance has corrupted teaching (Herman et al., 1992; Glazer & Brown, 1993).

Accountability for Complex Learning

In contrast, portfolios of students' work require analysis, investigation, experimentation, cooperation, and demonstration of findings through written, oral, or graphic presentations. Authentic assessment strategies present problems that require students to think analytically and demonstrate their proficiency as they would in real-life situations. These assessment strategies hold schools accountable for helping students acquire the kinds of higher-level thinking skills and abilities needed in the world outside of school. They include many different types of tasks within many types of settings. Some require students to respond to other students' questions. Others require students to perform a science experiment using mathematical and scientific concepts. Many engage students in writing tasks requiring several days of work.

Accountability for Local Goals

Successful initiatives involve teachers in developing and scoring the assessment, in supervising development of student work for portfolios, and in comparing work of their students with those in other schools. Involving teachers in the process promotes ownership for educational goals, rather than the more traditional top-down approach to testing. By including portfolios as part of the testing program, the likelihood increases that the district's goals will determine the curriculum, rather than a high-stakes exam dictating what is taught, what programs are offered, how much state funding the school receives, and which administrators are retained.

If we are to hold schools genuinely accountable, the school community has to identify what it wants students to learn. Educational goals must be negotiated within our schools, districts, and states. At the building level, it is the principal's responsibility to bring the constituent members of the school community together to establish clearly defined objectives and agreed-upon forms of data gathering. Educational theory, political pressure, research, parental preferences, and teacher beliefs are accommodated to establish the vision, determine curriculum goals, and decide on forms of data gathering (Anthony et al., 1991). Does the community want to know about social and emotional growth that underlie students' learning or only cognitive growth? Attitudes, cooperation, problem solving, and use of knowledge can be assessed if stakeholders identify these characteristics as valuable instructional outcomes. When portfolios are used as a measure of accountability, they must reflect educational goals of the local district.

Pieces of the Assessment Puzzle

Program assessment is similar to a puzzle, with each piece being one indirect indicator of competence. This involves using a variety of measures, including standardized tests, teacher-created tests, observations, self-assessment, anecdotal records, work samples, attitudinal surveys, and examples of performances. The combination used in any portfolio results in a profile of achievement towards curricular goals. At best, any profile is an incomplete answer to the question, "To what extent are students obtaining a good education?" No single test or measure can define progress in absolute terms (Anthony et al., 1991; Glazer & Brown, 1993; K. Goodman, 1986).

POWER TO CREATE A DYNAMIC SCHOOL CLIMATE

Schools with a dynamic climate are those where learning is the main focus. Administrators, teachers, staff, and parents are learners, as well as the students. When all are learners, the school becomes a learning community where caring, collaboration, and curiosity are the norm. These characteristics are visible not only in classrooms, but also in staff lounges, school corridors, principals' offices, district offices, and school board meetings (Wortman, 1992; Pappas et al., 1990). As a comunity, we all share in constructing an environment in which learning occurs, and portfolios are one way to measure this learning.

School Vision

Principals assist in creating a dynamic environment by focusing on individual staff members' professional development, elevation of expectations, and intellectual stimulation. They challenge each person to improve and take risks (Kirby et al., 1992). Through changing the attitudes inside the building, schools begin to do a better job of educating students. To build a climate of inquiry, principals must foster community vision building.[9] Shared values, sentiments, and beliefs provide the needed cement for uniting people in a common cause. This cause or vision determines the school climate (Sergiovanni, 1992). Portfolio contents reflect the school's vision.

Collaborative Work Climate

A principal who builds a collaborative work climate enables the staff to evaluate popular practices, select those that fit students' needs, and determine how to implement them. This type of leadership provides the school with tools to continue improvement, regardless of curriculum, methodologies, or the person in the principal's office. Mayher (1990) believes that the greatest support one can expect from others is not readily adoptable answers, but the excitement and rewards of becoming part of a wider community whose members take the journey seriously and recognize the need for mutual respect along the way. They value individuality, coordinate collaboration, expect continuous improvement, model problem solving, encourage lifelong teacher development, and promote risk taking, which are all necessary in portfolio implementation (Fullan, 1991; Newman, 1990).

Learning Community

Signs of a healthy learning community include a safe social and emotional climate for staff, students, parents, and principals who feel comfortable in the school and know they are valued. Students and teachers are free to try out new ideas and techniques, knowing they can learn from successes and failures. The prevailing atmosphere is exciting, and school is fun. People who enjoy learning together are less likely to criticize one another (Wortman, 1992).

As students become more responsible for their learning and teachers grow to view their role as collaborative coaches, schools become less formal institutions and more communities for learning (Sergiovanni, 1992). The process for implementing portfolios has the potential to assist in transforming a school from a hierarchical organization to a community of learners. As this metamorphosis occurs, principals spend less time and energy controlling through rules, supervision, and evaluation, while spending more attention supporting, reinforcing, and facilitating teachers, students, and parents.

TROUBLESHOOTING

A great deal of confusion surrounds portfolios. Principals will have to correct misconceptions before portfolio implementation can begin. Below, you will find statements we have heard about portfolios. You might want to give it as a true/false test to your staff to initiate discussion about any of these misconceptions that your staff may have about portfolios.

- "I don't see any differences between portfolios, learning logs, journals, and folders teachers put together for conferences."
- "I think portfolios are large boxes of student's work that the teacher collects over the year."
- "Portfolios are containers."
- "Portfolios are to help kids get jobs. They are folders with attendance records, grade cards, job experiences, test scores, and lists of extracurricular activities."
- "In our state, portfolios are required to show student growth. We meet the mandate by giving students a sentence stem in September and they write a paragraph from the stem. We repeat the activity in May. That shows growth over the school year. That's a portfolio."
- "Portfolios are class notes."
- "Portfolios are the same as weekly folders that teachers send home to parents."
- "They are journals for the students to write about what they think we did in class."
- "Portfolios are one more thing to keep in the file room."

GLOSSARY

Alternative Assessment: assessments that require students to construct, rather than choose, responses to measure what they can do and know.

Assessment: data gathered to measure growth and development of learners.

Authentic Assessment: assessment activities that take place as a regular part of the classroom. They reflect learning and instructional activities of the classroom and those in the world beyond the school.

Benchmarks: criteria used to evaluate excellence.

Criteria for Selection: decisions by a team of teachers, students, and administrators to determine what is placed in a portfolio.

Evaluation: the interpretation and analysis of the data gathered during assessment. It also includes reflection and decision making about instruction and programs based upon the careful examination of the evidence produced by assessment techniques.

Evaluation Standards: criteria for judging the merit of the contents of the portfolio.

High-Stakes Tests: tests that are used as the basis for making decisions that may significantly affect the future of those taking them.

Kid Watching: ongoing classroom evaluation that allows for continuous instructional planning. Teachers are attentive to how students are progressing. They make decisions about what experiences and opportunities might be needed for learning to continue and for development.

Lifelong Learning: the notion that learning does not end at the completion of formal education. Learning continues throughout one's life through both formal and informal educational experiences.

Performance Assessment: activities where students are asked to demonstrate their knowledge or level of competence by creating a product.

Portfolio: a collection of student work gathered for a particular purpose that exhibits to the student and others the student's efforts, progress, or achievement in one or more areas.

Risk Taking: a frame of mind in which the individual is willing to give up security to try something that may not be successful because the consequences of failure have been minimized.

Stakeholders: all those who have a vested interest in students' education, including students, parents, teachers, staff, administrators, school board members, business leaders, and other community members.

ENDNOTES

1. By student participation in selection of portfolio content, we mean that students must have a role in deciding which items are placed into the portfolio and are responsible for explaining why they chose each item.
2. During self-evaluation, learners do more than simply record their accomplishments. They examine how they are learning, strategies they are using to accomplish goals, areas needing improvement, and future goals. Part of this process includes an explanation of the reasoning behind the inclusion of each item in a portfolio.
3. When using the term *employability,* we are referring to the use of portfolios to help high school graduates obtain a job by showing evidence of their personal

responsibility and collaborative abilities, as well as their academic performance. This type of portfolio reflects both out-of-school activities and those produced while in school.

4. Student ownership is a prerequisite to active participation and lifelong learning. Students must recognize relevance in what they are learning before they are willing to learn on their own.

5. The phrase *sage on the stage* refers to the teacher being the focus of learning in the classroom. The teacher directs how instruction is delivered, which is usually a lecture format with the teacher on the stage. The teacher selects what is taught, how it is taught, who will answer which questions, and how learning will be assessed. Teachers who are the sage on the stage are the experts, and students have little or no control over their own learning. We prefer teachers who are the guide on the side. These teachers provide a framework for learning, rather than making all the decisions.

6. Classroom inquiry consists of teachers and students conducting research on topics of interest in their classrooms. Topics can include areas such as teaching practices or content areas that students or teachers are wondering about. This research involves asking questions, searching for questions to ask, understanding our disciplines, collecting data and choosing the best procedures to analyze that data.

7. Teacher researchers are those who use classroom inquiry to find answers to their questions about their own teaching practices and the needs of students in their classrooms.

8. By authenticity, we mean the validity of the measure of a student's learning. When using only one measure, too much emphasis is placed upon the validity of the test. Any one assessment tool is only a snapshot of the complete picture of a student's learning at a particular time. To accomplish an authentic measure of learning, we need multiple assessments taken over time.

9. Vision building is the creation of an image of what the school can become and sharing the image with others to build support for change. It is based on the ability to visualize what might be, rather than what exits.

CHAPTER 2

Evolving Nature of Portfolios

Miss Kline's Concerns about Portfolio Assessment

There is always something else that the administration wants us to do. Isn't there a curriculum guide or manual that I can use so that I have the correct format to follow? Just tell me what to put into this portfolio so I can get on with my teaching. Since when has anyone ever asked me what I believe is the right way to assess students? The rules for teaching and assessment are always being changed by some politicians who have never seen the students I have to deal with. My kids come to school without proper rest, nourishment, interest in learning, or commitment to education in the home. These students won't stay focused on any lesson for long and often don't score well on tests. Everyone keeps mentioning anecdotal records and other alternative assessments, but they don't have thirty students to deal with, or they have a full-time aide in their classrooms. This just doesn't seem feasible to me. There's just not enough time to do everything. After all, some new governor will come into office and all this portfolio stuff will go out the window, anyway. Why can't the administration just leave me alone and let me teach? If I must use portfolios, then provide me with the information I need to do it easily and correctly.

THE MYTH OF "ONE RIGHT WAY"

MANY teachers we work with feel just like Miss Kline. More often than not, teachers are accustomed to having manuals and curriculum guides that tell them what to teach, how to teach it, and even what to say. These manuals are often accompanied with assessment materials[1] that teachers administer and objectively score according to the requirements in the guides. Until recently, teacher judgement has not been highly valued during assessment or teaching (K. S. Goodman, 1986; Y. M. Goodman, 1992; Wells and Chang-Wells, 1992; Heald-Taylor, 1989). It is little wonder that teachers feel they don't know what to do with portfolios and want a quick, easy cookbook approach where each step is prescribed for them.

Portfolios are more ambiguous than simply following a recipe. Flexibility is one of the greatest assets of portfolios, and it may also be one of its greatest problems (Valencia, 1990). Principals' jobs of implementing portfolios would be much easier if we could list exactly what contents are to be included, when to collect entries, where they are to be stored, and how to evaluate them. Without specific guidelines, teachers often feel overwhelmed and uncertain about what is expected of them and worried, too, that perhaps portfolio implementation is beyond their capabilities (Fullan, 1991). Teachers want to do it "the right way." However, a standardized formula would destroy teachers', students', and parents' evolving ownership and understanding that comes from making collaborative decisions about the contents, timing, storage, and evaluation.

Portfolios reflect the variety of visions, philosophies,[2] goals, standards, and needs of local school communities. Because of the many factors to take into account when using portfolio assessment, *there is no "one right way" for creating and using portfolios for educational purposes.*

Top-Down Mandates Don't Work

How do principals initiate and facilitate a change to portfolio assessment within their buildings? Until recently, principals have relied on a top-down autocratic model for changes. Principals' roles in this approach have been to deliver documents to teachers' mailboxes and encourage implementation. During the decade of the 1980s, we learned that top-down mandates[3] don't work (Heald-Taylor, 1989; Fullan 1991). State legislatures, local school boards, and administrators can demand change, but when the classroom doors close, tried and true practices continue to be the norm. Top-down models do not recognize that change occurs over long periods of time. Autocratic models seldom involve principals and teachers in academic development and rarely design curriculum or assessment that addresses a particular school's needs. In addition, top-down mandates discourage principals and teachers from participating in decision making and mutual problem solving. Furthermore, few provide the systematic inservice necessary to sustain success in portfolio assessment.

Increasingly, state legislators are mandating portfolio assessment. Fortunately, policies are often vague and ambiguous, leaving the details to be decided by local districts. Fullan (1993) maintains, "Governments can't mandate what matters, because what matters most are local innovation, skills, know-how, and commitment." Schools that have successfully implemented portfolios recognize that both top-down and bottom-up strategies are necessary.[4] They seek outside ideas, are sensitive to their communities, and engage in state-level policies proactively (Louis and Miles, 1990; Rosenholtz, 1989).

An Investment in the Change Process

Before any lasting change can occur, principals, parents, and teachers must have an investment in the change process that comes from the opportunity to participate in defining the change and the flexibility to adapt it to their individual circumstances (Kirby et al., 1992). True change is an evolving and often agonizing process. The more principals, teachers, and parents are actively involved in the decisions, the more likely the change will be successful.

Based on Michael Fullan's (1993) and Gail Heald-Taylor's (1989) suggestions for the change process, we recommend the following six developmental stages for success in portfolio assessment:

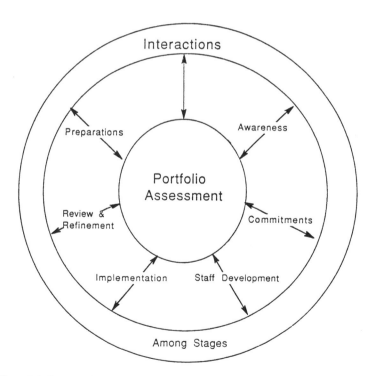

Figure 2.1. Reciprocal Interactions among Developmental Stages in Portfolio Assessment.

- preparing for portfolios
- developing awareness
- obtaining commitments
- providing staff development
- implementing portfolios
- reviewing and refining

This chapter will explain the first three developmental stages. Chapter 3 provides staff development ideas. The chapters in Part Two discuss implementation. Reviewing and refining are in the last two chapters. While we discuss the stages one at a time, the process of changing to portfolio assessment does not occur in a smooth linear fashion. The stages are constantly interacting with one another. What happens during one stage will affect movement toward the final goal of using portfolios in your school. New developments might occur during the implementation stage that necessitate more preparation, commitments, or staff development before you ever reach the reviewing and refining stage. Even at the reviewing stage, you will not be finished with your growth in using portfolios to assess student learning and instruction. The cycle is an evolving one that resembles the diagram presented in Figure 2.1.

DEVELOPMENTAL STAGES

Preparing for Portfolios

Before a school decides whether to embark on portfolio assessment, certain elements have to be present. You will need a great deal of background information, a school climate conducive to change, a problem-solving procedure, and commitment from your stakeholders. This stage will take from three to twelve months, depending on your situation. Avoid skipping an area because each element is critical to successful implementation of portfolios. Figure 2.2 illustrates the steps in preparing for portfolios.

As the school leader, begin by gathering background information. You want to be familiar with pertinent research and literature, local concerns, your staff's strengths, and your own leadership style.

Be Familiar with Effective Practices

You will find it necessary to have a firm foundation in the research and literature in effective instruction, the change process, problem-solving

PREPARING FOR PORTFOLIOS

- Be familiar with effective practices.
- Know the goals, standards, issues and concerns in your school district.
- Recognize the strengths of your staff.
- Know the strengths of your leadership style.
- Create a climate of trust, communication, and risk taking.
- Use problem-solving procedures.
- Be a principal-participant.
- Acquire the superintendent's support.

Figure 2.2.

procedures, collaborative decision making, and teacher mentoring. You will also need to build your knowledge in the area of portfolio assessment. After reading this book, you may want to read some of the resources listed in the bibliography. In addition, we recommend seeking additional information through conferences and workshops on portfolios. At the conferences, identify other administrators who are implementing portfolios. Consider starting a network of administrators who are interested in a similar implementation process. Within the group, you can share ideas, strategies, resources, and solutions to obstacles. Personal contact with another administrator who has implemented portfolios is extremely helpful in avoiding pitfalls. Visits to schools and discussions with administrators using portfolios are well worth the time and effort.[5]

Assess Local Goals, Standards, Issues, and Concerns

Another crucial knowledge base is knowing the goals, standards, issues and concerns in your local school district. Before making any changes, answer the following questions:

- What are the curricular goals and standards in your building and across the district?
- What program issues are current topics of discussion at your building, district, and state?
- What are your community's concerns about school goals, curriculum, and assessment?

Frequent contact with central office personnel, district curricular teams, and parents with students of different age groups will help answer these questions. Reading articles in state journals about curriculum goals, standards, and issues will also provide valuable information. Formal and informal parent meetings where concerns and issues are discussed are sources for you to gain insight into community perceptions. Parent surveys, such as the example provided in Appendix A.1, can also serve as a means of gathering additional data. From this combination of people and readings, you will be able to gain knowledge of the local attitudes toward curriculum and assessment.

Survey the Strengths of Your Staff

A third knowledge base consists of identifying the strengths of your staff:

- Have any teachers attended conferences or workshops about portfolios?
- Do some teachers currently use elements of portfolios?
- Are there some who are interested in doing so?
- Which teachers serve on curriculum committees?
- Are others interested in working with curricular goals?
- Who do the teachers view as leaders in innovations?
- Which teachers are influential with members of the community?
- Who is dissatisfied with the current assessment procedures?

Answers to questions such as these will help you assess your staff's readiness for an introduction to portfolios. Open communication with your staff and observation are the main ways to gather this information. Further data can be collected by using the teacher questionnaire provided in Appendix A.2. As teachers respond to the items, questions will arise that can be a catalyst for informal discussions about portfolios.

Know the Strengths of Your Leadership Style

The last piece of background information to gather is to know the strengths of your leadership style. Principals who lead change-oriented schools share several characteristics. They establish and exhibit risk taking in curriculum development and instruction, encourage innovation from teachers and students, and help build leadership skills in their staff. Effective change agents use a collaborative, collegial, and flexible style of administration. They are key players in reform, but they don't seek to control activities and plans. Attention is placed on team building, establishing trust, and obtaining commitment for the change within their school (Goldring & Rallis, 1993). To what extent do you exhibit these behaviors? The questionnaire in Appendix A.3 will help you identify your readiness to implement portfolios.

Create a Climate of Trust, Communication, and Risk Taking

A school climate of trust, communication, and risk taking is crucial to the success of educational change (Heald-Taylor, 1989; Y. M. Goodman, 1992; Wortman, 1992). Teachers can change only when they feel safe enough to risk failure. Parents can risk change only when trust exists. Teachers and parents respond more positively to change when they have principals who share ideas with them, listen to their problems, support their efforts, and actively participate in the implementation process (Fullan, 1993; Whitaker & Valentine, 1993). When teachers and parents feel the principal is working with them, taking risks, learning about something new, tolerating diversity of practices, and providing opportunities to make decisions, they are more likely to become committed to implementing portfolio assessment (Valencia & Place, 1994). Reinforce with your staff and community the message that you are listening to their concerns, trust their abilities, and will divert resources towards the common mission.

Changing to portfolio assessment is stressful for teachers. Many feel overextended from dealing with a wide variety of students with a wide variety of needs. Committing the time and effort to implement portfolios may seem impossible after a full day of teaching, especially for those who also have family and community responsibilities waiting to be fulfilled in the evenings. A few teachers have become complacent and satisfied with the status quo. Others would like to learn new skills but are reluctant to risk short-term failure to improve their expertise in assessment. Principals can respond to the various barriers to portfolios by increasing social support through collegial support teams.

Collegial support teams can act as a sounding board for teachers to examine their assessment practices, risk changing to portfolios, and validate their intuition. By engaging in dialogue with other teachers, they can begin to give up security and complacency and consciously come to trust their intuition. Members engage in an ongoing process of evaluating their own progress toward portfolio implementation and generating feedback to one another. This leads to improved practices and professional development (Bertrand, 1991).

Adults learn best in a supportive setting with others who are interested and excited about sharing in their learning. Teachers are more willing to try portfolios when the cost of failure is shared. They will try again and again where there is encouragement and some sense of control over what and how portfolios will be implemented (Bent, 1990).

If you are forming collegial teams for the first time, select teachers who are the most likely to be successful with portfolios and who would enjoy working together. You will want teachers who are positive, supportive, and competent. After their initial start, other teachers can join. Chapter 8 provides examples of successful collegial teams.

Utilize Problem-Solving Procedures

Another element that must be in place before implementation of portfolio assessment can begin is a problem-solving procedure. Effective principals are outstanding problem solvers who focus on solutions and generate ideas (Whitaker & Valentine, 1993; Leithwood & Montgomery, 1986). Regardless of causes, they avoid spending time and energy on blaming outside factors for problems within their school. Instead, principals, who are expert problem solvers, view problems in the context of the larger mission. They are able to clearly define the problem, identify deeper problems related to the problem at hand, and communicate the effects on the school's mission. They use collaborative problem solving with staff, students, and community to establish goals to resolve the problem (Leithwood & Steinbach, 1989; Fullan, 1991). Although there are a variety of problem-solving models, many of them share the steps listed in Figure 2.3.

For successful collaborative problem solving, regularly scheduled sessions are needed. Together, staffs and principals identify key obstacles to implementation of portfolios and brainstorm solutions. If an outside expert's opinion is needed concerning a specific dilemma, that person is consulted. The key is to develop a system in which both you and the staff have input into identifying and solving problems. Rosenholtz (1989) found that 87 percent of teachers in buildings where collaborative problem solving

---

STEPS IN COLLABORATIVE PROBLEM SOLVING

- Establish positive attitudes toward problem solving.
- Define the problem clearly.
- Gather information about the nature, causes, and extent of the problem.
- Brainstorm a variety of solutions.
- Decide on a plan.
- Implement the plan.
- Monitor and readjust the plan.

Figure 2.3.

was utilized believed that the principal was a good problem solver. Only 30 percent found the principal to be a good problem solver in buildings where teachers were not actively involved in finding solutions to problems.

Be an Active Principal-Participant

Still another key element is the principal's commitment to portfolios. If teachers perceive that the principal is not involved in the implementation process, they will feel that portfolios are just another top-down mandate. To support teachers and the implementation process, the principal must be an active participant in the learning and planning process. Teachers want their principal to attend inservices about portfolios with them, participate in matching portfolios to curriculum goals and standards, and communicate about portfolios with the school community (Valencia & Place, 1994; Goldring & Rallis, 1993). The key is to be an active participant in the planning and implementation process.

Acquire the Superintendent's Support

Schools that have success implementing portfolios have principals who acquire materials and consultative resources, arrange for teacher visitations, promote teacher mentoring, and provide time for teachers to attend inservice sessions. Many of the innovations were possible because the principals communicated regularly with the superintendents and convinced their superintendents to free up materials, consultative time, and professional development opportunities (Goldring & Rallis, 1993). Until the staff has had the opportunity to explore the need for portfolio assessment, the best approach is to arrange for informal discussions with the central office staff to lay the groundwork for a later formal proposal.

At this point, you are seeking approval and funds from the superintendent to bring portfolios to the attention of your staff and community. Part of gaining approval for the concept of portfolios is convincing the superintendent of the need for a collaborative approach to implementing change. By using this approach, staff and community will participate in making decisions regarding portfolio adoption. Whether they decide to commit to portfolios or if portfolios are mandated, all stakeholders must be involved in determining preferred types of inservices, experts to work with, and materials to use. Resources will be necessary to cover costs of sending teachers to conferences, visiting other schools that use portfolios, providing substitutes while teachers are away from the building, and inviting an expert to develop awareness of portfolio possibilities. Some districts are fortunate to have staff development funds allocated to each school, while others must request financial support from their central office. You are requesting to begin the awareness stage.

Developing Awareness

After preparing for portfolios, the principal must formulate a plan to increase awareness of the need to have alternative ways to assess student learning. Educational innovations are plentiful. Whether portfolios are mandated or not, it is the principal's job to clearly and convincingly show the administration, staff, and community how portfolios can fill educational needs of the school. Change requires ownership that comes from the opportunity to participate in defining the particular change and the flexibility to adapt it to individual circumstances (Goldring & Rallis, 1993). Teachers and parents will be more supportive if they are included before a final decision is made to implement portfolios.

Often, teachers do not see a need to change practices that they have developed over the years (Fullan, 1991; Heald-Taylor, 1989). Others may not be aware of the assessment options that are available. Some may have heard about portfolios but are unsure of the benefits. In states where portfolios have been mandated by legislatures, most teachers do not feel ownership or know how to implement them. In all cases, it is the principal's role to bring staff members to an awareness of the need to change assessment methods.

The temptation is to tell teachers how portfolios will revolutionize assessment practices. However, unless they first see the need to look for changes in traditional methods, telling will lead nowhere. As Mayher states (1990, pp. xii–xvi), "Nothing is harder than to put on new theoretical lenses that may help us see that the tried was not always true."

Rather than rush in with *the answer,* we recommend some proactive strategies. For example, at a staff meeting, initiate a discussion about assessment methods. You might start by saying something such as, "Last week, you filled out a questionnaire about assessment in our school. What do you think about our current methods of assessment? Are there gaps in traditional assessment that we could fill?" Listen to the responses and record the comments, questions, and concerns that arise. Tell them you will see what you can find to answer their questions and will set up a staff-room display of articles and books about assessment practices. Encourage teachers to discuss their opinions. Teachers respond to change in many different ways. Expect some to be resistant by defending existing assessment practices and enumerating obstacles against any and all alternative assessments. Others will be more receptive. They will begin to ask questions about assessment, request professional articles, and participate in informal conversations about options (Heald-Taylor, 1989; Friend & Cook, 1991).

Once a general awareness has formed, discuss with the staff the idea of pursuing portfolios as a schoolwide effort. If the staff as a whole is more resistant than interested in portfolios at this time, it is better to delay proceeding until their interest increases. In the meantime, continue to support teachers who are willing to learn more about portfolios.

Parents and community members should also be included during the awareness phase. Often, school communities have become accustomed to traditional assessment methods that may not have changed since community members were students. The use of traditional assessment methods by the media to evaluate and compare school districts reinforces the importance of standardized tests. Newspapers report scores on mandated tests to compare school districts and to inform parents of the rankings of local school districts. Some communities are more willing to question the traditional methods of measuring school success than others.

Communities vary greatly. Some communities support innovations, others block changes, and many are apathetic. However, in cases involving conflict, dissenting community groups nearly always prevail (Fullan, 1991). Conflict avoidance is a common characteristic of school boards and administrators. Many school boards will back away from a change rather than face citizens who oppose it. The key is to prevent opposition from forming. Usually, communities support portfolios if they are part of the initial dialogue. Begin this discussion by reporting the data from the parent/guardian questionnaire. As with the staff, have information available about portfolios for parents to read. Invite them to discuss their opinions with you.

Obtaining support from parents and community groups is one of the primary tasks of planning and implementing new programs (Fullan, 1991; Goldring & Rallis, 1993). It is the principal's role to broaden the number of people committed to portfolio assessment. Vision building is a method of broadening support for this change.

Vision Building

A vision is a clear description of the ideal school. Building a vision begins by identifying beliefs and aspirations of what school should be and then by implementing changes to achieve the ideal. Visions of assessment are based on beliefs about curriculum content, student ability, and teacher accountability. Once the community shares an image of what the school should be, the principal and staff decide how to create the conditions to attain it (Eisner, 1991; Kaufman & Herman, 1991). This vision directs the purpose and guides the changes.

In the hit Broadway play *The Music Man*, Professor Harold Hill drew a visual image of seventy-six school children playing trombones as they led the parade down the main street of Muncie, Indiana. He described the colors of the uniforms, the sounds of the music, and the reflections from the sun glistening on the brass trombones. By describing the marching band in detail, parents were able to imagine what they wanted for their children. They were emotionally moved to obtain the resources needed for a marching band.

Similarly, you can begin to describe your vision of school assessment. As you do so, invite others to add their details. Deciding what really counts in school is the first step. Assessment should measure the skills and qualities that the community believes are valuable. Obtain viewpoints from all those involved in the school and representatives of the constituencies in the community (Kaufman & Herman, 1991). You are building the foundation for portfolios by making the public and all persons associated with the school aware of their beliefs about student learning and evaluation. Later, you will use discrepancies between "what is" and "what should be" to convince others that changes in assessment are needed. Ask questions such as: In your ideal school, what will students and teachers be doing, thinking, and feeling? How will the classrooms look? Will the students be smiling, talking, and laughing or sitting quietly, concentrating, and writing? Or will they be doing both? The more detailed the vision, the more likely others will be able to "see" it. One word of caution: unlike the music man, don't promise more than you can deliver. Although the community would like to imagine that all students could be National Merit Scholars, attainment of such a vision is unlikely.

For change to be successful, everyone must agree on a common vision. Visions are built from the bottom up and from the top down. Without input from stakeholders, it remains the principal's vision of "my school's assessment." Conversely, without leadership from the principal and superintendent, the vision will lack clarity and focus. Vision building requires listening to stakeholders' beliefs, evaluating strengths and weaknesses of the current assessment program, and clarifying the purposes of assessment. As tedious and grueling as it is, top-down and bottom-up communication must be in place at all times (Doyle & Pimentel, 1993).

The Parent and Teacher Surveys in Appendix A.1 and A.2 are an excellent starting point. Any changes in assessment must reflect teachers' and the community's convictions and inviolate commitments (Friend & Cook, 1991). After asking parents and teachers to complete the questionnaires, share the results from their input in memos, newsletters, newspapers, and speaking engagements. Articulate their beliefs about assessment in clear, concise terms. Let everyone know you are searching for an ideal vision that better reflects stakeholders' beliefs about assessment.

Next, collect information from state and national levels that might affect assessment. You will want to identify governmental laws and regulations that may dictate or limit assessment changes, forecasts and trends in assessment practices, economic and demographic trends for your state, and political attitudes toward local initiatives (Kaufman & Herman, 1991).

Principals have the complex task of integrating assessment beliefs of various school constituencies, state and federal regulations, and external factors. The community's beliefs, tempered with reality, give a realistic vision of what can be. Figure 2.4 shows the relationship between beliefs, visions, and realities.

Advisory Committee

Successful principals use an advisory committee to write the assessment vision. By investing time and effort in building the vision, you are basing assessment on the beliefs of a broad number of people.

We recommend forming an advisory committee of fifteen to eighteen members who represent every component of the school community. The composition of the committee must reflect the makeup of the school's con- stituents (Friend & Cook, 1991; Kaufman & Herman, 1991). Teachers, parents, classified staff, students beginning with intermediate grade levels, and community members form the planning team. Figure 2.5 is an exam- ple of a representative committee.

Committee participants must also reflect the racial and socioeconomic balance of the school. One method is to select members by neighborhoods as well as by roles. Teachers, parents, students, classified staff, and com- munity members who live in different areas within the school's boundaries are more likely to be representative of the school's composition. An addi-

---

DETERMINING A REALISTIC VISION

Teacher + Community Beliefs = What Should Be

Incompatible Beliefs + Regulations + Funding = What Exists

What Should Be + What Exists = What Can Be

Ideal + Reality = Realistic Vision

Figure 2.4.

Oak Falls High School

Oak Falls, Michigan 48856

Vision of Assessment
Advisory Committee

Ms. Walker	Parent
Mr. Vasquez	Parent
Ms. Donley	Parent
Mr. McNeil	Parent
Ms. Martinez	Teacher
Ms. Nelson	Teacher
Ms. Jackson	Teacher
Mr. Kuffmann	Teacher
Mr. Lutz	Paraprofessional
Mrs. Jackson	Paraprofessional
Mr. Lyons	Community member
Mr. Krueger	Community member
Jason Anderson	Student
Melissa Mashita	Student
Erik Lee	Student
Ms. Gonzales	Principal

Figure 2.5. Example of a Vision of Assessment Advisory Committee.

tional benefit of geographic selection is that neighbors tend to communicate with one another and will talk about the committee's vision building.

Another characteristic of team members must be taken into account—the personality mix. Each member must be willing to set aside special interests and pursue common interest. It is essential that all agree to subordinate personal interests and seek consensus (Friend & Cook, 1991).

Begin recruitment for committee membership with an article in the school newsletter. The article seeks volunteers to help formulate the school's vision of assessment. Include in the article a description of the task, when the committee will meet, a deadline to apply, and a request for volunteers from different neighborhoods. Their task will consist of reconciling discrepancies between what should be and what exists. Information from the teacher and parent surveys and external factors will be used.

Vision building usually takes three meetings that last approximately two hours each. More can be accomplished if the meetings are spaced tightly and held to strict time limitations (Friend & Cook, 1991). A sense of time restraints helps keep the team's attention focused. After the vision is written, the staff will be responsible for determining what changes need to be made in assessment practices to achieve the vision.

Wait a week for people to volunteer before you begin recruiting. After a week has passed, select members who meet the criteria of being representative of the school's composition and who will work well together. Parents, teachers, and business people are more likely to serve when they know the meetings will follow an agenda, remain on a time schedule, and end within three sessions with a completed statement.

Followup with a letter that restates the purpose of the committee, dates and times of meetings, a list of members, an agenda for the first meeting, and any readings that might offer clarifying information.

The First Advisory Committee Meeting

The principal begins with a brief overview of the process of implementing changes in assessment. Include the scope of the team's role in vision building and the responsibilities of staff and school board. It must be absolutely clear that they are an advisory committee, not a policy-making committee.

It is essential to establish the ground rules by reviewing group building roles such as the focuser, clarifier, encourager, and time keeper. Depending on the sophistication of the committee members, you may need to elaborate on characteristics of group dynamics. Stress that the meetings will be open, honest, and respectful. Everyone who was selected can offer a valuable contribution towards formulating a clear vision.

Their task is to write a vision of assessment that integrates the beliefs of the various stakeholders and external factors. The principal's role is to provide the data and guide the team to identify areas of differences and agreements. Using the data from the parent and teacher questionnaires, summarize the beliefs of parents and teachers about assessment. What are their similar beliefs about assessment? How do they differ? Charting them such as in Figure 2.6 is one way of organizing the data. Beliefs that are common to both groups will begin to emerge. Emphasize similarities and areas of agreement so that you adjourn the meeting with a sense of cohesiveness.

The Second Advisory Committee Meeting

At this meeting, introduce factors that might hinder or restrict attain-

---

STAKEHOLDER BELIEFS ABOUT
LEARNING AND ASSESSMENT

We believe:

- Schools are responsible for preparing students to be productive members of society.
- Learning and assessment occur simultaneously.
- Assessment measures what students know.
- Students have a variety of valuable talents.
- Differences enrich learning.
- Every student is entitled to a nurturing environment.

Figure 2.6.

ment of teachers' and parents' beliefs of an ideal assessment program. Include such things as incompatibilities in beliefs, state and federal factors, and any internal weaknesses that might affect implementation of an ideal vision of school assessment.

Many parents might want teachers to assess their child's self-esteem, leadership skills, and organizational ability. Other parents may believe the school should restrict assessment to paper and pencil tests of academic skills. Similarly, some teachers might want to expand assessment and others might want to maintain the status quo. The committee decides which beliefs are incompatible and which ones are similar.

Examples of state and federal factors that must be considered might be

- The state Department of Education requires a standardized, minimum competency test for graduation.
- Colleges require SAT or ACT scores from applicants.
- Funding for professional development has been reduced.
- The state Department of Education is considering increasing the number of Carnegie Units required for graduation.

The committee might want to chart the incompatible beliefs, regulations, and other factors that could hinder attainment of an ideal vision of school assessment. Figure 2.7 is an example of factors some schools have identified.

Factors That Might Hinder Attainment of the Ideal Vision

- Beliefs incompatible with portfolios
- State and federal regulations
- Internal weaknesses

Figure 2.7.

The Third Advisory Committee Meeting

The final meeting is to write a vision statement that incorporates all the information. The principal's task is to keep the group focused, encourage creativity, and attain consensus. This is the most difficult session for the committee. Looking at the whole provides the foundation for a realistic vision of what can be. The process requires analysis, synthesis, and brainstorming to arrive at a vision of assessment that maximizes the school's potential to assess learning (Friend & Cook, 1991; Kaufman & Herman, 1991). By basing the vision on beliefs and realities, you are more likely to have others accept the vision and to be able to attain it.

Within a few days of the meeting, share the results with the superintendent, staff, and parents. Ask team members to communicate the vision with as many people as possible. Politically, visions are accepted more favorably if they are "our vision" rather than "my vision." Figure 2.8 shows visions from several districts.

VISIONS OF ASSESSMENT

- We believe students learn and demonstrate this learning in a variety of ways.

- We believe assessment is part of the daily classroom instruction.

- We believe students should be able to demonstrate what they know in multiple ways.

- We believe parents, teachers, and the community are part of assessing student learning.

Figure 2.8.

Obtaining Commitments

The success of implementation is dependent upon commitment from central office staff, as well as from staff and parents. At this stage, you want your superintendent to be an advocate for portfolios. Write a proposal for a three-year plan to present to your superintendent. In it, outline the need for alternative assessments, ways portfolios will fill the need, and resources needed for implementation such as time, materials, and money. It is the superintendent and central office staff who combine access, internal authority, and resources necessary to seek funds for a particular program (Fullan, 1991). It is important to clearly ask the superintendent to provide the support listed in Appendix B.1.

Administrative support includes obtaining school board approval. Ask the superintendent for advice on when and how to approach the board. Usually, school board members feel accountable for student learning, legal issues, and budgets. The evidence you present to the board should include information on the consistency between portfolio assessment and the current research on teaching, learning, and assessment (Lieberman, 1991); assurances of confidentiality of the information in the portfolios; and a realistic budget. Board members must recognize that portfolios are a cost-effective way to meet a significant need of the school. When principals have the combined efforts of the school board and central office actively working together to promote a change, they are able to achieve substantial improvements (Fullan, 1991; Slotnik, 1993). Appendix B.1 contains an example of information a principal presented to her school board. You may revise the information and use it with your board.

A combination of strong advocacy on the part of teachers, administrators, school board members, parents, and community leaders is ideal. Even in states and districts with portfolio mandates, implementation of changes occur only when stakeholders support them.

When you ask your staff to formally make a commitment, remember they are deciding on a focus that will take extra work over two or three years, so expect an outpouring of honest concerns and legitimate questions that will have to be addressed (Heald-Taylor, 1989; Friend & Cook, 1991). It is important to be honest with them, letting them know what specific resources have been promised from the central office. Realistic expectations are especially important if the resources are less than ideal, so that trust is not compromised.

Schools who have implemented portfolios have found a variety of ways to stretch their budgets. In several schools, teachers have stopped purchasing spelling books. Students learn to spell from word lists associated with topics studied in class by writing portfolio entries. Other schools have shifted some money from copy paper to pay for expandable folders for students. Teachers at another school became garage sale junkies to attain used filing cabinets from businesses who were remodeling.

Small districts may want to form a consortium with other small districts in the same area. They can divide the cost of a consultant, videos, reading materials, and other resources needed to prepare teachers.

In one district, the high school department heads delegated their administrative tasks to everyone in the department. The money allocated for department head stipends was reserved to hire substitutes while teachers attended school improvement meetings.

Providing Staff Development

Once commitments have been established, you are ready to begin providing staff development. During the development stage, the stakeholders determine their focus, set goals and objectives, find available resources, and locate experts who can assist them in implementing portfolios. Chapter 3 provides more details for each of the staff development sessions.

Implementation

By implementation stage, stakeholders have determined a focus for portfolio assessment, set goals and objectives, found available resources, and located experts to assist them. During this stage, the team develops a school-based implementation plan, proceeds with that plan, and continues further staff development. During implementation, your job is to support people who are acting and interacting to make significant changes in assessment.

Implementation involves the first experiences of putting portfolio assessment into practice. It is not a linear process. Rather, events at one stage affect decisions made at previous stages and continue to interact through the process. Figure 2.9 shows the reciprocity of this relationship. Implementation takes a minimum of two to five years before portfolios can become an integral part of the curriculum.

Reviewing and Refining

Reviewing and refining are not something done at the end of the year. Rather, they are part of every stage as stakeholders try to improve the fit between portfolios and the characteristics and resources of the school. The principal is responsible for monitoring the process of implementing portfolios, as well as the effect on students' academic progress.

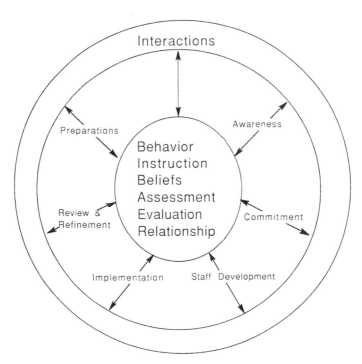

Figure 2.9. *Reciprocal Interactions among Development Stages and Variables Affecting Portfolio Assessment.*

During all stages, the staff members informally and formally evaluate their progress towards implementation. Rarely does the process go smoothly. In fact, Fullan (1991) points out that, if there are no problems, then there are no substantial changes. When people try something new, they often suffer what Fullan (1993, p. 749) calls "the implementation dip."[6] Things get worse before they improve, as people grapple with the meaning and skills of the change. Usually, problems become more apparent after teachers begin portfolio assessment (Black, 1993).

The principal's role is to enable problem solving by getting people talking on a regular basis and supplying them with the information and resources they need at that time (Fullan, 1991). Additional inservices, materials, assistance, and time might be needed. Modifications might also have to be made in the plans and logistics. Teachers usually find they have to experiment for awhile before they can develop portfolio strategies that fit their own teaching style, subject area, and classroom (Black, 1993). This is the evolving nature of portfolios.

TROUBLESHOOTING: NO CONCLUSIVE RESEARCH

To date, evidence on the use of portfolios is consistent with current research in teaching and learning. They provide a clearer connection between what is taught, what is learned, and what is assessed (Lieberman, 1991). Multiple-choice tests reinforce the drill-and-practice instruction that is based on outmoded learning theory. Portfolios require active construction of mental models or schemata by the learner, while traditional multiple-choice tests break down learning into constituent, prerequisite skills (Shepard, 1991; Marzano et al., 1993). Traditionally, learning has been a process that involves students repeating presented information in reports or on quizzes and tests. Portfolios, on the other hand, require students to use analysis, investigation, experimentation, cooperation, and written, oral, or graphic presentation of findings. They include may different types of tasks over time. Rather than imitative behavior, we look for what students' can create, demonstrate, and exhibit. Portfolios allow students to internalize and reshape information. By actively working with the information, new cognitive structures called schemata, or mental models, are developed. The emergence or refinement of new cognitive structures enables students to rethink and understand their individual worlds. Portfolios are based on theoretical learning principles that are neurologically sound (Caine & Caine, 1991).

Schools, districts, and states have developed portfolios in an effort to make schools genuinely accountable for helping students acquire the skills and abilities that they will need in the world outside of school (Darling-Hammond, 1991). Educators, legislators, business leaders, and parents are beginning to recognize that educational goals must reach beyond the scope of traditional subject areas to include goals such as decision making, problem solving, collaboration, and citizenship (Marzano et al., 1993). Kentucky, Maine, Minnesota, Pennsylvania, Virginia, and other states have revised their educational goals to combine traditional academic outcomes with lifelong competencies. For schools to be accountable for these goals, assessments have to include evaluation of academic knowledge, as well as outcomes that relate to lifelong learning. Traditional tests measure knowledge and skills of a particular discipline such as math or language arts. Lifelong goals such as collaboration are difficult to measure with paper and pencil tests. Portfolios that contain teacher observations of students working together, checklists of attitudes, and student self-assessments are better able to grasp a student's ability to work with other students. Chapter 4 examines the goal of self-assessment in portfolios. Identifying and agreeing on specific performance standards is part of the process of developing portfolios and will be described indepth in Chapter 3.

It is still much too early in the movement to point to research that shows statistical correlations between portfolios and increased student learning. Vermont is pilot-testing a system for using student portfolios of writing and math to obtain an overview of student achievement and assess the quality of programs (Arter, 1990). The RAND Corporation has completed an attitudinal survey of principals in the pilot schools. The results are promising. Universities such as SUNY and New Mexico State are using portfolios for students to demonstrate the writing competency requirement and to assign grades in composition classes (Arter, 1990). Many teachers at all grade levels are using portfolios to show indicators of student growth. Students select their best pieces of writing and explain their criteria for choosing each entry. Teachers report empirical evidence that students become more adept at making substantive writing revisions, recognizing quality, and accepting responsibility for their learning (Herter, 1992; Ballard, 1992; Cooper & Brown, 1992; Arter, 1990; DeFina, 1992). So far, there are no experimental studies to show that portfolios are an effective means of improving learnng.

It is too soon to predict if alternative assessments will falter or flourish. This developing system of accountability has the potential to be a powerful force in reforming schools. The extent of its success will depend on the combined commitments of teachers, administrators, school board members, parents, and community leaders to continuously make revisions in procedures to match the local school's needs. This requires all stakeholders to put energy and resources over a period of time into portfolio implementation. It is the principal's responsibility to sustain the interest.

GLOSSARY

Brainstorming: a technique used to solve problems by generating ideas.

Collaborative Decision Making: decision making where all of the stakeholders are represented, each has an equal voice, and consensus is used to arrive at decisions that are beneficial to all members.

Collegial Support Team: a group of peers that support and encourage members of the group. A type of collaborative decision-making group.

Effective Change Agents: people who are successful in gathering backing, resources, and followthrough from stakeholders in managing change in their schools.

Efficacy: the power to attain desired results.

Empowerment: granting authority to others to make decisions.

Group Building Roles: behaviors of participants that assist a group in achieving its goal.

Lifelong Goals: goals that are needed to be successful in one's life after leaving the formal school setting or classroom.

Reflective Thinking: a way to examine one's work to recognize patterns and connections in one's behavior.

Schemata: the organizational system that the brain uses to process and retrieve information relevant to a topic under consideration. The brain uses prior knowledge to integrate new information with what is already known.

School Climate: the general attitude of the members of the school community toward each other and learning.

Self-Actualizing: when one has the ability and confidence to make the most of one's potential.

Systematic Inservice: a type of staff development that occurs over a period of time. Periodic training is available prior to implementation, during implementation, and after teachers are using portfolios.

Teacher Mentoring: a support system that is provided for teachers who are attempting to implement changes in their classrooms. The principal and other teachers provide assistance, demonstrations, a sounding board, and encouragement as a teacher risks both successes and failures in innovations.

Teacher Intuition: a feeling of how students are doing and what they are ready to learn.

Vision Building: identifying beliefs and aspirations of the community's ideal image of what could be.

What Can Be: the ideal vision tempered with realistic conditions to form a vision that is possible to achieve.

What Exists: current conditions based on internal and external data.

What Should Be: the ideal vision shared by stakeholders.

ENDNOTES

1. Traditional assessment measures are norm-referenced, criterion-referenced, textbook manufactured tests, and other forms of multiple-choice or single answer tests. They share the common assumption that there is one or more correct responses to each item. They also tend to occur at particular times of the year with one chance to perform. Student work is evaluated in isolation, rather than in context of regular classroom activities. Traditional assessment

measures alone cannot give a true picture of the capabilities of a student and what has been learned.

2. When we use the phrase *philosophies of learning,* we are referring to the belief systems that teachers and others hold about what should be taught, how it should be taught, what materials best support the desired learning, what roles teachers and students should have during learning, where learning occurs, and how learning should be measured.

3. Top-down mandates occur when politicians, superintendents, or principals use their position power to force changes. These mandates can only work when subordinates follow directions and fulfill the mandates. Often, those not involved in the decision making do not see the change as belonging to them, and resistance is high.

4. For more information on each of the educational practices mentioned in this paragraph, we recommend that you read the suggested references.

5. Top-down and bottom-up strategies come from opposite ends of the teaching profession. The top-down strategies are similar to top-down mandates because they are initiated by those in power such as the principal, superintendent, or politicians. Bottom-up strategies refer to changes that are initiated from those involved directly in classrooms such as teachers and students or from the community. Ideally, these two types of strategies must work together before significant and lasting changes in education can occur.

6. Implementation dip is a label given by Michael Fullan and Matthew Miles to explain the documented problem of things getting worse before they become better. When implementing complex reforms, such as changes in assessment, participants go through a period of difficulty, anxiety, and frustration. It takes time to learn new ways to assess student learning. As teachers and students begin to understand the process of portfolio assessment, they will become better at doing it.

CHAPTER 3

Getting Started

Mrs. Smith

I've got sixty kindergarten students. I don't have time to discuss assessment issues. If I could find another hour in the day, it would not be for more meetings. By the time we take off coats and boots, go to the bathroom, have our circle time, and work on a letter in the alphabet, it is time to begin getting ready to go home by putting on coats and boots, matching lost mittens, and lining up for the right bus. Then, I clean up for the next group and start all over with the afternoon session. By three o'clock, I'm exhausted. I haven't sat down for a minute. Now you want me to come to meetings to decide how we can measure what the children have learned. And you even want me to help decide how to allocate the budget for this. That's your job. I'm paid to be a teacher, not an administrator. Let me do what I do best—teach. You do what you were trained to do. Just tell me when to give the readiness tests and how much money I have in my budget.

I've been in this district seventeen years. Administrators hear about these things and jump on the band wagon. In two years, no one will remember the phrase ''alternative assessment'' much less ''portfolios.''

Perhaps these changes are fine for older children, but my little ones already have too much crammed into a day. If they don't learn all the letters in the alphabet and numbers from one to twenty, they won't be able to do first-grade work. I can't fit one more thing into their day or into mine.

Mr. Hansen

I have 173 students a day and three different preps. I don't have time to discuss assessment issues. When do I have extra time for meetings? Every week, I give a math quiz that I have to grade. I sit up until ten or eleven at night grading papers. Now you want me to grade portfolios? No way. I have to get these kids ready for college algebra, not writing. Let the English teachers use portfolios. If we spend time writing in math class, SAT scores will drop. Then you'll be on my back about lower SAT scores. Show me proof that portfolios raise SAT scores, and I'll consider using them. Otherwise, no thanks. I'll stick to teaching algebra and using chapter tests like I've always done. I already have too much to do and not enough time.

INTRODUCTION

MRS. Smith and Mr. Hansen are typical of many teachers. They are hard-working, dedicated individuals who are concerned about preparing their students for the next grade level and for high-stakes tests. They have seen popularity-driven innovations dilute achievement. Past trends such as New Math and Open Classrooms have made many educators skeptical of un-proven practices. It is the principal's job to show the Mrs. Smiths and Mr. Hansens how to make portfolio assessment a worthwhile investment of time, resources, and effort.

In this chapter, three staff development sessions are presented that will enable teachers to begin implementing portfolios. During the first staff in-service, teachers identify what they want to measure. Entries in portfolios should reflect the learning goals of the school. For example, if your school's vision of student learning includes developing communication skills, then students will place written and oral entries into portfolios that show communication skills. The second session consists of deciding how to measure school goals. Will they show communication skills with writing samples and lists of books read, or will they also accept art, music, and drama as forms of communication? Finally, staff members will have to develop performance standards. This involves agreeing on criteria for making decisions about student learning. By the end of the three sessions, your stakeholders will have defined and adapted portfolios for their school.

Each staff development session will take several hours. If possible, schedule half-day sessions to allow enough time for teachers to focus and become involved in the topics. When the sessions are divided into an hour at a time and spread over several weeks, part of each session is wasted on reviewing and refocusing. Three half-day sessions utilize teachers' time more efficiently than nine or twelve hour-long sessions.

Consider establishing a small committee to develop an inservice plan for the remainder of the year. The plan should be balanced between formal presentations by experts who use portfolios and discussion sessions to allow staff to share some of their successes as well as their concerns and questions. If any key researchers are scheduled to be nearby, try to make contact with them in advance and arrange for them to visit your school. It is important to be aware of teachers' needs by planning flexibility into the staff development sessions to realistically accommodate the implementa-

tion of portfolios. Be sensitive to your teachers. Give support as they indicate need, provide encouragement when they are frustrated, and celebrate with them when they share successes. Only by developing a
long-term implementation plan and closely monitoring its growth can we
bring about significant improvement in our current instruction and assessment (Unia, 1990).

STAFF DEVELOPMENT SESSION 1: IDENTIFYING WHAT'S IMPORTANT

Portfolios are more than a collection of students' work. To be beneficial,
they must reflect progress towards the school's learning goals. In other
words, portfolio contents must match the knowledge, skills, and attitudes
that teachers are teaching and those that students are expected to learn
(Herman et al., 1992). Questions such as, "How am I (or we) doing?" "How
can I (we) do better?" cannot be asked until your school determines what's
important, what deserves focus, and what we expect as good performance.

In Chapter 2, we discussed vision building. What is your school's vision? What do you want students to know at each grade level? These learning goals drive the curriculum planning, daily instruction, and portfolio
assessment (Herman et al., 1992). The first staff development session is to
identify ways to assess academic skills, concepts, social skills, and attitudes that stakeholders believe are important for students to know. Portfolios need to contain examples of student work in the areas identified as important goals during the vision-building sessions.

For example, if stakeholders identified communication skills as a learning goal, then portfolio entries will reflect students' knowledge, skills, and
attitudes in writing, speaking, using word processing, following directions, listening, and expressing feelings through art, music, dance, and/or
drama. Another area might be competence in the basic skills of math and
science. Still another component of many school visions is citizenship.
The vision of what a school can be defines what is important for students
to know and for teachers to teach. Portfolio entries document progress
toward the school's vision of learning.

Connecting Portfolios with the Vision

During the first staff development session, display the chart of the
school's learning goals. Some learning goals frequently found in schools
are listed below.

Students in Franklin Schools will learn to

- communicate effectively in written, visual, and spoken lanuage
- compete and produce in a global economy
- exercise the rights and responsibilities of citizenship
- apply knowledge in diverse situations
- display innovative and creative ideas and activities

Some states, such as Kentucky, have defined the learning goals for all students. Others allow individual school districts to establish local definitions. In either case, you may want to review the definitions of each learning goal with your teachers. One way to arrive at a common definition is to select one goal and brainstorm with your staff a list of academic skills, concepts, social skills, and attitudes that constitute this goal. This list is the learning objectives. What do you want students to be able to do in this area? For example, what strategies and skills are part of communication? Certainly, speaking, listening, writing, and reading are part of communication. During this meeting, unless it is state-mandated, your staff and parents can decide if they want to include other modalities of communication such as accessing and transmitting information through technology, communicating thoughts and feeling through the visual and performing arts, and communicating through numbers and symbols. We recommend that you limit the learning objectives to a reasonable number such as ten or less. If you have too many, it will be difficult to focus on the major skills, concepts, and attitudes. It is best to eliminate less important ones to allow more instructional time for the most significant knowledge and skills. The questions listed in Figure 3.1 can guide the discussion for each learning goal.

QUESTIONS TO DEFINE A LEARNING GOAL

What important basic academic skills do I want my students to be able to do?

What important concepts should all students know about this goal?

What social skills are beneficial in this area?

What types of problems do I want them to solve?

Figure 3.1.

We recommend that you use these questions to ensure that everyone involved clearly understands the concepts and skills that make up each learning goal.

An example of a definition of the learning goal of communication skills is listed below. A good communicator

- understands and makes him/herself understood
- conveys information clearly and concisely
- communicates effectively for a variety of purposes
- communicates in different mediums
- expresses his/her needs, desires, and opinions
- accesses tools, information, and strategies from a variety of resources
- communicates effectively with diverse audiences

Overcrowded Curriculum: Less Is Better

Most teachers are similar to Mrs. Smith and Mr. Hansen in having too many students and not enough time to add one more thing to an overcrowded curriculum. In an era characterized by school accountability, an explosion of information, and global competition, teachers are under unprecedented pressures of accountability. Instead of trying to teach everything, the following process attains a balance between the current overcrowded curriculum and content that is essential, enduring, and relevant.

A process that we call a Three-Way Rotation[1] is a method that involves having the whole staff achieve consensus rather quickly and painlessly. Place staff members into at least four small groups with three to eight members in each group. The number of groups depends on the size of your staff. It does not matter how many groups you have, as long as you keep the size of each group small enough to allow participation from each member. The group will need a recorder, a piece of notebook paper, a large sheet of a tagboard, and a marking pen.

All groups take the same learning goal and brainstorm every possible component of the goal. They simply list all suggestions without asking questions or making judgements. Allow fifteen minutes for the brainstorming. At the end of brainstorming, each group should have a full page of academic skills, concepts, social skills, and attitudes that compose the learning goal. Figure 3.2 is a list of communication skills developed by teachers at a middle school.

During the next two steps, your staff will narrow the number of components to a workable number of learning objectives. The final list will contain a coherent set of well-understood concepts and skills that provides a solid base for further learning. To be useful, the list of learning objectives

---

COMMUNICATION SKILLS

writing
speaking
computer skills
reading
listening
reading for information
grammar
non-verbal
writing letters
art
music
drama
creative writing
giving directions
giving feedback
expresses ideas
empathy
expresses ideas for many purposes
uses a variety of ways to communicate
makes feelings known appropriately
expresses needs
communicates with different audiences
conveys information clearly
persuasive writing and speaking
logically debates ideas
accesses information and resources
develops a final product such as a story, report, song, piece of art...
uses the right tools for the type of communication
spelling
library skills
research reports
cooperative group skills

Figure 3.2.

must be limited in number and lasting in significance (Ahlgren & Rutherford, 1993).

Keep your staff in the same groups. Have each group pass their list of
objectives to the group sitting to their right. Each group will have another
group's list. They have five minutes to cross out any skills, knowledge, or
attitudes that are not essential. They are to focus only on those aspects that
reflect their highest priority of learning objectives, such as shown in
Figure 3.3. They may not alter the wording or go to the group for clarification.

At the end of five minutes, each group again passes the lists to the next
group on the right. This time they have fifteen minutes to narrow the list

and rank the most important objectives of the learning goal. The number of components should be between five and ten items. Only the key elements that are consistent with the best current understanding of the field and that will stand the test of time should remain. Again, they must not rewrite or combine the objectives.

After fifteen minutes, call time. Rotate the lists to the group on their right. This time, the group has five minutes to write the top five to ten objectives on the large tagboard paper and display the results for all groups to see. Figure 3.4 shows a middle school staff's ranked lists.

By comparing the lists, the most important objectives emerge. Usually, the lists are strikingly similar. Now that the list has been narrowed, the final step is to restate the learning objectives into statements that reflect es-

---

COMMUNICATION SKILLS

writing
speaking
computer skills
reading
listening
reading for information
grammar
non-verbal
writing letters
art
music
drama
creative writing
giving directions
giving feedback
expresses ideas
empathy
expresses ideas for many purposes
uses a variety of ways to communicate
makes feelings known appropriately
expresses needs
communicates with different audiences
conveys information clearly
persuasive writing and speaking
logically debates ideas
accesses information and resources
develops a final product such as a story, report, song, piece of art...
uses the right tools for the type of communication
spelling
library skills
research reports
cooperative group skills

Figure 3.3.

RANKED LIST OF ESSENTIAL COMMUNICATION SKILLS

4. listening
1. expresses ideas for many purposes
6. uses a variety of ways to communicate
8. makes feelings known appropriately
2. communicates with different audiences
9. conveys information clearly
3. accesses information and resources
7. develops a final product such as a story, report, song, piece of art...
5. uses the right tools for the type of communication

Figure 3.4.

sential skills, knowledge, and attitudes without omitting a key component that is necessary for further learning. At this point, ask the whole group if any objectives can be combined or reworded to be more inclusive. Figure 3.5 is an example of a final, reworded list.

Although the staff has narrowed the curriculum to focus on a small number of learning objectives, some teachers will still be concerned about lack of time. At this point, you may want to remind them that portfolios combine instruction and assessment into the same activities. Students will be spending less time testing and more time learning.

The nature of portfolio assessment lends itself to capitalizing upon assessment opportunities inherent in the classroom. Rather than gathering new data to assess attainment of a goal, teachers need to recognize how to use information generated by daily instruction. Instructional time consists

---

A GOOD COMMUNICATOR

- Understands and makes him/herself understood
- Conveys information clearly and concisely
- Communicates effectively for a variety of purposes
- Communicates in different mediums
- Expresses his/her needs, desires, and opinions
- Accesses tools, information, and strategies from a variety of resources
- Communicates effectively with diverse audiences

Figure 3.5.

of involving students in tasks that require complex thinking, planning, and evaluating. Assessment time involves solving the problem, making good decisions, and explaining the results. Assessment activities and instruction are integrated into one task (Valencia, 1990).

For example, a student might select a composition written in English class as an illustration of her competence in communication skills. The composition was part of the regular class assignments. From these assignments, each student may be asked to choose one example to place into her portfolio to be used as evidence of her ability to meet the standards of written English. The only additional class time required for portfolio assessment is the time needed for students to look through their compositions, decide which ones are their best work, tell why they believe they are good, and place them into portfolios. The entire process takes less time away from instruction than writing a separate composition on Fridays to be used to give grades to students.

A series of photographs showing steps in developing science or social studies projects, combined with a self-assessment piece and teacher feedback, is another example of entries into portfolios that can be used for assessment. Rather than adding to the curriculum, teachers are being asked to view instruction and assessment within the same activity.

You may need to remind teachers that the purpose of this staff development session is to identify what skills, concepts, and attitudes to assess. In Chapter 4, you will find numerous assessment options to use. Instead of dwelling on how to measure what students have learned, it is essential to keep the staff focused on what to measure. It is sufficient to reassure them that portfolios will allow them to combine instruction and assessment. Therefore, less is better.

Reducing Barriers across Disciplines

Many of the learning goals cross disciplines. Let's go back to communication skills. Students must demonstrate communication skills in all disciplines. In math, science, social studies, physical education, music, on the playground, in the lunch room, and before and after school, students must understand and make themselves understood; convey information clearly and concisely; communicate effectively for a variety of purposes; communicate in different mediums; express their needs, desires, and opinions; assess tools, information, and strategies from a variety of resources; and communicate effectively with diverse audiences. The forms and styles of communication are different in the different settings and disciplines. Reading a social studies textbook critically calls for a different aspect of communication than encouraging a teammate to catch a fly ball. Each broad discipline has certain characteristic communication styles, thinking patterns, and understandings (Gardner & Boix-Mansilla, 1994).

A number of professional organizations such as The National Association of Elementary School Principals and Science for All Americans recommend that all curriculum be taught in an interdisciplinary, cross-connected method to facilitate connections among ideas (Ahlgren & Rutherford, 1993). Many schools base curriculum around broad themes and issues. If your school is organized around themes or issues, it will be easier to assess the various aspects of each learning goal. If you lead a school that is subject-centered, with coordination, you can still obtain portfolio entries that illustrate the various objectives of each learning goal.

Your staff, as a group, can decide who will be responsible for assessing each learning objective of communication skills. Perhaps, the staff will divide the goal across disciplines, with each teacher contributing one portfolio entry. For example, the English teacher could require one example of conveying information clearly and concisely. The science or social studies teacher can have students access tools, information, and strategies from a variety of resources. The band, music, drama, debate, or student government teacher/sponsor can require one example of communicating effectively for a variety of purposes. The homeroom or advisor/advisee teacher could add an entry that illustrates expressing his/her needs, desires, and opinions. Together, the entries show the student's ability to understand and make him/herself understood in different mediums. Assessment across disciplines is more comprehensive than the same number of entries taken in one class.

Not everything can or should be assessed across all disciplines (Ellis and Fouts, 1993). At the K–12 levels, the goal of displaying innovative and creative ideas and activities lends itself to being assessed more easily in social studies, language arts, and the arts than in mathematics and science. You may not want to reward creative multiplication. However, creative approaches to solving a situational math problem might be appropriate. Common sense should prevail.

The process of deciding what knowledge, skills, and attitudes to assess forces teachers to talk across disciplines and grade levels. Reduction of barriers is essential to understanding the various objectives of each learning goal.

STAFF DEVELOPMENT SESSION 2: CHOOSING EVIDENCE TO EVALUATE

By this session, you should have a list of the knowledge, skills, and attitudes that define your learning goals. These components of the learning goals are the learning objectives. This session involves designing tasks that assess the learning objectives. The performance tasks may take a variety of forms. They can be short test-like tasks to assess specific knowledge and skills or lengthy, complex tasks to assess broad knowledge, processes, and attitudes (Hart, 1994). There is no right way to assess students (Herman et al., 1992; Anthony et al., 1991).

Matching Assessment to Learning Objectives

Ask your staff to create a list of ways for students to demonstrate knowledge, skills, and attitudes for one learning objective. You may want to write their suggestions on an overhead, a large flip chart, or a white board. Adhere to the rules of brainstorming by not questioning or discussing any of the ideas. Figure 3.6 is a list of ideas generated by teachers of ways to assess one learning objective of effective communication skills: "expresses ideas clearly."

Ask staff members to divide into small, interdisciplinary or grade-level groups to repeat the process for another learning goal. Assign each group a different goal. Going back to our examples, have one group brainstorm ways to assess the degree to which a student can compete and produce in

---

WAYS TO ASSESS "EXPRESSES IDEAS CLEARLY"

standardized tests

teacher constructed tests

self-assessments

check lists

observations

letter writing

story writing

written and oral reports

parental observations

illustrations

awards

publications

Figure 3.6.

a global economy. Another group will identify ways to assess the extent to which a student exercises the rights and responsibilities of citizenship. Two other groups will take the other two learning goals.

Unless you have a very small staff, you will want to divide the groups into subgroups, and each subgroup can be responsible for one objective. In other words, assign part of the communication group to brainstorm ways to assess "understands and makes him/herself understood." Another subgroup can do "conveys information clearly and concisely."

A word of warning: authentic assessment is, by definition, the orchestration, integration, and application of skills in meaningful contexts. We cannot become lost in assessing the mire of subskills. In doing so, we would reduce assessment to isolated skills and miss the purpose of authentic assessment (Valencia, 1990).

After brainstorming ways to assess each objective, groups or subgroups are asked to look at the list and identify assessment procedures that would be appropriate to place in portfolios. Because performance assessment requires considerable time and energy, you will want to focus on a relatively small number of assessments that measure your major learning objectives. At this point, identify assessments that would cover key elements of the objective. The procedures must yield information about students that is worth the effort and time to obtain it. Each group may go through the process for their assigned learning goal. For example, for the communication goal, the following assessment procedures could be included in a portfolio:

- photographs of demonstrations
- self-assessment
- behavioral checklists
- documented teacher and parent observations
- writing samples
- audiocassettes or videocassettes of oral reports and demonstrations
- photographs or lists of student participation in speech, debate, band, forensics, dance, student government, computers, and so on
- lists of awards recieved

Have each group display the assessments that could be placed in a portfolio. Many will overlap. As a group, your teachers can decide how many measures and which measures they will be required to collect. You will want several indicators for each objective. Usually, the more measures one has, the greater the reliability of the conclusions (Valencia, 1990). One way to increase consistency while not overwhelming teachers is to have two types of evidence—required evidence and supporting evidence.

A Good Communicator...

Student Learning Goal: Students in Franklin Schools will
Communicate effectively in written, visual, and spoken language.

A good communicator:
(Definition of student learning goal = learning objective)
- Understands and makes him/herself understood
- Conveys information clearly and concisely
- Communicates effectively for a variety of purposes
- Communicates in different mediums
- Expresses his/her needs, desires, and opinions
- Accesses tools, information, and strategies from a variety of resources
- Communicates effectively with diverse audiences

Required portfolio entries of a good communicator:
(ways to assess a good communicator)
- Photographs of demonstrations and projects
- Self-assessments
- Behavioral checklists
- Documented teacher and parent observations
- Writing samples

Supporting evidence of a good communicator:
(additional ways to indicate a good communicator)
- Audio cassettes or video cassettes of oral reports and demonstrations
- Photographs or list of student participation in speech, debate, band, forensics, dance, student government, computers, etc.
- Lists of awards received

Figure 3.7.

Required and Supporting Evidence

Required evidence consists of structured activities or checklists that are required of all students at a grade level or in a program, such as all first graders reading into an audiotape at the beginning and end of first grade or all ninth-grade English students selecting their best piece of writing from each marking period to include in their portfolio. Some authors refer to this type of portfolio as "indicator systems" (Arter, 1990). A list of various types of measures or indicators is required, such as attitude surveys, number of books read, writing samples, norm-referenced test scores, and teacher checklists. This type of assessment enables administrators to evaluate programs and curriculum, as well as being for teachers to make comparisons among students.

Supporting evidence is additional documentation selected either by the student, teacher, or parent to add to the portfolio. It allows for individualization, uniqueness, and depth that is typically missing in traditional assessments. Information from supporting evidence is not used to make comparisons of programs, grade levels, or students. Rather, it is an opportunity to learn more about individuals (Valencia, 1990). Supporting evidence can include awards, the development of a project such as examples of ongoing work with all drafts, and comparisons of recent work with an earlier effort. Supporting evidence ensures a variety of indicators of learning and offers a more complete picture of a student's development.

Your staff has now identified student learning goals that are based on the community's vision of what students should know, defined the goals in the form of learning objectives, and identified ways to assess the objectives in portfolios. Figure 3.7 is an example of what a staff has done with one strand of the goal, "Students in Franklin Schools will communicate effectively in written, visual, and spoken language."

STAFF DEVELOPMENT SESSION 3: CREATING PERFORMANCE STANDARDS

During this staff development session, teachers will explicitly define the standards to judge portfolio entries. By establishing standards, portfolios can be standard setting, rather than a standardized assessment tool (Hart, 1994). Creating performance standards involves building a common understanding of the expectations and criteria that indicate progress toward attainment of the learning goals.

Authentic assessment has raised concerns about unreliability, inconsistency, and inequity across classrooms, schools, and districts. By creating performance standards, consistency of scores can improve (Valencia, 1990; Hart, 1994). Performance standards will enable your staff to clearly describe what constitutes excellent, good, average, and poor work for their students. Also, you will want to collect several entries for any particular goal. Usually, the more measures one has, the greater is the reliability of the conclusions. Sufficient data exist in most classrooms to provide reliable assessment.

In an effort to improve consistency across classrooms, new scoring tools and methods are being developed to assess performance standards (Hart, 1994). Two tools that can be used are benchmarks and scoring rubrics. Benchmarks specify the tasks, attitudes, and applications that are expected along the way toward attainment of a learning goal. They define quality work for a given grade level. A rubric is a set of observable criteria used to rate students' work. The scoring rubric assigns a value that describes the level of performance within a grade level. Rubrics guide us to look for certain criteria or indicators of student learning.

In the first staff development session, your staff defined their learning goals. The next session dealt with identifying ways to demonstrate each goal. During this session, they will establish criteria of growth toward the goals. Figure 3.8 illustrates the steps. Clear expectations of student achievement are essential if students, teachers, administrators, and parents are to work toward the learning goals.

Benchmarks for Attaining Learning Goals

Benchmarks are used to determine progress toward the learning goals. They are markers or informal norms developed to assess how far along a

---

Steps in Establishing Performance Standards

Learning Goals = Student outcomes

Learning Objectives = Essential skills, concepts, and attitudes to attain the learning goal

Performance Tasks = Evidence to assess the learning objectives

Performance Standards = Benchmarks and rubrics

Benchmarks = Progress toward the goals

Rubrics = Observable criteria for evaluating students' work

Figure 3.8.

FORMING BENCHMARKS

- Begin with the learning objectives from session one.
- Describe the performance of experts in the discipline.
- Define the types of problems experts can solve.
- Show samples of excellent student work.
- Identify the developing characteristics of outstanding samples of primary, intermediate, middle school, and secondary students' work.

Figure 3.9.

student is toward attainment of the learning goals. In the example of effective communication, a first grader who "clearly and effectively communicates the main idea or theme and provides support that contains rich, vivid, and powerful detail" is not the same as a senior in high school who is expressing ideas. Similarly, a high school student's ability to effectively communicate in a variety of ways will not be the same as that of a primary student. Benchmarks are samples of student work that illustrate common expectations of children's, preadolescents', adolescents', and adults' abilities to communicate. Benchmarks are based on standards in the discipline. They reflect an absolute standard or mastery approach that describes attainment of learning goals (Herman et al., 1992).

For this session, you will need to bring examples of experts' work for each discipline and samples of student work from your school. The process involves establishing a clear understanding of desired performance levels for each goal. Show your staff how the discipline defines quality performance. What behaviors are important in the discipline? In reading, students are expected to comprehend what they are reading, know the meaning or words, retell stories, read for information, recognize the purpose of the author, and others. Benchmarks describe the development of these behaviors. Figure 3.9 lists the steps in forming benchmarks. These characteristics of outstanding primary, intermediate, middle school, and secondary students' work are the benchmarks of progress. Other work will be judged against these benchmarks. Have your staff bring samples of their students' work and identify the developing characteristics in the samples. It is important to spend time discussing each characteristic to arrive at a common understanding of the benchmarks.

Criteria for Attaining Outcomes

When your staff can identify and apply benchmarks, you are ready to begin defining criteria to use to evaluate student performance. Figure 3.10 is an overview of the steps involved in establishing criteria. It does not matter whether or not you will "grade" portfolios. Grading will be discussed in Chapter 7. At this time, it is important to identify specific behaviors that indicate degrees of student progress.

Gather sample criteria from state and local assessments and from curriculum experts who have developed models. Lists of criteria standards are readily available and can usually be adapted for your school. Several national groups have developed standards for their disciplines, such as the National Science Foundation, the National Mathematics Foundation, and the National Reading Association. Some states have rating forms of standards in math and language arts. The Vermont mathematics portfolio is one of the best known samples of portfolio assessment criteria. Many school districts have developed criteria for their student learning objectives. We recommend gathering samples and tailoring them to match local needs.

Bring samples of students' work that demonstrates the range of performance within your school. Ask each teacher to bring samples from their best, average, and struggling students.

ESTABLISHING CRITERIA

- Define what important behaviors exist in each benchmark.
- Identify the criteria used by other assessment models.
- Examine samples of students' work to determine the range of performances.
- Form descriptors for the important characteristics.
- Select samples of student work that reflect the criteria.
- Practice applying the descriptors to determine if the criteria are correct.
- Revise criteria.
- Practice applying the descriptors until everyone agrees on the interpretations.

Figure 3.10.

Write clear descriptors of the important characteristics. Rubrics, a popular buzzword, are descriptors of behaviors that demonstrate attainment of an important characteristic. To be usable, these rubrics must be clear descriptors of observable behaviors. For example, reading is one form of effective communication. Some behaviors that would indicate a youngster is becoming a beginning reader would be, "holds the book properly, turns pages left to right, points to beginning or end of story, and points to front and back cover (Midland Public Schools, 1994).

Practice applying the descriptors to more samples of student work. Are the rubrics usable? Do they clearly define the progress toward an objective, encompass the range of student work, and differentiate between students (a practical guide to alternative assessment)?

To be useful, rubrics must have the following characteristics. A rubric must

- communicate clearly the desired standard of achievement
- describe specific and observable behavior
- create a logical progression toward an objective
- reduce the likelihood of inaccurate scoring
- help students know in what ways they can improve
- be usable for the entire school year to show improvement over time

Revise your descriptors. Rarely, if ever, are the rubrics clear and usable on the first, or even second, draft. The key is to have carefully selected words with a common meaning.

A combination of clear rubrics and examples of student work further reduces ambiguity. Providing samples of student work that illustrate the criteria is a concrete way to reduce subjectivity. This is often done in writing assessments. Teachers are given copies of student essays that exemplify each rubric (Herman et al., 1992). The essays illustrate criteria such as, "the essay is logically organized; it has a clear statement of purpose." Teachers, students, and parents can better understand these rubrics if they have samples that typify each criteria.

Practice applying the descriptors until everyone agrees on the interpretations. Teachers need time to practice this in a group setting where they can discuss each descriptor or rubric, argue about how to apply it, and arrive at a common understanding of the terms.

The next step is to decide what categories to use to rank the work. Scales can be descriptive or evaluative. Descriptive scales use fairly neutral terms to label student performance, for example judgements about task completion, task understanding, or the appearance of certain elements are descriptive scales.

The Midland Public Schools in Michigan used the example in Figure 3.11 of descriptive scales to score kindergarten students' performance in the learning objective, "uses language to communicate thoughts, ideas, feelings, and experiences."

Evaluative scales judge performance and competence based on an underlying standard of excellence. Grades are the most common example of evaluative scales. Descriptors such as, "excellent, good, minimal" are evaluative. The California Department of Education (1989) uses the following scale to score statewide essay-type mathematics problems:

Exemplary Response   Rating = 6
Competent Response   Rating = 5
Minor Flaws but Satisfactory   Rating = 4
Serious Flaws but Nearly Satisfactory   Rating = 3
Begins but Fails to Complete Problem   Rating = 2
Unable to Begin Effectively   Rating = 1
No Attempt   Rating = 0

Your staff will also have to decide on the number of categories they want to use to differentiate among students. Many schools use three categories such as outstanding, average, and poor, while others prefer a four-level rating scale of achievement such as superior, adequate, minimal, or inadequate. Some schools use the categories of applied the knowledge, understood, partially understood, or misunderstood. A few, such as the

---

MIDLAND PUBLIC SCHOOLS
Kindergarten Assessment

Uses language to communicate thoughts, ideas, feelings, and experiences.

Not Yet	Developing	Achieving
Speaks in one or two word combinations.	Speaks in phrases and short sentences.	Speaks fluently using sentences.
Has limited vacabulary.	Often omits descriptions.	Uses details and descriptive words in verbal communication.
Does not use oral language to express self.		

Figure 3.11.

California Department of Education in the above example, use more than a four-level scale. In general, the number of divisions on a scale depends on what decisions you will be making about students. If you want to use the assessment to show who needs additional work on the skill, who needs to continue at the normal pace, and who needs enrichment, then a three-point scale will suffice. On the other hand, if you are using the assessment to select ten students to represent a school at an "Olympics of the Mind" competition, you will want a scale that will provide more differentiation among students. In general, to save time and effort, limit the number of scale divisions to only those that are necessary.

Clearly defined criteria and scales can reduce the subjectivity of portfolio assessment. Still, unrecognized biases can slip into the definitions of criteria, the specifications for performance, and application of the criteria to individual pieces of student work (Herman et al., 1992). Care must be taken not to assess students on criteria and variables over which students have no control such as culture, sex, or socioeconomic background. Before this staff session is completed, review the criteria for ethnic, gender, and socioeconomic bias.

Holistic and Analytic Criteria

Benchmarks and rubrics can be applied in two ways—holistic scoring and analytic scoring. Holistic scoring is based on an overall impression of the student work and produces a single number. This type is often used to score large-scale assessments such as Vermont's portfolio assessments or California's assessment program where all students at a specified grade level demonstrate the same performance task. Analytic scoring is more time-consuming but yields more information. Analytic scoring measures more than one criteria in a single task. Separate scores are assigned for each criteria. Because it is more detailed than holistic scoring, it is often used for diagnostic purposes and to identify strengths and weaknesses within instructional programs (Hart, 1994).

Portfolio assessment has the distinct advantage over standardized tests of taking multiple measures over time. To be valid, the benchmarks, criteria, and scoring must represent the most relevant or useful dimensions of student work (Herman et al., 1992). The preceding staff development sessions are designed to bring differing perceptions together that when combined, formulate clear and usable ways to assess student strengths.

Many schools, districts, and consultants have developed benchmarks and rubrics for their learning objectives. The example located in Appendix B.2 might give your staff a starting point. Do not adopt performance standards without modifying them to fit your school's uniqueness. Also, it is essential that your staff go through the process of developing and applying criteria to clearly understand the meanings and practice applying the rubrics in a group setting. Otherwise, your assessments will lack reliability.

In the example in Appendix B.2, the learning goal of effective communication has been separated into five learning objectives. They are expresses ideas clearly, effectively communicates with diverse audiences, effectively communicates in a variety of ways, effectively communicates for a variety of purposes, and creates quality products. A parallel form was also created for student self-assessment. Chapter 4 provides more detail about the importance of self-assessment.

Each student learning goal will need a list of learning objectives with clear standards that describe the behavior of students who are in the process of learning. Your staff will have to develop or adapt a list for each goal. Subcommittees can work on different goals as long as the entire staff meets to practice applying the criteria. With important, clear, and usable rubrics, you will have a strong base for assessment.

TROUBLESHOOTING: AMBIGUITY VERSUS CREATIVITY

A problem you may encounter is the contradictory tug between giving teachers a template of identical assessment tasks, specific standards, and clear scoring rubrics across the school district and allowing for individual differences, a variety of ways to demonstrate students' strengths, and tailoring the portfolios to match the needs and styles of students within each class. The question is how do we balance ambiguity and allow for creativity? Teachers who are uncomfortable with ambiguity say to us, "Just tell us what to put in them with the assessment tasks and give us a key to score them." If you do this, you will lose the richness that comes from teachers discovering their own way.

Assure your staff that there is not one right way to develop portfolios and that the staff will continue to meet regularly to discuss portfolios after implementation begins. You are not leaving them on their own without continual assistance. Support teams, mentoring, and staff development will be ongoing.

Creativity involves risk taking, failures, persistence, and adjustments. You should expect some teachers to feel more confident and therefore take more risks than others.

In Chapter 7, there is a section on dealing with resistance. The methods for overcoming fears about implementing portfolios can be applied when dealing with ambiguity.

GLOSSARY

Analytic Scoring: measures of more than one criteria in a single task. Separate scores are obtained for each criteria.

Benchmarks: markers or informal norms to assess how far along a student is toward attainment of a learning goal. They are based on standards in the discipline.

Descriptive Scales: categories to describe task completion, task understanding, or the appearance of certain elements that are characteristic in attainment of a learning objective.

Evaluating Scales: categories used to judge performance and competence based on an underlying standard of excellence.

Holistic Scoring: a single score that is based on an overall impression of the student's work.

Learning Goals: the concepts, academic skills, social skills, and attitudes that stakeholders want students to know by the time they graduate. They are sometimes referred to as broad student outcomes.

Performance Standards: the expectations and criteria that indicate progress towards attainment of learning goals. Benchmarks and rubrics are part of performance standards.

Reliability: the degree to which the same results repeat themselves over time. In evaluative authentic assessment, it is the consistency in judging student work.

Required Evidence: structured activities or checklists that all students at a grade level or in a program must enter into their portfolios.

Rubric: a set of observable criteria or indicators used to rate students' work. Descriptors of observable behaviors.

Scoring Rubric: a value that describes the level of performance within a learning objective. Indicators of degrees of student progress.

Supporting Evidence: documentation selected either by the student, teacher, or parent to place in the portfolio to add individualization, uniqueness, and depth. It is used to learn more about individuals.

ENDNOTE

1. We learned the Three-Way Rotation from K. Hugh Rohrer who is a professor at Central Michigan University. It is an effective technique to arrive at consensus in a relatively short time. We have used it in many different situations.

PART TWO

CONSTRUCTING

*Constructing is the actual implementation of portfolios. This section con-
tains practical advice for using a variety of tools, self-reflection activities,
and types of portfolios commonly found in schools.*

CHAPTER 4

Clarifying the Role of Self-Assessment

Mrs. Norwood's Self-Reflections

Amazing as it seems to me now, I once truly believed that it was my job to fill those empty heads and use worksheets for assessment. I am proud to say, I have a new perspective of myself and how children learn. I have learned how to celebrate knowledge. Now I learn from my students. I encourage them to challenge themselves and measure their own growth. I have become a facilitator of learning. I no longer limit their capacities to learn. I am no longer the keeper of knowledge. I no longer believe in one correct process or answer. I know that it was my head that needed filling. I will continue to assess myself through "kid watching," education, and interactions with my peers.

Miss Hafner's Goals

As a teacher, I want the best learning environment I can create for my students. To do this, I need to read the research that is out there about how children learn and how to best assess it. Then I need to create that environment in my classroom. By creating a safe, "no risk" environment for students and allowing them to become part of both learning and assessment, I am hoping to encourage learners to take chances while learning about the world around them. We must allow time for children to explore and practice skills for lifelong learning. We must also provide a safe atmosphere for their explorations so they are willing to take risks needed to grow. Only then will they love learning for its own sake. The secret lies in respecting and supporting each learner we touch. Someone once said, "A bird does not sing because it has an answer; it sings because it has a song." I hope that, through my own searching, changing, and growing, I can let the students that I teach sing their own songs.

INTRODUCTION

THROUGH their reflections about their own teaching and assessment, teachers are coming to know that they are learners in their beliefs about teaching, their instructional decisions, and their use of assessment. The focus of this chapter is the importance of self-assessment by students, teachers, and administrators. We examine ways to assist learners in documenting, assessing, and reflecting on their learning and conclude with an exploration of problems, issues, and concerns that may arise when educators and students begin to assess themselves as learners.

TRADITIONAL EVALUATION

Administrators, teachers, and students have often overlooked the value of teaching learners how to determine the worth of their own efforts. At all levels of education, the merit of student input into evaluating learning has been largely ignored. Graves (1991) asserts that "with each successive year, from kindergarten through high school, students participate less and less in evaluating their own work" (p. 3). Assessment has often been something done to them and students have become experts at playing the game of providing teachers with what was expected of them (Tierney et al., 1991; Graves, 1991; Anthony et al., 1991). Their questions frequently seek specific information about teacher's criteria for grading assignments, such as

- How many pages does it have to be?
- Can it be double-spaced?
- Do I have to type it?
- Does spelling count?
- What do I need to get an A?
- What is good enough to pass?

Many educators, especially those who have not participated in self-assessment practices, frequently question whether students are capable of honest or critical self-assessment.[1] Others contend that even young children are natural evaluators (Ministry of Education, 1988; Anthony et al., 1991; Froese, 1991; Fullan, 1991; Graves, 1991; Hettershiedt et al., 1992; Kohn, 1993; Dudley-Marling, 1995).

STUDENTS' CAPACITY FOR CRITICAL SELF-EVALUATION

Both researchers and practitioners who do involve students in self-assessment techniques find that students are not only capable of critical, perceptive, thoughtful self-evaluations, but are also highly conscientious and frank in assessments of their learning products and processes (Rief, 1990; Tierney et al., 1991; Gordon, 1992; Kitagawa, 1992; Hill & Ruptic, 1994; Dudley-Marling & Searle, 1995). After all, the students did the work and are the experts on themselves. Learners who are familiar with self-evaluation usually assess themselves accurately and are more likely to find fault with their performance than administrators, teachers, peers, or their parents. In addition, assessment of oneself has far more meaning and impact than the same evaluation by others (Wilson, 1992; Pigdon & Woolley, 1993). Fu (1991) provided the following example to demonstrate information that can be gathered from students' knowledge of their learning in her reflections about one bilingual child's self-assessment:

> Xiao-di's self-assessment shows that he knows when he has really learned and when he has not. He knows what he cannot do, what he has learned to do, and what he wants to improve. He has a sense of his past, his present, and his future. When others assess his work, no matter from what perspective, they would miss the perspective that Xiao-di sees himself as a learner. (p. 182)

When Bruce Kutney (1993) has his seniors develop their essays about world literature, he does not accept any final revisions unless students include another piece of writing on the title page. This extra piece must not only tell him which specific parts were revised, but must also explain exactly what was done to improve them. He finds that this forces his students to clarify what they are doing while they are doing it. Two of the student efforts that he shared are as follows:

> I rewrote the top section of page three because my point was unclear. In paragraph three I better explained status quo and true punishment by replacing them with similar phrases that are more clear. At the end of paragraph four I added a statement that explained why criminals should be forced to live rather than be executed. My final major edit was to rewrite the top of page 8. I explained my point about the law being flawed by telling how I think human error messes up interpretation of the law. (p. 64)

> The first place I had to make revisions was in my introductory paragraph. The first sentence was a bit wordy and was in passive voice. I changed it so it was in active voice. Also in this paragraph my thesis wasn't clearly stated. I changed it so it expressed my opinion that justice is unattainable. I the second paragraph I used the example of mercy killing and how Gilbert didn't receive justice. I didn't give a strong enough argument as to why he didn't. I strengthened this by adding more ideas from the text. Then when I went on to talk about Mersault I again did not give enough support to show that he did not receive justice either. I again added some ideas from the text. By adding more examples I feel that this strengthened the argument that they did not receive justice. (pp. 64–65)

As Mr. Kutney (1993) analyzed students' self-assessments of their essays, he found that they were actively involved in their writing through making both revision and editing changes. An equally important commonality was that these students made changes based on the content of their writing in response to texts they had read and not on some formula for responding to writing rules.[2] We agree with Mr. Kutney that these examples indicate a kind of thoughtfulness and self-assessment that we would like students to be able to do more and more often.

Just as Mrs. Norwood, Miss Hafner, Ms. Fu, Mr. Kutney, and other teachers in many school communities use assessment as an integral part of their teaching and learning, self-evaluation is a natural part of student learning. Children will engage in evaluation with or without help from others; therefore, it is imperative that our school communities assist and respect learners in their efforts to personalize assessment to meet educational and personal needs (Reardon, 1991; Kohn, 1993; Campbell et al., 1994; Dudley-Marling & Searle, 1995).

THE CRUCIAL ROLE OF SELF-ASSESSMENTS

Authorities in the field of portfolio assessment agree that self-assessment must be one of the underlying foundations of portfolio implementation (Arter, 1990; Harp, 1991; Tierney et al., 1991; Glazer & Brown, 1993; Hill & Ruptic, 1994; Valencia et al., 1994; Hewitt, 1995). *Without student self-assessment, portfolios become merely another storage area for student work.* Instead, students are actively involved as they organize their portfolios, select and arrange contents, provide rationales to accompany their selections, reflect upon what they have learned, create goals for future work, and share their accomplishments with others.

Kohn (1993) maintains that having students help determine the criteria for judging their work and then self-assessing that work on those standards accomplishes several goals. Students are given more control over their learnng and education. It makes assessment and evaluation seem less punitive. Students are provided with significant benefits from thinking about learning experiences themselves. Even more traditional approaches to testing can be improved by consulting students about what the test should measure, when it should be given, and under what conditions. In a democratic society, there is really no reason why schools or teachers need to make these decisions for students.

CLARIFYING SELF-EXAMINATION TERMS

Many authors of portfolio literature use the terms self-assessment, self-evaluation, and self-reflection interchangeably; however, Hill and Ruptic (1994) maintain that these are separate, but interwoven, processes. They view self-assessment as having learners examine both the processes and products of their learning. Sample questions that encourage students to use self-assessment include

- How do I learn best?
- What works for me when I study problem solving in math?
- What social studies concepts are still hard for me to grasp?
- What is getting easier for me in the writing process?
- What strategies work best for me when I am reading my science text?
- What can I do to remember what I have learned?
- How am I part of the group?
- What am I doing to contribute to the group?

Self-evaluation involves more appraisal of learning and occurs more often at the end of projects, grading periods, or terms. Students are frequently asked to make judgements about how well they are performing. Sample questions that encourage self-evaluation include

- How did I do on my science project?
- Did I learn what I need to know about cultural diversity through this social studies unit?
- How have I changed as a math student this year?
- In what areas do I still need to do more work?
- What do I do well?
- What can I do when I come to words that I don't know how to spell?
- What do I do when I am having trouble understanding what I am reading?
- How does this project demonstrate what I have learned?

Self-reflection encompasses the widest array of introspection. During self-reflection, students examine not only the products and processes of their learning, but also their emotions and thoughts about what they are learning. They need to explore not only what and how they are learning, but also why they are learning it (Kohn, 1993; Hill & Ruptic, 1994). Sample questions that encourage self-reflection include

- What did I enjoy learning the most when we studied the environment of the rain forest?
- How do I feel about what I learned about prejudice when we read about Martin Luther King, Jr.? Why do I feel this way?
- What types of books am I interested in reading next?

- What have I learned about myself as a problem solver?
- What is my favorite piece of writing?
- Why do I like this piece of writing the best?
- What are my reading interests outside of school?
- Why did I choose this topic to write about?
- How can I reach my reading goals for this semester?

Whether you and your teachers choose to consolidate these three areas of self-examination or deal with them separately, the information gained by questions similar to these can be invaluable in understanding student learning. When students examine their learning, they are actively involved and less likely to view education as something done to them. They are more apt to value learning as something they will be engaged in for the rest of their lives.

FOSTERING INDEPENDENT, LIFELONG LEARNERS

If one of our goals as administrators is to assist students in becoming independent, lifelong learners, then students must become decision makers. Students must not only be involved in assessment to learn criteria for developing sound judgements, but must also be responsible for self-assessment to develop ownership of what they learn (Caine & Caine, 1991; Froese, 1991; Kohn, 1993; Dudley-Marling & Searle, 1995). One way to assist students in gaining ownership of learning is through discussions of reasons and criteria for assessment.

If another ultimate goal is to assist our students in becoming adults who think critically, make wise choices, and know the criteria that they used to reach their decisions, then students must be provided with numerous opportunities to evaluate themselves at all grade levels. Students need to be encouraged to monitor, reflect upon, assess, and evaluate their own achievements, learning strategies, progress, products, and efforts (Tierney et al., 1991; Y. Goodman, 1992; Glazer & Brown, 1993; Armstrong, 1994; Dudley-Marling & Searle, 1995). As Kohn (1993) maintains, there is a positive relationship between having children critically examine their progress and teaching them how to learn.

In Sara Kraley's kindergarten classroom, students were asked to complete the self-evaluation form found in Figure 4.1. They could use invented spellings and drawings, or they could dictate their responses to her. This form was used after the class had completed a six-week thematic unit about the zoo. Mrs. Kraley found that her kindergartners could easily communicate what they had learned. These young students knew what their best

KINDERGARTEN SELF-EVALUATION FORM FOR THEMATIC UNITS

Unit: _____The Zoo_____

Name:_____ Date:_____

I learned:

I made:

I wrote:

I read:

The best part was:

My best work was:

Figure 4.1.

work was and had definite opinions about the best parts of the unit. Through their self-assessments, she was able to form a better picture of what they remembered about the unit and which lessons had the most impact on them.

You may wish to expose your teachers to forms such as those found in Appendix C. The form in Appendix C.1 can be used to discover strategies that students use to learn concepts related to a topic. This form asks students to identify which content area reading strategies they use. These strategies would be helpful in learning from reading materials in any curricular area because good readers apply reading strategies before, during, and after reading subject matter content. The form in Appendix C.2 can assist primary teachers in examining student attitudes about learning and school. Appendix C.3 provides an example of a form designed to encourage learners to share their reflections about what they learned from completing an assignment, project, or other work in any area of the curriculum.

DEVELOPING STUDENT OWNERSHIP AND GOAL SETTING

When principals encourage teachers to stress self-evaluation in their classrooms, students can experience ownership of their learning. Figure 4.2 provides an example of one way to help students take ownership of assessment of their learning through choices in how they will demonstrate what they have learned. This form can be modified with less choices for lower grades, teachers who are just beginning to provide students with shared responsibility in control of learning, or when students are first beginning to make choices. Sometimes, too many choices are overwhelming at the beginning for teachers and/or students. As both teachers and students become more comfortable with alternative ways to measure learning outcomes, more choices can be added to the form. Older students may be able to use a wider array of assessment options. Some options that could be added for students in intermediate grades through secondary school are

- doing a photo essay
- putting on a demonstration
- creating a statistical chart
- developing an interactive computer presentation
- engaging in a debate
- producing a videotape
- developing a musical
- making a mind map
- choreographing a dance

```
┌─────────────────────────────────────────────────────────────┐
│        CELEBRATING LEARNING THROUGH STUDENT CHOICES           │
│  To show that I know_____, I would like to:│
│                                                               │
│  _____ Draw a picture                                       │
│  _____ Write a report                                       │
│  _____ Make a scrapbook                                     │
│  _____ Build a model                                        │
│  _____ Do a play                                            │
│  _____ Create a group project                               │
│  _____ Make a chart or graph                                │
│  _____ Keep a journal                                       │
│  _____ Interview others                                     │
│  _____ Make a mural                                         │
│  _____ Do an oral report                                    │
│  _____ Set up an experiment                                 │
│  _____ Lead a class discussion                              │
│  _____ Create a rap or song                                 │
│  _____ Teach it to someone else                             │
│  _____ Make a semantic map                                  │
│  _____ Do a project not on the list: _____      │
│  How I plan to do this:                                       │
│                                                               │
│                                                               │
│                                                               │
│                                                               │
│  Student _____Date_____.         │
│  Teacher_____Date_____           │
└─────────────────────────────────────────────────────────────┘
```

Adapted from: Armstrong, T. 1994. *Multiple Intelligences in the Classroom.* Alexandria, VA: Association for Supervision and Curriculum Development, p. 125.

Figure 4.2.

- making a data retrieval chart
- using a venn diagram to compare and contrast information
- creating a time line of events

Another way to help develop student ownership is through contracts where projects and assessments are negotiated between teachers and students. Janice Huffman uses a contract for her seventh- and eighth-grade students' picture books in her English course. Students then assess themselves on how well they have followed their contract, and she assesses their drafts and final products. One student's contract is provided as an example in Appendix C.4.

Jane Shippee's fourth graders chose to evaluate their letters to their favorite authors by developing a rubric. Before they began writing their letters, they brainstormed as a class what would be an acceptable letter, what would be an outstanding letter, and what type of letter would need more work. Their rubric for writing a friendly letter is provided in Figure 4.3. When the students wanted to have commas and indented paragraphs as part of the criteria for outstanding letters, Miss Shippee commented that they had not yet studied commas or indenting paragraphs. The class reminded her that they were creating criteria for an *outstanding* letter, and they strongly felt that these were standards for an outstanding letter. They were also sure that the highest quality letters should also meet all the criteria for an acceptable letter. It was clear that these students have an understanding of quality work. Many of them chose to include a copy of their letter and its graded rubric in their portfolios.

Once students have a sense of ownership of learning, they are more likely to value education, to set realistic academic and personal goals, and to work toward accomplishing those goals. Self-reflection, self-assessment, and self-evaluation are all forms of metacognition, which assists students in developing a better understanding and awareness of themselves as learners, which, in turn, enables them to set attainable goals. The self-evaluation form in Appendix C.5 could be used by students after they have read a book and completed one or more responses to the literature. On this form, learners are asked to reflect upon what they have learned, their strengths and weaknesses, and their goals for future readings.

The form in Figure 4.4 was used in a middle school mathematics classroom but can easily be adapted for use in intermediate elementary grades or in more advanced mathematics courses. This form provides information about learner's perceptions of themselves as mathematics students. They are asked for preferences, their assessments of their strengths and weaknesses, and their goals. The teacher has the opportunity to discover what is important to each student.

RUBRIC FOR WRITING A FRIENDLY LETTER

Name_____ Date_____

Letter: Favorite Author

Level 3   Paragraphs are indented

Spelling is correct

Commas come after day in date, in greeting and in closing

All the criteria from Level 2 have been met

Level 2   Paper has margins.

Capitals are at beginning of sentences, dates, names, and
important places.

Letter has five parts: date, greeting, body, closing, and name.

Sentences are clear.

Level 1   Work is sloppy

There are missing capitals and periods

Capitals are misused

Maybe some sentences are not clear

Figure 4.3.

```
┌─────────────────────────────────────────────────────────────┐
│        MIDDLE SCHOOL MATHEMATICS SELF-EVALUATION SHEET        │
│  Name_____Date_____   │
│  How do you feel about yourself as a math student?            │
│                                                               │
│                                                               │
│  What areas of math do you enjoy the most? Why?               │
│                                                               │
│                                                               │
│  What areas of math do you enjoy the least? Why?              │
│                                                               │
│                                                               │
│  What do you believe are strengths as a math student?         │
│                                                               │
│                                                               │
│  What are your weak areas in math?                            │
│                                                               │
│                                                               │
│  What goals will you set for yourself as a math student?      │
│                                                               │
│                                                               │
└─────────────────────────────────────────────────────────────┘
```

Figure 4.4.

Rita Kirby developed the form in Appendix C.6 to assist high school students in establishing concrete goals that they could accomplish during a marking period. On this form, students not only list their goals, but also explain how they will attempt to accomplish them and how they will measure whether the goal was achieved. As students attempt to reach their goals, positive changes occur. As their efforts are recognized by principals, teachers, parents, and peers, evaluation becomes meaningful and can be used as an instructional tool, and students become aware that their opinions and contributions to the assessment process are valued by the school community (Fullan, 1991; Ching & Slaughter, 1992; Kohn, 1993; Valencia et al., 1994; Dudley-Marling & Searle, 1995). As Wilson (1992) notes: "We show children our values by the way we respond to what they write. If they are to be honest and to feel free to criticize in their written evaluations, they must trust their teachers and know that their responses will be taken seriously" (p. 67).

FACILITATING STUDENT KNOWLEDGE OF THEIR LEARNING

When schools provide students with numerous opportunities to reflect upon and evaluate themselves, they develop skills that allow them to come to terms with their learning styles, abilities, skills, strategies, strengths, and needs (Baskwill & Whitman, 1988; Tierney et al., 1991; Gordon, 1992; Harp, 1993; Hill & Ruptic, 1994). Because self-assessment in portfolios is not arbitrary in creation or implementation, it becomes part of the everyday life of classrooms and is reality-based.[3]

A middle school science teacher discovered that one of her inclusion students not only knew his best learning style, but also knew how to use this knowledge to his advantage even though he has multiple disabilities, including being legally blind, having cerebral palsy, and needing a brain shunt. When the teacher administered a learning styles preference test to her classes, Matt's responses indicated a strong auditory learning style. After the first test of the semester, Mrs. Hook had her students write a response, explaining how they felt they had done on the test, what they had done to study for it, and what self-evaluation meant to them. Many students predicted inflated test scores, reported studying alone, and had studied the wrong materials. One girl thought self-evaluation was a type of punishment or a grade. However, Matt not only accurately defined self-evaluation, but also explained that he had studied for the test through listening to tapes of the chapter, typing on the computer, having his parents read to him, and reciting materials back to them. He knew what worked best for him, and his teacher gained insights into his learning also.

WEEKLY EVALUATION

Name_____Topic _____ Date___/___/___

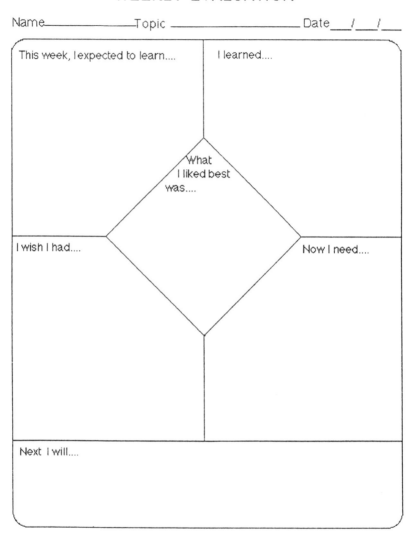

Figure 4.5.

Through self-assessments, portfolios provide students with a means of identifying patterns in their learning growth during the school year and throughout their academic careers (Baskwill & Whitman, 1988; DeFina, 1992; Short & Kauffman, 1992; Hill & Ruptic, 1994). One way to monitor progress over long periods of time is to involve students in self-assessments from the time they enter school. They can then reread their portfolio entries to gain a perspective of their growth and knowledge of their learning (Wilson, 1992; Hansen, 1994; Valencia & Place, 1994). The form in Appendix C.7 can provide primary teachers with students' insights into strengths, weaknesses, and views of themselves as readers and writers.

Many teachers use a weekly review to gauge how well students have learned concepts in a particular subject or in general. The form in Figure 4.5 is one that a fifth-grade teacher used during a social studies unit about Native Americans of the southwestern United States. This form provides information about students' knowledge about the topic, what each student felt was important, any misconceptions developed, areas of interest, topics needing further explanation, and goals for further learning. Students often chose to place this form in their portfolios to demonstrate growth over the course of the unit.

ENCOURAGING STUDENT RESPONSIBILITY

Your school community can encourage students to take responsibility for their learning by expecting them to participate in assessing themselves. Students who have taken responsibility for their learning realize that what they accomplish in school and in the world beyond the school doors is determined by what they choose to learn. This can only happen in schools that have an atmosphere where students are invited to become increasingly involved in learning through activities such as selecting topics for reading, planning themes and projects in various subject areas, choosing topics for writing, and evaluating their own efforts in ways that are purposeful to them (Tierney et al., 1991; Dudley-Marling & Searle, 1995). When others do all the evaluations, students often feel they have nothing to do with why or how they got a specific grade (Graves, 1991). However, when they participate from the start in creating the assessment measures, criteria, and standards that will be used as guidelines, the evaluations belong to them as well as to teachers and administrators (Weaver, 1994).

One of the ways that Jan Eversole's fifth graders are involved in developing criteria for their projects is through creating rubrics together. Through these rubrics, students have a voice in how their projects will be evaluated and know what standards will be applied to them. They are then responsible for part of their evaluation through using the rubric to self-assess and through turning it in with the project. The form could later be placed in their portfolios to demonstrate their accomplishments. Figure 4.6 is a rubric that the class developed to assess their character mobiles after reading *The Lion, the Witch, and the Wardrobe.* Appendix C.8 contains a form that the class developed to examine the process of completing projects.

Rita Kirby created the form in Appendix C.9 to assist senior high students in demonstrating their personal management skills of responsibility,

SELF—EVALUATION

Name	Date
Project Name	

	low		med		high
I used my work time wisely:	1	2	3	4	5
My project is neatly done:	1	2	3	4	5
I followed directions:	1	2	3	4	5
Overall appearance of my project:	1	2	3	4	5
Total points earned: (add all four scores together)					
Percentage: (Divide total points by 4)					%
Comments:					

Figure 4.6.

organization, flexibility, and career development in the area of knowing personal strengths and weaknesses. The form provides a place for students to record what they have done to indicate responsibility in learning and gives them guidelines for what responsible behavior in learning involves.

ESTABLISHING PREREQUISITES FOR SELF-ASSESSMENTS

Whenever students take ownership of an activity, they will usually spend more effort on completing the task to the best of their ability. Therefore, it is reasonable to give students a major role in compiling and evaluating their own work to place in portfolios. However, it is unreasonable to simply assign the task without telling them why it should be done and how to do it, as often happens when portfolios are mandated (Anthony et al., 1991; DeFina, 1992; Y. Goodman, 1992). Self-reflection will not flourish without the understanding and nurturing of classroom teachers and their administrators. Before students can take more responsibility for their learning and assessments, teachers must release some of the control over decision making about both instruction and assessment so that students will be willing to risk accepting more responsibility for learning. This will not happen unless teachers are willing to accept a certain amount of ambiguity in the beginning of implementing portfolios. Teachers are more willing to take these risks when they feel that their principal supports and encourages them to do so. Before portfolios can be used as a means of self-assessment, our school communities must provide for student ownership, student-centered classrooms, a noncompetitive atmosphere, and portfolios that are customized to meet the needs of all your community's stakeholders (Tierney et al., 1991). Principals who are knowledgeable and supportive are crucial in ensuring that these prerequisite be met.

SUMMARIZING STUDENT BENEFITS FROM SELF-EXAMINATION

The following reasons for using student self-examination can assist you in providing a rationale for their inclusion in portfolios and classroom practices for parents, community members, and other stakeholders. Self-assessments, self-reflections, and self-evaluations are critical to student portfolio implementation because they assist students in

- gathering a collection of meaningful work
- examining a variety of work
- reflecting on the content of what they have learned
- thinking about ideas presented in their work

- examining the processes of learning various concepts
- considering the amount of effort put forth
- recognizing purposes for what they are learning
- finding personal relevance in their work
- developing ownership for their work
- reflecting on their strengths and needs
- identifying their own progress over time
- understanding their versatility as learners
- taking responsibility for their learning
- making decisions based on sound judgements
- setting personal goals
- becoming independent learners
- feeling that others value their opinions and insights

WHY SHOULD YOU ENCOURAGE YOUR TEACHERS TO USE SELF-ASSESSMENT?

Self-assessment can provide teachers with information in several areas. Students' self-assessments provide teachers with an opportunity to gain a better understanding of how each student is progressing as a learner and provide feedback about instructional practices and curricular issues related to the classroom. Teachers profit from using self-assessment techniques themselves to evaluate their own progress in instructinal practices, curriculum choices, and assessment methods. Through self-reflection, they can explore their values and beliefs about teaching, which, in turn, shape practices used in their classrooms. Finally, their self-assessments can contribute to your understanding of their teaching philosophies, range of classroom practices, assessment tools used to measure classroom teaching, goals for teaching, and personal learning goals.

INFORMATION PROVIDED BY STUDENT SELF-ASSESSMENT

Supplying students with opportunities and skills needed for self-assessment is time-consuming, demands a great deal of teacher modeling, requires careful instructional planning, and necessitates acquiring new skills in evaluation; however, the knowledge that can be gained about student learning is undeniable (Tierney et al., 1991; Fu, 1991; Pigdon & Woolley, 1993; Hill & Ruptic, 1994). Self-evaluation contributes to a better understanding of students as learners and people because only the learner can relate information about how much effort went into a project, what

HOLOCAUST UNIT EVALUATION SHEET

Name_____ Date_____

Minimum assignment: Read Number the Stars
                                        Read second Holocaust book
                                        _____ Number the Stars journal
                                        _____ Number the Stars picture
                                        _____ Compare/contrast sheet for
                                                Movies (Venn Diagram)
                                        _____ Holocaust folder (2nd book)
                                        _____ Assessment sheet

Quality work is work that is finished on time, is written in your best handwriting, makes sense to the reader, and shows you used higher-level thinking skills.

Keeping those points in mind, on which of these assignments did you do quality work? Put a "Q" by the assignments that you feel were quality examples of your work.

On which assignments could you have done better? Put a check mark by those you feel you could have improved. What would you need to do to make this assignment quality work?

The second Holocaust book that I read was:

Additional books that I read:

What project or activity did you like best in this unit? Why?

How can we make this unit better for next year's students?

What project or activity should be added to this unit?

    _____ more art   _____ more writing

    _____ speakers/guests   _____ more group discussions

    _____ videos   _____ cooperative learning groups

    _____ other ideas:_____

Figure 4.7.

obstacles were encountered, and what knowledge the student obtained during the process. The form in Figure 4.7 is an example of one way to discover this information. Sue Horgan and Nancy Cantrell developed this evaluation sheet for their sixth graders to evaluate themselves and the Holocaust literature thematic unit. The form provides information about student's efforts and their opinions about the unit.

Through examining student self-assessments, administrators and teachers are able to discover what learners believe they have achieved. This information can then be compared to how the teacher perceived their level of achievement (Ministry of Education, 1988). Dana Hook uses the form in Appendix C.10 as a self-evaluation of students' weather maps for her middle school students. During this project, students became meteorologists and informed their classmates about the weather conditions present on their map. The form asks them to evaluate their roles in the project, how well they cooperated, and the grades they should receive.

When you encourage your teachers to collaborate with students and assist them in reflecting on their work, teachers can gather additional information about students' strengths as learners, how they learn best, and those areas that require further development and instruction (Paulson et al., 1991; Radger et al., 1991; Glazer & Brown, 1993; Hill & Ruptic, 1994). In summary, student self-assessments provide instructional information such as

- students' interest, enjoyment, and engagement in projects
- students' understanding of the nature and purpose for assignments
- amount and kind of help students received from others
- most significant information students felt they learned
- students' perceptions of their strengths and needs
- what students found to be the most challenging aspects of tasks
- students' goals for improvement on similar assignments or projects
- students' problem-solving abilities
- students' knowledge of content area concepts in all curricular areas
- students' ability to apply metacognitive strategies

RATIONALE TO ENCOURAGE TEACHER SELF-EVALUATION AND REFLECTION

Since a major purpose of both self-evaluation and education is to enable an individual to function independently, intelligently, and productively, self-assessment is not only a worthy goal for students, but must also be an essential component of everyday life for teachers. If your teachers expect students to self-assess their learning and progress, then your teachers must also be encouraged to demonstrate and practice self-assessment (Routman, 1991; Howell & Woolley, 1992; Glazer & Brown, 1993; Hill & Ruptic, 1994; Valencia et al., 1994; Porter & Cleland, 1995).

Self-evaluation implies trusting teachers and students as learners. This is often one of the hardest parts of evaluating the learning process. Teachers frequently find self-assessment to be a difficult component of evaluation because it is not something they have often been encouraged to do with traditional assessments, teaching, and policies (Goodman, 1986; Heald-Taylor, 1989; Fullan, 1991; K. S. Goodman et al., 1992; Wells & Wells, 1992; Five, 1995).

In addition to serving as a model for student self-evaluation and reflections, self-assessment demands that your teachers examine their own beliefs because, when they reflect upon what they choose to evaluate, they also discover what they value (Routman, 1991; Sparks-Langer & Colton, 1991). Those values are part of your teachers' belief systems or philosophies that determine what and how they teach, as well as how they assess learning. As a principal, you are in a role that can influence teachers' belief systems. Encouraging teachers to reflect upon their teaching and assessment practices forces teachers to examine whether there is congruence between what they claim to believe and what actually occurs in their classrooms. Hill and Ruptic (1994) recommend having teachers start with their philosophy and goals before examining outcomes, teaching practices, and assessment tools. The form in Figure 4.8 can be used for this purpose.

On the other hand, Cambourne and Turbil (1994) maintain that teachers often cannot deal with their philosophies until they have first examined their teaching practices. In their staff development model, Cambourne and Turbil have had teachers list their practices or teaching episodes, the time each episode typically lasts, and what the teacher and students do during each episode. Figure 4.9 is an example of a form that could be used to document this information.

Once teachers have documented their teaching episodes, they analyze each one by asking themselves why they chose to use this practice, what benchmarks or markers they can observe during the episode, and how they can measure these benchmarks. By examining why they chose each of these and what meaning can be derived from them, teachers begin to focus on their values and beliefs, which then lead them to stating their philosophies and to setting goals to support or change their teaching practices and assessment methods. Figure 4.10 is an example of one form that could be used to examine teaching episodes.

Another reason to encourage teachers to engage in self-evaluation and

TEACHING PHILOSOPHY AND GOALS

NAME_____ DATE_____

1. Learning is best facilitated when_____
_____

2. I believe my role in teaching is to_____
_____

3. I believe that students' role is to_____
_____

4. The main goal in education must be _____
_____

5. By the end of the school year, I want my students to learn _____
_____

6. My curricular goals for this school year are_____
_____
_____

7. My teaching and/or professional goals for this year are _____
_____
_____

8. This year I hope to learn_____
_____
_____

9. I believe assessment should_____
_____

10. I believe evaluation should_____
_____

11. This year I will measure and describe student growth through _____
_____
_____

Adapted from: Hill, B. C. & Ruptic, C. 1994. *Practical Aspects of Authentic Assessment: Putting the Pieces Together.* Norwood, MA: Christopher-Gordon Publishers, Inc.

Figure 4.8.

EPISODE RECORDING SHEET

Episode	Time Frame	What Happens

Adapted from: Cambourne, B. & Turbil, J. eds. 1994. *Responsive Evaluation: Making Valid Judgments about Student Literacy.* Portsmouth, NH: Heinemann, p. 21.

Figure 4.9.

Evaluating Episodes

Episode	Reason for episode	Benchmarks	Assessment tools

Adapted from: Cambourne, B. & Turbil, J. eds. 1994. *Responsive Evaluation: Making Valid Judgments about Student Learning,* Portsmouth, NH: Heinemann, p. 23.

Figure 4.10.

reflection about their teaching practices is to assist them in making sure they are providing appropriate curriculum, strategies, and resources for learners in their charge. Evaluation of assessment data is only effective when it is used to make informed decisions for planning how to teach information or strategies students need to learn next (Ministry of Education, 1988). Educators have too often fallen into the trap of assessing for no particular purpose, collecting information they already have, or gathering data that will never be used for any instructional purposes (Clark, 1987; Woodward, 1994). Indeed, we have often heard teachers complain about spending over a week administering standardized or mandated tests, not receiving test scores until after the school year is finished, and finding that they already knew the information that the results provided for students they were no longer teaching. As an administrator, you can help district policymakers examine testing programs to ensure that assessment is meaningful in your school community.

TECHNIQUES FOR ENCOURAGING TEACHERS TO SELF-REFLECT

We have found several assessment techniques to be valuable when encouraging teachers to engage in self-reflection and self-evaluation. Sometimes it is helpful for teachers to have a checklist to take stock of personal goals (Ministry of Education, 1988; Routman, 1991; K. S. Goodman et al., 1992; Glazer & Brown, 1993; Hill & Ruptic, 1994; Porter & Cleland, 1995). A list of possible personal assessment questions are

- Am I noticing and commenting on what students are doing well and are capable of doing?
- What am I currently doing to demonstrate learning in my classroom?
- Did the strategies I provided help to clarify and/or extend student understandings?
- How did I help the students learn?
- Can I identify each student's strengths and weaknesses?
- Was my feedback appropriate?
- Am I equally respectful of all students, regardless of culture and background?
- Are children in my classroom feeling successful, regardless of their abilities?
- Do I make time for the things that I value?

Questions that may assist your teachers to reflect on various teaching behaviors during daily instruction might include

- Am I reading literature aloud to students every day?
- Am I an effective model for my students?
- Am I providing time and choice daily for students to read and write on self-selected books and topics?
- Do I promote a love of learning in my students?
- Do I reflect satisfaction in what I am doing and excitement in my teaching?
- Do I provide a supportive learning environment?
- Are my questions allowing for varied responses and interpretations?
- Was my assistance to those students who need extra help effective?
- Are my expectations high for all students?
- Are my responses to students, both orally and in writing, specific and helpful?
- Do I check students' prior knowledge in content area topics?
- Do I provide regular opportunities for students to share and collaborate?
- Do I encourage higher-level thinking skills?
- Have I provided a balance of whole-class, small-group, and individual instructinal opportunities?
- Am I encouraging students to solve their own problems and take ownership of their learning?
- Is the work students are doing meaningful and purposeful?
- Do I enable students to be part of the decision-making process for instructional purposes?
- What do I want students to look like at the end of the semester?
- Are my students too dependent on me?

Questions that you can use to encourage your teachers to evaluate their progress in using student portfolios might include

- Have I set my goals for using portfolios in my classroom?
- Are my evaluation procedures consistent with my philosophy and teaching?
- Have I included students in making decisions about how portfolios will function in our classroom?
- Do students know and understand how they will be evaluated or graded?
- Am I providing opportunities for students to reflect on their progress?

- Have I tried assessment techniques that allow me to measure the process of learning, as well as the products that students produce?
- Am I communicating effectively with parents and administrators?
- Am I reaching my goals for using portfolios?
- Are there changes that I need to make?

One effective way to ponder these questions and others is through having your teachers keep a journal or write briefly on a question at a staff meeting. Writing provides a means of documenting what teachers do, clarifying their beliefs, and examining how their efforts meet their goals (Ministry of Education, 1988; Sparks-Langer & Colton, 1991).

Working with colleagues in a team teaching situation or as part of support or mentoring groups also encourages continual and immediate reflection, feedback, and refinement (Wells & Chang-Wells, 1992; Valencia et al., 1994; Porter & Cleland, 1995). Teachers can share their written reflections, samples of student work, forms they have created or found, and artifacts from portfolios. Through sharing their self-evaluations, they can help each other by discussing their doubts about how things are going, examples of risk taking, problems they have encountered, and successes they have had in portfolio implementation. Chapter 9 explores using support or mentoring groups in further detail.

Teachers can also use audiotaping or videotaping to examine what is happening in their classrooms in instruction and assessment. After listening or viewing the tapes, they can jot down their reflections. Another way to evaluate these tapes is to have students provide their input on how effective the lesson was. Teachers can tell students what they noticed and then have students provide suggestions.

Whichever means of self-reflection or combination of the techniques described appeal to you and your teachers, self-evaluation is a vital part of the portfolio assessment process for teachers as well as students. Some guidelines that can assist your teachers in beginning to use self-assessment include

- Engage in self-assessment slowly.
- Don't try to assess everything at once.
- Focus on a limited number of areas or skills to begin.
- Strive for openness and honesty in examining yourself.
- Try different approaches or a combination of approaches until you find one or more that seems comfortable to you.
- Make a regular schedule to engage in self-assessment until it becomes a habit.

- Find others with whom you will feel comfortable sharing your thoughts.
- All self-assessments do not need to be shared with others.

WHY SHOULD PRINCIPALS ENGAGE IN SELF-ASSESSMENT?

Principals who are instructional leaders in the change process for their school communities realize that leaders cannot expect a culture for change without participating and reflecting along with their staff. Administrators who are supportive of risk taking for their teachers do not ask them to use assessment techniques that they have not also tried. Teachers respect principals who are willing to take risks with them. By participating in self-assessment, you can model the process for your staff and students (Hutchinson, 1991; Sunstein, 1991). The form in Appendix A.3 can assist you in determining your readiness as a change agent in the portfolio process.

Another reason for actively engaging in self-assessment is that it forces us to examine our own beliefs and values in teaching, learning, and assessment. Both teachers and principals use their previous experiences and reflections to make decisions each day. The knowledge and information we have gained from our previous experiences are reflected in the decisions we make. By using self-reflection, we bring this knowledge to an awareness level that allows us to evaluate the decisions we make about what stances we take on what will be taught in our schools, best practices in teaching, and assessment practices that can effectively measure student learning (Hutchinson, 1991; Wibel, 1991). Participating with teachers in using forms such as the one in Figure 4.8 and using the process described by Cambourne and Turbil (1994) to examine your routines can assist you in developing your philosophy, goals, and beliefs of assessment.

Self-assessment can also be used to assist you in judging your effectiveness in the various roles that you must assume as an administrator, including those in school business management, educational leadership, personnel management and evaluation, conflict resolution, and public relations. Journal entries or narrative writing is usually the best method for this type of self-reflection. William Wibel (1991), a middle school principal, found that writing reflections served as a release valve and that his attempts at problem solving on paper sometimes prompted solutions that he could use later at school. He felt that his writing helped him deal with some of the dilemmas of his position and empowered him to find solutions.

The following model of professional reflections, adapted from Killion and Todnem (1991), can be another way to use self-reflection to assist you

Reflection Process

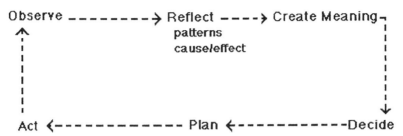

Observe -------→ Reflect ----→ Create Meaning⌐
⋀   patterns   ¦
¦   cause/effect   ¦
¦   ¦
¦   ¦
¦   ¦
¦   ↓
Act ⟵------------ Plan ⟵----------- Decide

Adapted from: Killion, J. P. & Tondem, G. R. 1991. "A Process for Personal Theory Building," *Educational Leadership.* 48(6):14–17.

Figure 4.11.

in your many roles as an administrator. The first step is to observe what is happening in a situation. Then reflect or self-evaluate to find patterns or causes and effects. Next, you create meaning from what you have observed and evaluated. Once you have made sense of the situation, decide what needs to be done or what the problem is. After this decision, you will need to devise a plan of action. When you have created your plan, your next step is to act or follow through on it. This leads you back to observation to determine how well your plan is working, and then the cycle begins again with revisions to your plan or a new area of focus. This model for the reflection process is depicted in Figure 4.11.

The habit of self-reflection takes time and practice for teachers, students, and administrators to acquire. However, the benefits that self-assessment holds for each of these stakeholders are similar because all three groups are lifelong learners who need to assess where they are in their own learning, how they got to that point, and where they are going next. This is a process that will take patience, effort, and risk taking in a safe environment.

TROUBLESHOOTING: NO ONE SAID IT WOULD BE EASY!

When teachers first attempt to have their students engage in self-assessment, the results are not always what they hope to receive. When Mr. Kutney (1993) had his high school English students begin using self-assessments, he found that they had a difficult time writing about themselves as writers and attempting to clarify their strengths and weaknesses.

They did not have strategies for change, lacked the vocabulary they needed, and had little insight into their own writing. Mr. Kutney felt they were unskilled at self-assessment because they had not had enough opportunity to do so in the past. To help students become better at examining their writing, he modeled the process often and had conferences with students to assist them in finding their strengths and needs.

Mrs. Hook also found that her middle school science students had no idea what self-evaluation meant. She was especially disappointed that a student thought self-evaluation was a form of punishment or a type of grade! She discovered that, before her students became better at self-evaluation, she needed not only to explain what it meant, but she also had to provide numerous examples of how she uses self-evaluation in her teaching and how students might use it to assist them in doing a better job of learning. Mrs. Hook provided many think-alouds and mini-lessons that integrated self-assessment into her teaching before students began to improve in their self-assessments. When she first began working with self-assessment, most of these students told her that they had never been asked to do this before, and after all, it was the teacher's job to give them grades.

Another problem that sometimes surfaces when students are first asked to self-assess is that they might provide the answers that they think teachers want to hear. They are often unwilling to take risks until teachers have provided them with assurances and actual proof that their honesty is valued and used to assist them in becoming better learners. It takes time and patience to develop this trust (Hill & Ruptic, 1994; Valencia et al., 1994; Dudley-Marling & Searle, 1995; Porter & Cleland, 1995).

It is important to remember that we can usually do a task before we can talk about how we did it or even how well we did it. Children from a variety of cultures or different levels of affluence will vary also in their ability to use the language that they need to successfully engage in self-reflection and goal setting. These students will also vary in their ability to answer questions that focus on their learning process (Matthews, 1992). One way to assist students is to provide sentence stems for them to finish. Various teachers have found some of the following to be helpful:

- This week I discovered . . .
- I learned that . . .
- I could do a better job on . . .
- I liked . . . because . . .
- I am confused about . . .
- This week, the most important thing I learned was . . .
- I used these strategies to help me understand . . .
- I feel I did a good job on . . .

- I want to learn more about . . .
- Next, I will . . .
- To make my project better, I would . . .

Two final guides for using self-assessment include using only language that your learners understand on your self-assessment forms and making sure you do not overuse this type of assessment. Sometimes, there can be too much of a good thing; students do not need to use self-assessment for everything (Hill & Ruptic, 1994).

GLOSSARY

Data Retrieval Chart: a type of matrix or graphic organizer that has topics along one side of a grid and characteristics on the other axis. Information is placed within each box of the grid to demonstrate knowledge of subject matter.

Episode: parts or portions of a block of instruction. For example, episodes of a language arts block could include whole class instruction on a strategy, silent sustained reading, literature discussion groups, teacher modeling, writer's workshop, and sharing time.

Lifelong Learners: teachers, students, and administrators who do not stop learning at the completion of formal education. They continue to learn throughout their lives through both formal and informal educational experiences.

Metacognition: being able to know about how one thinks or knows information. Thinking about one's own learning and learning processes.

Mind Map: graphic representation in which art is combined with phrases to demonstrate connections between facts or ideas. Mind maps are used to demonstrate knowledge and reflection on subject matter.

Ownership: having control over one's learning and behavior.

Risk Taking: a frame of mind in which the individual is willing to give up security to try something that may not be successful during the first attempt because consequences of failure have been minimized.

Rubric: set of observable criteria or indicators used to rate students' work with descriptors of observable behaviors.

Self-Assessment: form of metacognition that focuses on both processes and products of learning but usually focuses more on the ongoing process of learning.

Self-Evaluation: form of metacognition that focuses more on the end product, is more summative in nature, and involves more appraisal.

Self-Reflection: form of metacognition that focuses on a thoughtful contemplation of learning, is more aesthetic in nature, and focuses on emotions as well as thoughts.

Theme: integration of curriculum subjects around a focus topic that is usually science or social studies related or around a piece of literature. Themes range in duration from two to six weeks as a rule, although some schools use year-long themes.

ENDNOTES

1. When assessment is referred to as critical assessment, we mean that the material is examined with criteria in mind, with a rationale for the evaluation of the material, and more than superficial comments such as, "It was my best work because I like it," or "It's funny."
2. When students use a formula for responding to writing rules, they are responding simply to the grammatical and mechanical aspects of writing such as where punctuation marks need to be placed or whether the text has proper subject/verb agreement. They may also be using formulas, such as that the writing must contain a paragraph of introduction, a paragraph stating the problem, and so on.
3. When assessment is reality-based, it is authentic, in that it takes place in the regular classroom and resembles activities that students preform in the daily routine of the classroom. Reality-based assessments make sense to both teachers and students because they measure important tasks and the results have meaning.

CHAPTER 5

Choosing from Multiple Sources for Data Collection

Mrs. White's Reflections on Options for Change

When I first started making changes in teaching and assessing children three years ago, I was learning as much as they were. It was like I had been thrown overboard and couldn't find the shore. I kept swimming but didn't know what direction to go. There were so many options available that I was overwhelmed at first. Now I feel I've found the shore and I'm making a landing. Things are coming together. If I had to go back to the way we used to teach and assess, I would feel like I was locked in a box and the key had been thrown away.

Mrs. Nothlyne's View on the Need to Change Assessment

Often, in the race to "improve" the educational system, we lose sight of our children and our goals. We let curricular restrictions and demands dictate to us what will be done, rather than putting the needs and readiness of the learner first. Because of this, we have not always been successful. We have created "readers" who do not read and "writers" who do not write. If our goal is to nurture children to grow into strong, mentally healthy adults who are lifelong thinkers and learners, then we must change the way we look at the students and environment in our classrooms.

INTRODUCTION

PORTFOLIO assessment involves making multiple decisions. Just the array of possibilities can be overwhelming for those just beginning down the road to portfolio implementation; yet many teachers feel exactly as Mrs. White and Mrs. Nothlyne do and are not satisfied with the status quo or traditional methods of assessing students. This chapter provides a range of

105

assessment options and artifacts for possible inclusion in your school's portfolios.

Once you and your stakeholders have defined your parameters, chosen what evidence will be evaluated, and created performance standards, you are ready for teachers and students to select techniques that best reflect guidelines your stakeholders have created. Encourage your teachers to select only one or two new assessment options to implement at any one time. Even the most experienced, innovative staff member can become frustrated by attempting to implement too many changes at once. Although your teachers will select a variety of different strategies, depending upon personal knowledge, readiness for change, personality styles, and student needs in their classrooms, they must be able to explain why they chose any particular one to include in portfolios used in their classrooms and how it satisfies your school's guidelines.

SELECTING FROM ASSESSMENT OPTIONS

Alternative assessments frequently placed in portfolios include informal tools such as anecdotal records, checklists, interviews, surveys, questionnaires, inventories, journal entries, logs, and classroom rubrics. Student work samples and artifacts from classroom activities are often selected for inclusion in portfolios. Many school communities use portfolio items that represent students as a whole. These items include materials that come from students' lives outside of the classroom as well as those from school. Traditional assessments such as tests that are teacher-made, provided by text publishers, state-mandated, or standardized are more formal tools and may sometimes have a place in a portfolio (Herman et al., 1992; Rhodes & Shanklin, 1993; Hill & Ruptic, 1994; Valencia et al., 1994).

ALTERNATIVE ASSESSMENTS

In the following sections, anecdotal records, checklists, interviews, surveys, questionnaires, inventories, journal entries, logs, and rubrics are explored. These tools are considered alternative assessments because they originate in the classroom and require students to construct, rather than choose, responses to measure what they can do and what they know.

Anecdotal Records

Anecdotal records are notes written during or after an observation of a student. The best notes are brief, yet descriptive, and capture an event with enough detail so that it can be considered again at a later time but without becoming a long and involved narrative. Anecdotal records need to be dated so strengths, weaknesses, needs, progress, learning styles, and patterns over time can be examined. Depending upon reasons for the observation, settings for kid watching can vary from whole class to group work to individual conferences, yet the focus for anecdotal records remains on individual students.

How to Collect Anecdotal Records

There are different ways to encourage your teachers to begin collecting anecdotal records. It is often helpful to have teachers examine their daily schedules for times students are engaged in independent practice or group work when they are not actively teaching or supervising. These time periods provide excellent opportunities for making anecdotal comments. One way to begin is by focusing on only one context or content area, while another is to observe one or two students a day or a small group of four or five students a week. Encourage teachers to use clipboards for jotting down their notes as they circulate through the classroom or sit with a small group. Some of your teachers will be comfortable jotting notes in front of students after they have explained what they are doing and why they are doing it; others will prefer to step aside and jot down their comments in private. However, the process of keeping anecdotal records must be kept simple, or your teachers won't continue it. The simplest storage systems for anecdotal records work best (Routman, 1991; Rhodes & Shanklin, 1993; Armstrong, 1994; Hill & Ruptic, 1994).

One way to store anecdotal records is to use a three-ring binder with dividers to store comments. Several pages can be allocated for each student for the teacher to write comments about various subject areas or to paste labels and sticky notes. To aid in managing the procedure, student names can be listed in alphabetical order and/or color coded. Advantages of using a binder are that everything is in one place; sheets can be added or removed as necessary; individual sheets can easily be placed into students' portfolios; and other types of assessment tools can easily be added. Disadvantages include that they are bulky and materials may have to be handled twice before being organized (Anthony et al., 1991; Routman, 1991; Rhodes & Shanklin, 1993; Holland, 1993; Hill & Ruptic, 1994). Figure 5.1 is an example of one type of form that could be used in three-ring binders. This form can be adapted to meet needs of teachers at various grade levels.

Another way to store comments is to use a spiral-bound notebook with

Name_____Date_____Grade_____

Reading	Writing	Math	Science	Social Studies

Other Comments:

Figure 5.1. Anecdotal Record Form.

a tab inserted for each student. Tabs can be color coded for each day of the school week. One way to help your teachers check to be sure they are making notations for each student several times a month is to have them divide their classes into five color coded groups. When they are taking anecdotal notes on any day, they can concentrate on the five or six students in a particular color. Once again, the anecdotal records are in one place, and color coding helps keep the notebook organized. Potential disadvantages include that the number of pages for each student is limited; transferring notes to the notebook can be time-consuming; it is more difficult to place appropriate anecdotal comments into students' portfolios; and it is difficult to add other assessment tools (Baskwill & Whitman, 1988; Routman, 1991; Hill & Ruptic, 1994). The form provided in Figure 5.1 could also be used for taking notes in a spiral-bound notebook. The example in Appendix D.1 is another format that could be used in either type of anecdotal note storage system.

Another way to manage anecdotal records is to use folders for each child or for different teaching episodes such as writing workshop, literature circles, mathematics, and so on. Advantages of folders include the following: they are more portable; teachers can focus on one subject area at a time; materials can easily be taken out at conference time to be placed in portfolios; and other assessment tools can easily be added to them. Main disadvantages are that there are more items to keep track of, organization can take more time, and they take more storage space (Baskwill & Whitman, 1988; Hill & Ruptic, 1994). The two forms mentioned earlier in this section can also be used with folders. The format provided in Appendix D.2 gives another option that could be used in any of these three methods for organizing anecdotal records.

Another alternative form for organizing anecdotal records is to use a large sheet divided into small squares, with one square per student. This collection page should be kept in an easily accessible place to record observations in writing or on small sticky notes. If sticky notes are used, the sheet can be xeroxed when it is full, and then the sticky notes can be discarded. Sticky notes can also be transferred to an individual student's sheet, placed in chronological order, used to examine patterns, or used to assist when writing narrative progress reports. For larger classes, legal size paper allows more space to include all students on one sheet. Advantages of using one large sheet for storing anecdotal notes include that it helps teachers make sure each student has something recorded regularly; students needing more observations can be more easily detected because they do not have many comments in their squares; sheets for individual students can easily be placed in student portfolios; and the smaller space limits comments to brief notes. Disadvantages include keeping track of a single sheet, which could become misplaced; sticky notes could fall off the master sheet before it is xeroxed; and other assessment tools would need to be kept separately (Anthony et al., 1991; Hill & Ruptic, 1994; Woodward, 1994). The form in Appendix D.3 is an example of this format for keeping anecdotal comments. Teachers can write their comments directly in each square, or they can place small sticky notes over them. It can be used for whole class observations, individual student comments, focused topic observations, thematic units, or specific subject areas.

Another method of storing anecdotal records is using file cards. Teachers should be encouraged to use the 5 × 8 inch size to have enough space to write information about students. One way to use these is to keep a card for each student on a ring. Another method is to layer them on a clipboard like a flip chart, with each student's name showing. When cards are full, they can be placed in a file box or directly into portfolios. Cards can be kept handy in a pocket or on a flip chart for each content area. They are easily portable, can be placed in portfolios without transferring information, and take little storage space; however, they can be misplaced if not filed after being completed, and management could be a problem if teachers do not have the time or inclination to be well organized (Hill & Ruptic, 1994). Sample file cards in Figure 5.2 are related to a science thematic unit entitled "Wonderful Water" that was used in a second-grade classroom. Note that comments reflect what students did, rather than judgements of their behaviors toward learning.

Technology brings teachers the capability to use a computer for still another option in storing observational comments. Word processing programs allow notes to be transferred to individual student files or portfolios. These notes can later be transferred to narratives for progress reports, conferences, or permanent records. Some programs allow integration of word processing, spreadsheets, and databases for additional capacity to sort and classify information for reporting. Advantages include greater versatility in using information from observations and minimal use of storage space when using a hard drive. Disadvantages include the fact that many teachers are not comfortable with computers, some schools do not have access to computers or software needed to use them, computer diskettes can create a storage problem, and files can be inadvertently erased or mislabeled (Armstrong, 1994; Hill & Ruptic, 1994; Hewitt, 1995).

One technique that works well for taking notes is the use of stick-on or "Post-it" notes. Sticky notes are often used in combination with the techniques described previously in this section. Teachers can label each sticky note with a student's name or initials and carry them in a pocket or on a clipboard. Plenty of blank notes should also be kept available to make comments that are spontaneous for students not scheduled for observation.

Crystal P.   **Water Unit**

4/27/94 Worked well in her group. Shared that water is used to wash clothes, cook with, & drink. Reported group list to class.

5/4/94 Explained her water wheel to Mrs. Jones. All the necessary parts of the water cycle were in her drawing.

5/11/94 Volunteered to read her Water Poem- Good expression and contained three facts about water.

Jordan A.   **Water Unit**

4/27/94 Contributed that water is good for swimming. Said he did not want to be the recorder for his group. Did not contribute any other uses for water. Did agree to keep track of who gave which uses for water.

5/4/94 Shared his water wheel with classhelper. Had only the part provided on the sheet - no additions of his own.

5/11/94 Wrote three lines with facts about water. Chose not to share his poem with the class but did share it with his partner.

Figure 5.2. Examples of Anecdotal Notes on File Cards.

Stick-on notes can be easily transferred to file cards, individual large sheets, folders, pages in spiral-bound notebooks, or pages in three-ring binders. Topics for focus of observations or questions about student learning can be jotted at the top to label the note. Yellow "Post-it" notes can be copied and stored in portfolios. Advantages include that they are easy to carry and can be transferred easily. Main disadvantages are that, after a while, they lose their stickiness, can become lost, and can accumulate if they are not organized and stored soon after they have been used (Anthony et al., 1991; Routman, 1991; Rhodes & Shanklin, 1993; Hill & Ruptic, 1994; Woodward, 1994). Figure 5.3 provides examples of comments on sticky notes that a kindergarten teacher jotted while observing students during center time.

An alternative to sticky notes is pregummed mailing labels. Labels can be kept in various places, including grade books, on a clipboard, and in other accessible locations. They can be used for the same purposes as sticky notes, but they will not blow off and they stick better. There are sheets of blank labels that can be run through a copy machine so that students' names or topics can be placed on labels ahead of time. A main disadvantage of gummed labels is that they can only be moved once (Baskwill & Whitman, 1988; Holland, 1993; Hill & Ruptic, 1994; Porter & Cleland, 1995). Comments on the mailing labels in Figure 5.4 were taken during a literature discussion group and contain goals to meet individual needs.

Your teachers will need to experiment to find which combination of methods for taking and storing anecdotal records works best for them. There is no one right way. As your teachers begin taking anecdotal records, they will need your encouragement and trust so the task will not seem like just more extra work. Many teachers have found that, as they become comfortable with kid watching, they know their students much better than before. Encourage them to start small and to keep in mind that their first attempts may be short and infrequent, but even taking anecdotal records twice in a nine-week period can provide teachers with valuable information (Routman, 1991; Hill & Ruptic, 1994; Dudley-Marling & Searle, 1995).

What Information Can Be Collected

When your teachers begin to collect notes for their anecdotal records, there are some general principles that they will need to consider. Kid watching or observations should occur in authentic situations that are a normal part of classroom instruction. For example, a student's participation in peer revision should be observed while students are working to revise their writing. Effective anecdotal records describe a specific event

10/14/94   Jessica
Journal Center:
Showed Teala how to
write "MAMA." Said
"MAMA spells Mom
because it starts with
M."
- Knows the sound and
   letter for "M."

10/14/94   Teala
Journal Center:
Drew a picture of her
mother. Asked Jessica
how to spell "Mom."
Copied "MAMA"
from Jessica's journal.
- Can form upper case
   M & A

10/14/94   Brandon
Math Patterns Center:
Shared ink pad and
stamps with others.
Could alternate two
stamps in the same
color
- work on patterns in
   more colors and in
   varied patterns

10/14/94   Jamal
Math Patterns Center:
Told others about his
patterns. Can name
colors. Could use two
colors to make
patterns of two.
- needs to explore new
patterns in more color
combinations

10/14/94   Shari
Reading Center:
Chose Mrs. Wishy-
Washy. Read the book
from memory to Alicia.
- knows directionality;
   points near words;
   work on sight words
   & letter recognition.

10/14/94   Frank
Reading Center:
Looked at pictures in
"The Farm" Began at
the back of the book.
Laughed in appropri-
ate places
- work on directionality
   & pointing to words

Figure 5.3. *Examples of Anecdotal Comments on Sticky Notes.*

9/20/96 Literature Study Group   Jennifer S.
Novel: Bridge to Terribithia

Shared material from the text. Remembers details
and identifies motive of main characters. Can find
the main idea.
Goal: To risk personal opinions and reactions to
     the text content.

9/20/96 Literature Study Group   Paul G.
Novel: Bridge to Terribithia

Makes good predictions using cues in the text.
Reads ahead to confirm predictions and modifies
them.
Goal: Continue to work on character development
     and valuing the opinions of others.

9/20/96 Literature Study Group   Saul W.
Novel: Bridge to Terribithia

Interacts well with the group. Values opinions of
others and contributes his own opinions.
Goal: Work on asking higher level questions and
     confirming predictions.

Figure 5.4. Examples of Anecdotal Notes on Mailing Labels.

or product, report information rather than evaluating or interpreting it, and relate the material to other facts known about the student. Although many teachers tend to examine students' learning by what they are not doing, anecdotal comments should begin positively with something the student can do. After a positive beginning, teachers may then include student needs or deficits. By beginning with positive comments, teachers can help students and parents feel more comfortable with the evaluation process. Encourage your teachers to check their notes by asking themselves whether they would be comfortable having others, including the student, read them. If not, perhaps they should reevaluate how they write their comments. A final principle is that anecdotal records should be geared toward reflections about teaching and learning (Anthony et al., 1991; Routman, 1991; Rhodes & Natherson-Mejia, 1992; Holland, 1993; Armstrong, 1994).

Range of information that can be collected in anecdotal records is unlimited. Teachers can note points about students' learning behavior, attitudes, and choices. Notes might record information about silent reading choices; writing choices during writer's workshop; how often students volunteer to share their work; which oral or written language skills a student has mastered; whether student needs should be handled individually, in a small group, or as a whole class focus for learning; whether a student has completed assigned work; how much effort was put into a presentation; accuracy of work; or incidental notes about health or extracurricular interests (Simms, 1994). Other notes could record observations during reading circle discussions, author's circle, peer conference, and throughout the school day (Holland, 1993). Other options include recording information on comprehension, which strategies students employ, comments students make about their own learning, goals for each student, specific behaviors in different contexts, conversations, skills or strategies taught, and breakthroughs (Holland, 1993; Wilcox, 1993; Hill & Ruptic, 1994; Porter & Cleland, 1995).

Anthony et al. (1991) remind us that there is usually so much happening in a classroom that teachers find it helpful to be selective in what they choose to record. There are two basic ways to collect anecdotal records. One is spontaneous, when a teacher simply has materials at hand and records interesting or important behaviors as they are observed. The second is planned observations that are focused on predetermined areas, criteria, or benchmarks (Anthony et al., 1991; Hill & Ruptic, 1994; Valencia et al., 1994). Teachers can focus on questions they would like to have answered, such as

- How well do students communicate their ideas during group work?

- How are students solving problems during science experiments?
- What processes are students using to solve mathematical equations?
- Are students sharing their personal insights and opinions during literature response groups?
- Do students respect reactions and opinions of others?
- Are students willing to take risks in their writing?
- What strategies are students using on their own?
- What do students find to be frustrating in reading or writing?

Teachers can also be encouraged to use the criteria and curricular benchmarks that your school community has targeted as exit standards for their students. Teachers can target one or two benchmarks in a subject area to observe over a period of time and write comments on progress made by each student. Social behaviors such as cooperative learning skills, leadership skills, completing work, initiating projects, or participation in discussion can also be noted. The more comments reflect benchmarks established by your school community, the more valuable your teachers wil find them in noting progress, learning, and patterns over time.

Benefits of Using Anecdotal Records

Because the nature of anecdotal records is entirely up to the teacher, they can be used to record details about virtually anything that seems significant (Rhodes & Shanklin, 1993). Since teachers have a unique opportunity to observe children in the process of learning, constraints of time and effort that anecdotal records exhibit are worth the effort. Anecdotal records allow teachers to be specific and accurate in conferences with students, parents, and administrators. They can serve as benchmarks for noting student progress and for setting instructional goals, as objective sources of documentation, and for sources of information for writing reports about student progress (Anthony et al., 1991; Routman, 1991).

When used as one source of putting together pieces of the assessment puzzle, anecdotal records can help your teachers form a more complete picture of individual students from a variety of contexts. Continuous examination and evaluation of patterns in anecdotal records can help your teachers plan for instructional needs of each student. Routman (1991) included the following as a sampling uses for information gained through anecdotal notes:

- evaluating individual students' learning
- making instructional decisions for individual students

- making instructional decisions for small groups or the entire class
- discovering which students need additional instruction
- finding patterns in student behavior
- providing documentation of learning for the school community
- assisting teachers in evaluating their own teaching

Concerns about Anecdotal Records

If anecdotal records are to be useful for instructional planning, your teachers will need to be experts in what to look for, and this takes training and practice. Many teachers have difficulty finding the time necessary for taking notes when they are not directly teaching because this is a departure from the transmission model of teaching during which teachers dispense knowledge and students listen. Some teachers are reluctant to place anecdotal records in cumulative records because they fear that future teachers will not value their comments. Sometimes, teachers tend to focus only on those students who have problems or those who are producing exceptional work, while "average" students tend to slip through the cracks with few anecdotal comments or observations. A final possible problem is that teachers will often take detailed notes but not have time to analyze them to examine their teaching practices and, therefore, continue with what they have been doing, regardless of contradictory information provided in their anecdotal records (Rhodes & Shanklin, 1993; Wolf, 1994; Woodward, 1994).

Checklists

For many teachers just beginning to use observation as an assessment tool, checklists are less formidable than anecdotal records. There are many commercial checklists available that have been created by experts in a field or by experienced teachers. Sometimes, teachers who are novices at taking anecdotal records find that they repeatedly record the same information for certain subjects or topics. You might want to suggest that they create a checklist for common traits in a subject or unit and continue recording comments for individual students on aspects of learning that are difficult to represent on a checklist or that apply only to that student (Routman, 1991; Rhodes & Shanklin, 1993; Hill & Ruptic, 1994).

Checklists usually contain a list of learning traits or descriptors to observe and a system to mark the occurrence or quality of each during observation. Purposes of checklists include keeping observations focused, providing a way to document information that requires a minimum of writing, providing consistency across observations over time, and allowing teachers to customize assessment to match their instructional focus (Cockrum & Castillo, 1991).

How to Create Checklists

Checklists developed by teachers during instructional planning are most appropriate since they will best reflect targeted outcomes in their classrooms and needs of their students. Some of the best checklists are those that provide students with an opportunity to assist in creating and monitoring them. Adding anecdotal comments to checklists increases their usefulness in instructional planning (Routman, 1991; Rhodes & Shanklin, 1993; Wilson, 1993). Jane Shippee uses the checklist in Appendix D.4 to keep track of student ownership in her fourth-grade classroom. Having students value and take responsibility for their own learning is one of her major goals for the year. This form can be used to observe the whole class, small groups, or individual students and allows growth in student ownership to be documented and analyzed over time.

Rhodes and Shanklin (1993) provide the following suggestions when creating checklists:

- Avoid becoming overwhelmed with too many items or descriptors on a checklist.
- Select only those traits or descriptors that are most important at the time.
- Review and change items several times during the year.
- Consider constructing different checklists for different students with the aid of a word processor.
- Remember that checklists should always fit instructional purposes, and these will change over time, context of use, texts, and from student to student.

Teachers use several different checklist formats. Rhodes and Shanklin (1993) provide three formats for retelling checklists that can easily be adapted to any topic or subject area. The format in Figure 5.5 is a multiple-setting checklist for individual student's reading behavior. When your teachers use one form per student, it will be easier to identify progress or differences in each student's performance across time and different contexts. Teachers fill in the top with the date of the observation and a context for it. Your teachers can customize the form by filling in descriptors for their focus for observations. Finally, they will need to develop a marking system to fill in the squares. One system provides a plus to indicate that

Name _____

Checklist Items	Date and Context					
Willingness to accept an approximate meaning of an unknown word.						
Using context to approximate the meaning of an unknown word.						
Uses prior knowlege to predict.						
Uses meaning to confirm predictions.						
Uses letter/sound relations to decode unknown words.						
Self-corrects miscues that disrupt meaning during oral reading.						

Notes

Date:

Date:

Date:

Date:

Adapted from: Rhodes, L. K. & Shanklin, N. 1993. *Windows in Literacy: Assessing Learners K-8.* Portsmouth, NH: Heinemann, p. 239.

Figure 5.5. *Reading Checklist.*

the student demonstrates a trait to a large extent, a check to indicate the trait is demonstrated to some extent, a minus to indicate the trait is not yet present, and a blank space or zero to indicate that the item was not observed in this setting. Some reasons the behavior may not be observed are that it was not appropriate to the setting, the context was not conducive to the behavior, or the teacher was not present when the behavior occurred. Notes at the end are provided to document details that are not part of the checklist but are important for instructional planning, meeting student needs, or documenting student accomplishments.

A second format shown in Appendix D.5 can be used for individual students when teachers want to analyze criteria on a regular basis or for students whose progress concerns them most. Some reasons teachers may want more documentation are to provide information for others or to plan instruction more effectively. Data on checklists can be compared over time to find patterns of strengths and weaknesses. This example provides an opportunity to observe writing. Your teachers can change the descriptors to those that reflect their interests and concerns. This form provides a space to write comments for each descriptor.

The third format provided in Appendix D.6 is designed to observe a group of students in a single setting and can be used to collect information about students during group work such as cooperative learning discussions on a project in science. This type of checklist is more challenging because the teacher must focus on more than one student, but it does provide a way to document how individual students function in a group. As with the other two formats, teachers can change the descriptors and marking system to match their needs, focus, or concerns.

Ways to Use Checklists

The number of specific uses for checklists may be unlimited, since any learning event can have a checklist designed to facilitate its observation and evaluation. Cockrum and Castillo (1991) provide the editing stage of the writing process as an example for creating and using a checklist:

- Mechanical aspects of writing such as use of capitals, use of punctuation, and so on are placed on a checklist.
- A marking system for levels of attainment is also placed on the checklist.
- Teachers examine a student's writing sample by using the checklist at a later date.
- Teachers can use the checklist to evaluate the effect of the learning environment on the student's use of writing mechanics.

- The student can fill it in before having an editing conference with the teacher.
- Together, student and teacher can determine which writing mechanics the student has mastered and which ones need to become goals for attainment.

Checklists can be used during or after instruction. Armstrong (1994) noted that they are useful in developing an informal criterion-referenced assessment system to keep track of important skills or content areas that students have achieved and for indicating progress toward each goal. Checklists that have been created by experts in reading and writing can be used to assist teachers in looking at readers and writers in different ways. Checklists are helpful for efficiency in recording the same information for students while anecdotal records capture information that cannot be reduced to a checklist (Rhodes & Shanklin, 1993). Routman (1991) advocates using narratives and anecdotal records but does feel that checklists are useful for checking early literacy behaviors when they are combined with narratives and anecdotal comments and for putting students in charge of their own learning.

Benefits of Using Checklists

Checklists allow teachers a quick overview of a student's progress or performance in each targeted area and may be used to inform other stakeholders of what kinds of behaviors are valued. They also provide a guide for teachers during future observations. Commercial checklists are available so teachers don't have to create every assessment tool (Anthony et al., 1991; Routman, 1991; D. Goodman, 1992). While teachers do not need to totally create their own checklists for each teaching episode, sorting and sifting through both commercial and teacher-made checklists can be valuable in providing a clear picture of what to expect from students developmentally. However, other people's checklists seldom exactly fit this year's group of students or instructional needs. Teachers who have created their own checklists have found the most valuable aspect to be the process of selecting items to use as descriptors. This process requires your teachers to clarify what behaviors, processes, and products indicate successful learning in a specific context. After using a checklist for a while, teachers often find they have the information they want to observe in their heads as they become more efficient kid watchers and they begin to discard checklists in favor of other assessment tools (Baskwill & Whitman, 1988; Routman, 1991; K. S. Goodman, 1992; Rhodes & Shanklin, 1993; Woodward, 1994).

Concerns about Checklists

Some checklists only allow for recording presence or absence of certain skills, with no way to record any real progress. At best, these checklists can only indicate the number of times a particular behavior is observed or a goal is achieved. They cannot adequately reveal individual progress (Woodward, 1994). One of the dangers is that teachers may spend most of their time focusing on the list to be checked, rather than on students, and my easily miss learning that is occurring. Encourage your teachers to remain alert to significant behaviors that may not be covered in their checklists (Anthony et. al., 1991; Routman, 1991).

Since checklists are set up in linear patterns, teachers can believe the skills or items are sequential and must be taught in order. Checklists are meant to be guidelines for assessment and *not* prescriptions for teaching (Baskwill & Whitman, 1988). Most checklists present learning in a fragmented fashion, and there is the danger that learning will be viewed in a simplistic manner. Your teachers will need to find ways to portray each student's learning performance, growth, and needs. Checklists only yield helpful information when they are geared to meet specific student needs (Church, 1991). Because assessment checklists are static and students are not, a single checklist will not work equally well for every student or for an entire school year. Students develop as learners, and teachers' goals for them change; therefore, checklists must also be revised. Challenging the format of a checklist helps bridge the gap between assessment and instruction (Rhodes & Shanklin, 1993; Hill & Ruptic, 1994).

Interviews

Interviews use open-ended questions that a teacher asks a student in a comfortable setting that is relatively free from interruptions. The teacher records responses on a form with blank spaces provided after each question. Interviews provide information about student perceptions about learning, specific topics or content areas, instructional practices, and their preferences. Figure 5.6 is a form that has been used to discover how primary children view the writing process. Interviews can also be used to discover students' attitudes about themselves as readers, writers, and learners. Your teachers can discover what prior knowledge students have about a topic or subject area, what students are most interested in both at school and at home, types of literacy events they choose to engage in, what kinds of materials they read, topics they might want to write about, or their future learning goals (Cockrum & Castillo, 1991; Y. Goodman, 1992; Rhodes, 1993; Rhodes & Shanklin, 1993). The interview form in Appen-

PRIMARY WRITING INTERVIEW

Student Name_____Date_____

1. Do you think you are an author? How do you know?

2. How do you feel about writing? Do like to write? Why/Why not?

3. What do you like to write about? Tell me about your favorite piece of writing.

4. What do you do when there are words you are not sure how to spell?

5. What is easy for you when you write?

6. What is hard for you when you write?

Figure 5.6.

dix D.7 can be used to explore student attitudes toward school and learning.

How to Construct and Conduct Interviews

Types of questions that are used on interview forms depend on the purpose for collecting the information. One factor to remember when constructing questions is that students may not always view them in the manner intended or may not understand what information is appropriate for answering them. The best interview questions are both reflective and nondirective. They require students to think about their answers and provide a glimpse of their thought processes. Nondirective questions avoid alerting students to incorrect responses, using double questions that provide too much information, or guiding students to a specific "correct" answer. Asking good probing questions while interviewing is not easy but can provide rich, meaningful information (Y. Goodman, 1992; Rhodes & Shanklin, 1993).

Interviews can be conducted as separate entities or as part of instruction. When interviewing, it is important to explain the purpose for the questions to help place students at ease and increase chances of receiving honest responses. Teachers who are skilled at interviewing watch students carefully to see if they understand and adjust questions accordingly. If they sense that the student is uncomfortable, they reach a stopping point and finish at another time. Interviewing two or three students during times when the class is working independently or in groups often provides information about those students and is often a good indication of what needs to be clarified or taught to the whole class (Y. Goodman, 1992; Rhodes & Shanklin, 1993).

Benefits of Conducting Interviews

One main advantage of interviews is that they are oral. Students frequently provide more elaborate information orally than in writing. Teachers can clarify or further extend students' responses through additional probing questions, which is not possible with written surveys, inventories, or questionnaires. Interviews allow teachers to get to know their students at the beginning of the year, to examine changes in student learning, and to examine their teaching over time. Through interviews, teachers can find data to assist them in designing appropriate strategy lessons and in gathering information to use in curricular decisions to relate what students already know and are interested in to new knowledge. A major purpose for interviews is to gain insight into how students view their own learning ability or feelings toward some learning event. Students participate in self-evaluation as they respond to the questions. Through interviews, your teachers can learn more about students' self-evaluations, their learning, and their choices for inclusion in their portfolios (Cockrum & Castillo, 1991; Y. Goodman, 1992).

Concerns about Using Interviews

Interviews are more time-consuming to administer than checklists or surveys. If they do not match or inform your teachers' instruction, they will not be worth the extra time they require. Teachers need time and practice to develop good interviewing techniques and questions that provide them with rich data about their students.

Rhodes and Shanklin (1993) identified common questioning errors that interfere with gathering valid information. Sometimes teachers guide students toward a certain answer through leading questions. When this happens, teachers are teaching, rather than assessing, because students are following their lead and may provide different responses than when nondirective questions are used. Another problem occurs when teachers paraphrase students' responses. When a teacher uses cueing or interprets student responses, students often repeat the teacher's view, rather than their own, later in the interview. Pressuring often happens when time is short and teachers try to hurry through an interview, but students clam up and provide little useful information. A final problem is overuse of praise, which only reinforces the teacher's role and the student attempting to give answers the teacher wants. Even when teachers ask good interview questions, students are often used to traditional questions and respond as if open-ended questions have right answers. Building trust for honesty is not easy and takes time to achieve.

Inventories, Questionnaires, and Surveys

Inventories, questionnaires, and surveys are interviews that are written, rather than oral. It is sometimes helpful to have students or parents respond in writing to preplanned questions and then follow up on interesting or confusing responses with an oral interview. Since these forms can be answered by an entire class at once, they are often used to save administration time (Cockrum & Castillo, 1991; Y. Goodman, 1992; Rhodes & Shanklin, 1993; Hill & Ruptic, 1994). These forms can be used for a variety of purposes, including

- Interest surveys or inventories provide insights into students' interests and hobbies.

- Attitude forms attempt to discover a student's general perceptions about school.
- Attitude surveys, questionnaires, or inventories can discover attitudes toward specific content areas.
- Forms can be used to determine prior knowledge before studying a topic.
- Parents can provide information about the student's learning at home.
- Self-evaluation is often measured through surveys, inventories, or questionnaires.
- Goals can be listed on inventories.

Constructing Inventories, Questionnaires, and Surveys

Inventories, questionnaires, and surveys are usually presented in short-answer format with open-ended questions. Figure 5.7 is an example of a questionnaire that provides information about students' prior knowledge, attitudes, and interests about the rain forest at the beginning of a unit used in a sixth-grade classroom. Appendix D.8 provides a form that uses a think-aloud procedure with open-ended questions to discover what strategies students use while they are reading.

A second format for questions is a forced-choice response format where students select from a given set of responses that best matches how they feel or think. Appendix D.9 presents a forced-choice format that uses multiple-choice responses on a reading/writing inventory for elementary students. This inventory allows teachers to examine students' literacy attitudes and interests. Another forced-choice format is a Likert scale, which elicits the degree of students' interests in subject areas or topics. Figure 5.8 contains an example of a Likert scale survey, which older students can use to self-evaluate skills they are using in their writing and to determine how much effort was put into the editing process. Your teachers may want to use a combination of these three formats of inventories, questionnaires, and surveys, rather than simply adopting one of them. Using a combination provides more data to reach a more accurate picture of students' responses (Cockrum & Castillo, 1991; Rhodes & Shanklin, 1993; Hill & Ruptic, 1994).

Benefits of Using Inventories, Questionnaires, and Surveys

The main advantage for using inventories, questionnaires, and surveys is that they require written responses, which can be filled in by a whole class at the same time or sent home for students and/or parents to fill out on

Rain Forest Questionnaire

Name_____Date_____

1. What are you interested in learning about rain forests?

2. Where do you think rain forests are located?

3. What kinds of animals live in the rain forest?

4. What kind of plants grow in the rain forest?

5. What do you think the climate is like in a rain forest?

6. Do you think rain forests are important to us? Why or Why not?

7. What kind of projects do you think we should create about rain forests?

8. Do you think rain forests are in danger today? Why do you think that?

Figure 5.7.

EDITING SURVEY

Name_____Date_____

Place an **x** on the line to show the editing strategies that you use.

| | Always | Sometimes | Seldom | Never |

1. I read what I have written over after I have finished.
$\longleftrightarrow$

2. I read my work to someone else.
$\longleftrightarrow$

3. I consider others' suggestions for improving my writing pieces.
$\longleftrightarrow$

4. I use details to support my logic.
$\longleftrightarrow$

5. I use original ideas.
$\longleftrightarrow$

6. I incorporate new vocabulary.
$\longleftrightarrow$

7. The relationship between my sentences is obvious.
$\longleftrightarrow$

8. My writing shows organization.
$\longleftrightarrow$

9. I have a consistent point of view in the piece.
$\longleftrightarrow$

10. I vary my sentence structure.
$\longleftrightarrow$

11. I check and correct misspelled words.
$\longleftrightarrow$

12. I use correct punctuation and capitalization.
$\longleftrightarrow$

13. I use accurate punctuation within sentences.
$\longleftrightarrow$

14. I use clear agreement with pronoun antecedents.
$\longleftrightarrow$

15. I use consistent verb tense.
$\longleftrightarrow$

Figure 5.8.

128

their own. This type of assessment takes much less time to administer than interviews, checklists, or anecdotal records. They can also be easily customized to elicit information that your teachers would find helpful in planning instruction. Attitude surveys can provide useful data about students' likes, dislikes, opinions, and feelings about various school subjects. If these are administered at various times during the school year, growth and change in attitude can be documented. Through inventories, your teachers can discover what their students know, what interests them most, kinds of materials they read, and range of topics they write about. Teachers can use this information to relate what students already know and are interested in to new knowledge and experiences. Questionnaires can uncover students' perceptions of the learning process, purposes for assignments, criteria for evaluating comprehension, and learning strategies for various content areas. Knowing students' interests can help teachers guide them to books, suggest writing topics, learn more about them, and provide a format for self-evaluation (Routman, 1991; DeFina, 1992; Y. Goodman, 1992; Rhodes & Shanklin, 1993).

Concerns about Inventories, Questionnaires, and Surveys

When lengthy oral interviews are simply given to students as an inventory, questionnaire, or survey, students become overwhelmed and often give shorter or different responses than they would orally. This is especially true of those students who have difficulty with writing. While forced-choice inventories provide one solution to this problem, Rhodes and Shanklin (1993) note that they have disadvantages also:

- Teachers cannot be sure that answers students chose are ones they would have given on their own.
- Identifying the best response among several may not be sufficient to know what students would choose to do when no alternatives are given in a real situation.
- Distracters could all be strategies students might use.

Another potential problem is that students may simply provide or choose the responses that they think the teacher wants, rather than giving an honest opinion. As Hill and Ruptic (1994) note, building trust is crucial to alleviating this problem, along with observations of students to judge whether their responses match their actions.

Journal Entries and Logs

Journal entries and logs can be notebooks or booklets with several blank pages stapled together with a front and back cover. Whether booklets or notebooks are used, dating and labeling the topic of each entry provides a framework that readers can use when examining data later (Cockrum & Castillo, 1991; DeFina, 1992).

Journal Entries

Journal entries are usually loosely structured, with students having the freedom to write anything they wish. Topics may or may not be related to school work. Two frequently used types of journals include dialogue journals and peer response journals. In dialogue journals, teachers and students exchange written responses, with both writers choosing any topics they wish. In peer response journals, classmates become pen pals. Both of these journal types encourage students to express their ideas and opinions, while providing teachers with insight into their students' writing abilities, thought processes, and cognitive processing (DeFina, 1992).

Logs

Logs differ from journals in the area of topic choice. In a log, learners usually respond to some agreed-upon topic. Logs can be as simple as a listing of books read, writing topics, or skills/strategies used in learning. Other types of frequently used logs include *reflection logs* and *learning logs* (Cockrum & Castillo, 1991; Routman, 1991; Tierney et al., 1991; DeFina, 1992):

(1) Reflection log: In reflection logs, students reflect on what they learned, what they still have questions about, and what they want to know more about in a particular subject or topic. How students felt about what they learned, what helped or hindered their learning, and their future goals are often other focuses of reflection logs (Routman, 1991; Pigdon & Woolley, 1993).

(2) Learning log: In learning logs, students usually communicate how and what they have understood about a concept or theme. Through this process, students examine and describe their learning processes. Students can ask questions, state hypotheses, make predictions, organize information, note whether this is new learning, make connections that link information, brainstorm ideas, record insights, make observations, and list future learning goals (Baskwill & Whitman, 1988; Routman, 1991; Tierney et al., 1991; Pigdon & Woolley, 1993; Simms, 1994).

Ways to Use Journal Entries and Logs

As Routman (1991) noted, use of writing to think about our lives, materials we read, and what we have learned is becoming more of a focus in classrooms every day. When kindergartners write their first journal entries, teachers have an opportunity to examine their level of writing development. Later, students can provide teachers with information about events, feelings, and people in their lives. They can keep literature logs and learning logs that hold class notes, summaries of materials read, observations from experiments, questions, and predictions as part of thematic units or content area classes in middle school.

Journal and log entries are usually treated as rough drafts that are examined for content and instructional purposes, rather than as finished products that are graded. A better practice is to have students look back through their entries as a way to evaluate their writing progress. Students can use logs to enter views of their learning. They might write how they feel about progress of a current project or what they hope to express in a story, and teachers can respond to them (Cockrum & Castillo, 1991).

Logs can be used to trace writing development by having students include a sheet to record an ongoing list of skills that they are using competently. These can be placed then into students' portfolios when they are full. As students become aware of what strategies and skills they are using in their writing, these should be jotted down on the list. Appendix D.10 is an example of a simple sheet that can be used for this purpose. Heald-Taylor (1989) suggested that teachers divide an 8-1/2″ × 11″ sheet of paper into four columns, which include responses to a draft, strategies the student uses well, strategies being worked on, and spelling that needs to be edited. When the teacher reads a draft of a piece of writing, information is documented on the sheet so that both the teacher and student become aware of personal growth. Eventually, items listed under column three should move to column two, as students gain proficiency in an area. This sheet can then be placed in students' portfolios and reported to parents. Figure 5.9 provides an example of a sheet that could be used for this purpose.

Learning logs can also be used to encourage self-monitoring and reflection. One way to introduce them as a tool for self-evaluation is to ask students to reflect on three things they have learned or one thing they found to be confusing at the end of a unit or activity. Students may then choose to share their responses with the class, a small group, a partner, or the teacher (Cockrum & Castillo, 1991; Anthony et al., 1991). Another way to begin having students reflect on their own learning is to provide them with

WRITING LOG			
Name_____			
Draft Responses	Strategies Being Used Well	Strategies Being Learned	Spelling to Edit

Figure 5.9.

prompts or lead-in phrases. Once students are comfortable with responding to prompts that have been provided for them, your teachers can encourage them to create their own prompts. Some samples of prompts for gathering information about learning styles, learning strategies, student preferences, student perceived strengths, areas they want to improve, and their learning goals are presented in Appendix D.11.

Nyla Simms (1994) has her students write their reflections on learning for ten minutes at least once a day while she monitors the class by reading their responses and taking anecdotal records. Students need many discussions and demonstrations of reflections before they are able to articulate how they learned something. She discusses with them how learning takes place in many ways such as through talking with others, reading, watching demonstrations, asking questions, listening to explanations, watching a video, or real-world experiences. Some content area teachers take five to ten minutes at the beginning or end of a class period to have students respond in their learning logs, which may be used in any subject area (Routman, 1991).

Students can be encouraged to include entire journals or logs as part of their portfolios or to copy parts of them to include. Another way to use learning logs is to give students ten minutes at the end of a week to review their logs and to write a summary of questions or comments about the week's learning, which will be placed into their portfolios. A third way to use them is to invite students to refer to their journals and self-reflections to help them pull their portfolios together or to reflect on their portfolios in their journals (Heald-Taylor, 1989; Tierney et al., 1991; Milliken, 1991).

Benefits of Using Journal Entries and Logs

Routman (1991) notes the versatility of journals and logs. They combine instruction and evaluation, can be used in any subject area, and are appropriate at any grade level. Baskwill and Whitman (1988) maintain that learning logs are especially useful in science, social studies, and mathematics because they provide an immediate view of how students are processing what is happening in the classroom and how they understand the information presented. Your teachers can use students' responses to answer questions such as

- Can students describe what they have learned?
- Can they make connections?
- Can they organize information into coherent thoughts?
- Are they receiving the same message that the teacher is sending?
- Are there concepts that need to be retaught or expanded?

The final benefit for using learning logs and journals is that they serve as a vehicle for meaningful reflection on learning and for self-assessment for students, teachers, and administrators (Tierney et al., 1991; Sunstein, 1991).

Concerns about Using Journal Entries and Logs

As with any assessment tool, there are concerns about using journal entries and logs. Because students are free to write about what they choose in journal entries, sometimes the content reveals private matters that students or their families may not want to share with others (Cockrum & Castillo, 1991). Issues related to privacy are discussed in Chapter 6 under accessibility.

Journal entries and learning logs take class time for demonstrations students will need before they can make reflections about their learning. If students place entire logs or journals in a portfolio, it becomes bulky; however, if they choose parts to include, time must be provided to discuss how to select passages and to actually have students select entries they want to include.

Routman (1991) cautions that teachers can become too involved in examining journals to find areas needing improvement in writing skills. An overemphasis on mechanics detracts from purposes and benefits for using logs and journals. Anthony et al. (1991) remind us that journals should not be overused or students will lose interest as they become a chore or busywork, rather than learning and assessment tools. Too much of a good thing can stifle students' willingness to participate.

Classroom Rubrics

Chapter 3 explained uses of rubrics for comparing student work within and across classrooms to measure benchmarks, while Chapter 7 discusses rubrics as an alternative to traditional report cards. Rubrics explained in this section are those that classroom teachers can use to evaluate student work. Depending on your teachers' needs, they may use commercial rubrics, adapt existing rubrics, create their own rubrics, or have students assist in their creation. These rubrics are part of everyday instruction and can be included in student portfolios along with those created by the school or district to measure benchmarks for learning goals of your school system.

Classroom rubrics are a clear set of guidelines for scoring student work. These guidelines are usually written in increasing order of difficulty. Each level is assigned a numerical value, which moves what might have been considered subjective judgements in the past to more clearly defined and defensible numerical scores (Davis, 1993). The purpose of classroom rubrics is to help teachers clarify their goals, process instruction, and involve students in self-evaluation.

How to Design and Use Classroom Rubrics

As your teachers begin to create and work with classroom rubrics, they will need your support and encouragement. First tries often require many revisions before teachers are satisfied that intended outcomes or standards are indeed being measured. Teachers are usually more comfortable brainstorming with colleagues while creating their first rubrics and bringing results back to share and revise further before using it again. First attempts are usualy too achievement-oriented, with little attention given to effort, growth, or improvement. Students can provide feedback about success of the assessment and suggest needed changes. Once teachers are comfortable with creating rubrics, they often have students assist in creating them because students will then know expectations for a project, piece of writing, report, or other assignment from the beginning (Routman, 1991).

Having your teachers use these rules for using indicators in rubrics will help develop classroom rubrics that will be meaningful assessment tools:

- Indicators must be relevant to standards, benchmarks, goals, and objectives.
- Indicators should be spelled out before students begin the work that will be evaluated with the rubric.
- Each level in the rubric should have at least three indicators.
- The first use of the rubric is to gather baseline data to set criteria for success.
- Rubrics should have specified levels of what will be considered as a success or incomplete work.

Rubrics have three or more levels of achievement. Many rubrics have a five-point scale. We have found it useful to begin with the level that demonstrates what a good paper, assignment, or project would look like. What characteristics would it have? What must it include? Then we move up to the next level. What would make this work truly outstanding? What additional features or qualities would make the work clearly superior to the good one? Next, we move down to the second level. Here, students have much of the concept or needed characteristics, but it is not quite there. What would this look like? After this, we focus on the project or work that is not acceptable. What would be the characteristics of this work? It could still have some good features, but most would lack quality work. A final level could be one that shows no effort, has major portions missing, or simply is not attempted.

Teachers can use classroom rubrics that they have created themselves for any subject area. Students can use rubrics for self-evaluations and to compare their results with those of the teacher. Examples of using classroom rubrics for student self-evaluation are provided in Chapter 4. In Chapter 8, examples of rubrics that are used for peer evaluations and parent input into evaluation are provided. Figure 5.10 is an example of a four-point rubric that was used in a high school social studies class. The focus of this rubric was on making decisions. Students have a clear indication of what is quality work, good work, passing criteria, and unacceptable work. The five-point rubric presented in Appendix D.12 was used for

---

Social Studies Decision-Making Rubric

Name _____ Date _____

4. All issues identified by the student are relevant.
   Student accurately and insightfully assesses the implications of each issue as favoring or opposing the decision.
   Student's explanation of his/her decision is thorough and completely consistent with his/her rankings.
   Student's work indicates insightful use of specific relevant information.

3. Student identifies relevant issues.
   Student accurately assesses the implication of each criterion as favoring or opposing the issue.
   Student's explanation of his/her decision is consistent with his or her findings and is complete.
   Student's work reflects meaningful use of relevant information.

2. Most issues selected by the student are relevant.
   Student usually accurately assesses the implication of each issue as favoring or opposing the decision.
   Student's explanation of his/her decision is partly unclear and/or not consistent with his/her chart.
   Student's work reflects some use of relevant knowledge.

1. Many irrelevant issues are selected by the student.
   The implications of each issue as favoring or opposing the decision is incomplete or inaccurate.
   The student's explanation of his/her decision is not consistent with his/her rankings or incomplete.
   Student does not use relevant information.

Figure 5.10.

problem solving in a middle school mathematics classroom. Indicators on this rubric relate to problem solving, communication, and computation. Again, the criteria for achieving each level are clearly articulated for the student.

Benefits of Classroom Rubrics

A well-designed classroom rubric can assist teachers in scoring students' work more accurately and fairly. It can also give students a clearer picture of what qualities their work should have. Students become aware of characteristics of quality work and are therefore in a better position to achieve it. Rubrics often include both process and products in varius contexts and can be used for any subject area at any grade level. They can be used by teachers, students, and parents with equal ease. Not only can students help create rubrics, but they can also use them for self- and peer evaluations (Routman, 1991; O'Neil, 1994). Your teachers can use them to assess standards or student demonstrations and use time effectively. There are several key points that make classroom rubrics a valuable alternative assessment tool:

- Criteria are explicitly stated and understandable.
- Awareness of criteria is easily obtained.
- Assessor is able to use time more efficiently.
- Student accountability in subject areas is enhanced.
- Classroom rubrics are easily modified to meet individual needs.
- Classroom rubrics are easily adjusted to meet grade-level objectives.
- Classroom rubrics are easily adjusted to meet the needs of an inclusion classroom.

Concerns about Using Classroom Rubrics

While classroom rubrics have many benefits, there are also concerns or cautions that apply to using them. One concern is that teachers need time to learn how to create rubrics that will match their instructional and assessment needs, rather than simply adopting those that are on the market, if your goal is to have them realize potential benefits to their instructional practices. Before teachers allow students to help create classroom rubrics or use them for self-assessment or peer evaluation, they must believe students need to be involved in their learning and assessment.

Sometimes, teachers learn how to use a new assessment technique and apply it to everything they teach. You may need to remind your teachers that every piece of work students produce does not necessarily need to be assessed or graded and that overuse of any one assessment tool lessens its effectiveness. Some classroom activities, assignments, or projects lend themselves better to being assessed through observations, checklists, learning logs, or inventories.

STUDENT WORK SAMPLES AND ARTIFACTS

Heald-Taylor (1989) maintains that work samples over time are one of the best ways to show growth in student learning. Samples and artifacts that can be included in a portfolio are limitless. Possibilities that we will explore include writing samples, conceptual maps, sketching to stretch, artwork, photographs, audiotapes, videotapes, projects, and awards. In this section, we provide descriptions of each, information they provide, or ways they can be used. Advantages and disadvantages of including work samples and other artifacts are explored at the conclusion of this section.

Writing Samples

Possibilities of writing samples to include in portfolios are limitless. Types of student writing samples your school community will want to include depend on purpose for the portfolio, type of portfolio being used, and audience for the work. In this chapter, we present examples of writing samples that many school communities, teachers, and students have included in portfolios of various types.

Multiple Drafts and Published Pieces

When students display a piece of writing from the first draft through to its publication, they can celebrate achievements and analyze writing development, decision-making abilities, and use of the revision process (Porter & Cleland, 1995). These writing samples also provide evidence of growth in mechanics of writing such as handwriting, spelling, conventions, grammar, and composition (Heald-Taylor, 1989).

Letters

Students may wish to include copies of letters they have written or received from others because they remind them of specific learning events (Porter & Cleland, 1995). DeFina (1992) notes that these shorter contexts are more easily assessed for knowledge of audience, purpose, format, and mechanics of writing.

Essays and Reports

Including different kinds of essays such as problem/solution statements in portfolios provides information about understanding of various genre and students' ability to write in a variety of styles. Reports demonstrate students' research abilities, organizational skills, reporting formats, and understanding of content material (DeFina, 1992; Hewitt, 1995).

Creative Writing

Whether it is a short story, an innovation of a story, or a poem, creative writing provides a way for students to demonstrate their imaginations, metaphorical thinking, and ability to use language innovations on a story. They can highlight students' comprehension of story line, understanding of characterization, ability to make predictions, and ability to establish a theme that relates to the original story. Poetry may represent students' understanding of various forms of poetry, figurative language, and ability to use alternative writing formats (DeFina, 1992).

Conceptual Maps

Conceptual maps, mind maps, and semantic maps are a way to represent links or relationships between concepts in visual form that can also incorporate art in a form that is often easier for students to understand. Sometimes, large posters are used to provide enough room for students to make connections between concepts. When students draw a concept map, they demonstrate what they know about a topic or field of knowledge. Concept maps use a combination of the student's prior knowledge and understanding of work that has been completed (Pigdon & Woolley, 1993). These maps can be used at all grade levels in any subject area. Conceptual maps can also be used as pretests and posttests to measure students' growth in learning.

Sketch to Sketch

Porter and Cleland (1995) allow students to place samples of this strategy in portfolios. Sketch to Sketch is an alternative form of communication about literature that students have read. Sketching an interpretation has provided their students with an opportunity to use their imaginations and to see many ways to interpret a text so they can take risks in their own interpretations. Armstrong (1994) recommends using sketching to demonstrate character development or the plot of a book to support multiple intelligences in the classroom.

Harriet White uses sketching to help her fifth graders comprehend both fiction and nonfiction. Students use character development diagrams, story grid maps, and large sheets of ABC's that are drawn to represent concepts about a unit of study in various content areas. These sketches are often used for assessment and included in her students' portfolios to demonstrate their knowledge of subject matter.

Artwork

Illustrations, sketches, paintings, doodles, dioramas, maps, comic strips, and other artwork should not be overlooked as a part of portfolios because they may have been the inspiration or rough draft for a piece of writing, an interpretation of literature, or a connection between one communication system and another. Not all students can express themselves best through writing. Including artwork allows visually or spatially oriented students to demonstrate their knowledge and understanding of content as well as writing does for the linguistically oriented student (DeFina, 1992; Armstrong, 1994).

Photographs

Photographs can provide an answer for including items that will not fit well in portfolios, such as three-dimensional projects, some of the artwork mentioned in the previous section, or science inventions. A Polaroid camera can be kept in the classroom for just this purpose.

Photographs can also be used to capture students using various strategies in the learning process that do not lend themselves well to other forms of documentation. For example, students might be photographed when they are taking risks, becoming more personally involved in learning, or investigating questions or ideas (Porter & Cleland, 1995).

Audiocassettes

Audiocassettes can be placed in portfolios for many different reasons. One frequent use of audiotapes is to record reading samples. Students can be involved by having them record why they chose the book that they read onto the tape and how the tape shows their progress as readers. Then they can record their future goals on the tape and/or in writing. As students listen to themselves reading on tape, they become better at monitoring their fluency and reading with expression (Hill & Ruptic, 1994). Baskwill and Whitman (1988) recommend having students read two selections on the tape: one they choose and one that the teacher chooses. The information collected will reflect both fluent reading on familiar text and use of strategies on more difficult unrehearsed material. Woodward (1994) suggests that parents, teachers, and students review the tapes periodically and note growth in learning. Sara Shriver uses the taped reading assessment sheet in Figure 5.11 with the Title I first-grade students. She uses this form once each semester and goes over comments with individual students and encourages them to help in the assessment process. Teachers of beginning readers may want to include running records along with the audiotapes, while teachers of more experienced readers may want to include a miscue analysis to explain a student's strengths and needs in the reading process.

Other material that may be recorded on audiocassettes includes retellings, jokes, riddles, stories, memories, opinions, musical ability, storytelling, a strategy for creating a rough draft piece of writing, an editing device that has been effective, a song that a student felt was significant in learning, changes in risk taking during group discussions, or a speech they gave (Baskwill & Whitman, 1988; Heald-Taylor, 1989; Armstrong, 1994; Porter & Cleland, 1995). Regardless of the way audiocassettes are used, each entry on the tape needs to be dated so that growth can be measured.

Videotapes

Another way to document those hard-to-record events is through videotaping. Videotaping can provide a greater context than simply taking photographs because they are not static and can provide visual data in addition to audio records. When students are videotaped while reading, teachers can note how the book was held; if students are using eye, voice, and print matching; whether pages are turned on cue; facial expressions; and other aspects of reading behavior. Videotapes can then be shared with parents to demonstrate what their children are doing during reading and to show growth in reading ability (Baskwill & Whitman, 1988).

Other examples of activities that lend themselves to videotaped documentation include acting out a role in a play, demonstrating how to perform a task, giving reports, participating in literature discussions, editing peer's writing in writer's workshop, and presenting projects created for various subject areas. Your teachers may also want to include videotapes of their teaching in their portfolios to demonstrate their teaching philosophy, strategies they teach, and classroom instruction (Baskwill & Whitman, 1988; Armstrong, 1994; Woodward, 1994).

Projects

Project work is another area that can be examined in the assessment pro-

Taped Reading Assessment Sheet

Student _____

Date _____

Name of Recorder _____

    1.   Familar Rereading   or   New Text

    2.   Teacher Selected   or   Student Selected

Name of Text_____

Level _____

Characteristic	+	W	–
Speaks clearly when reading			
Recognizes high frequency words			
Recognizes beginning blends			
Recognizes word endings			
Makes reference to question marks			
Reads with expression			

What do I need to do to help this student improve in areas of need?

_____

_____

_____

_____

(+) Student is successful

(W) Student is still working on this

(–) Student needs more help

Figure 5.11.

cess and included in student portfolios. Your teachers may find a contract system to be an efficient method of involving children in the evaluation process and of keeping track of the necessary recording. In Chapter 4, we shared a contract one teacher used when middle school students made picture books to share with elementary students. Sometimes, actual projects are too large to fit into students' portfolios. Then students may want to consider using photographs or videotapes to document their projects.

School Awards

Another artifact that students often choose to place in portfolios is awards they receive at school. Awards can include certificates of attendance, honors for academic performance, and special awards. For example, Michael Rose included his Martin Luther King Peace Award in his portfolio. He and some of his classmates received the award for a videotape that they chose to make as a culmination for the unit on prejudice that their class had finished.

Benefits of Including Work Samples and School-Related Artifacts

Including work samples and various school-related artifacts as a part of student portfolios provides teachers with a wider range of assessment measures to construct a more complete picture of a student's learning. These items allow teachers to focus on the process of learning as well as products. Often, students select which artifacts to place in their portfolios, and these choices provide more data to assess. Finally, having these items as options meets the needs of a variety of learners with different learning styles and preferences for cognitive processing.

Concerns about Including Work Samples and School-Related Artifacts

The main concern your teachers will probably express when these items are included as options for inclusion is that portfolios will become unmanageable with too many items. There is the risk that the portfolio can become simply a scrapbook, rather than an assessment tool, when too many of these artifacts are selected. They also make the process of evaluating portfolios more difficult. These issues are explored further in Chapters 6 and 7.

SAMPLES FROM OUTSIDE OF SCHOOL

Some options of materials from outside of school that some communities have chosen to place in portfolios include personal artifacts from students' lives, job-related artifacts, materials from organizations that students belong to, and learning evidence from athletic events. Possibilities for each of these areas are explored in this section along with benefits and concerns about including out-of-school materials in a portfolio.

Artifacts from Beyond Classroom Borders

Hansen (1994) contends that literacy and learning are not school property. If portfolios are going to represent learning, students must be permitted to include nonschool items. These items give insight into students' uses of literacy and learning outside of school. By encouraging students to include nonschool items in their portfolios, your teachers validate students' lives outside of school. Salvio (1994) reminds us that popular culture, film, television, family life, neighborhoods, catalogs, and comic books contribute in complex ways to what children claim to know, believe, and value.

Another source of out-of-school artifacts is parental input. Parents have valuable information to share about their children's learning outside of school. Chapters 8 and 9 explore ways that parents can be involved in portfolio assessment. One way to involve parents is to have them provide information that can be placed in portfolios.

Job-Related Artifacts

Job-related artifacts are especially useful for inclusion in an employability portfolio. In these portfolios, students showcase their skills for future employment, the military, or college admission. To provide evidence of an academic skill such as "writing in the language in which business is conducted," a student could include a letter from a past or present employer (Stemmer et al., 1992). Students can create resumes to demonstrate their employment experiences. They could also include recommendation or evaluations by employers.

Organizations and Sports

Students may include lists of organizations in which they participate, such as drama clubs, debate teams, future teachers, band, and athletics. Students can also include materials that originate in activities outside of school such as boy scouts, girl scouts, 4-H, volunteer groups, or church organizations. To document a teamwork standard such as "actively participating in a group," a student could include proof of membership in one or more such organizations (Stemmer et al., 1992). To satisfy some of the standards for an employability portfolio, Rita Kirby created the form in Figure 5.12 to evaluate students' teamwork skills in extracurricular organizations and the form in Appendix D.13 to measure these skills in sports.

Benefits of Including Nonschool Items

Including nonschool items in student portfolios provides a picture of the whole student and not just the view present at school, and it supplies a richer information base to examine in measuring student learning.

Extracurricular Evaluation by Advisor

Student's Name _____ Activity _____

___ Actively participates / is productive in group
___ Follows group rules and values
___ Listens to other group members
___ Expresses ideas to other group members
___ Is sensitive to group members' ideas and views
___ Is willing to compromise if necessary to best accomplish the goal
___ Is a leader or follower to best accomplish the goal
___ Works in changing settings with different people
___ Relates well with peers
___ (Other) _____
___ (Other) _____

Comments _____
_____
_____
_____
_____

Advisor's signature _____ Date _____

1 = Excellent
2 = Average
3 = Needs improvement

Source: Rita Kirby. 1994. *Portfolio Development Masters.* Handout of blackline masters. Mt. Pleasant, MI: Rita Kirby Portfolio Consultant.

Figure 5.12. *Sample Organizational Evaluation Form.*

Nonschool items can meet the needs of students with different learning styles and a variety of cognitive processing styles. Using these items is a way to involve parents and community members in portfolio assessment. Nonschool items can be especially useful in employability portfolios.

Concerns about Including Nonschool Items

The same concerns that surface when work samples and school-related artifacts are included in portfolios apply to nonschool items. Portfolios can become unmanageable, too bulky, and unfocused. The greater the variety of items in the portfolio, the more difficult questions of equity and comparability become. These are not unsurmountable problems, but they take time to work through. Chapters 6 and 7 will examine these issues in more detail.

TRADITIONAL TESTING

Marzano (1994) maintains that emphasis on new formats for gathering assessment and evaluation information is a necessary change; however, it does not necessarily imply that traditional forms of assessment are obsolete because there is no one answer to issues of assessing learning. He believes that the challenge to today's educators is to take the best that current research and theory have to offer and combine this with the best of what has been successful and useful in traditional testing. Murphy (1992) reminds us that a test in and of itself is neither valid nor invalid; it is up to the test user to decide whether a certain test is valid for use in a particular situation.

Teacher-Made Tests

Traditional teacher-made tests usually include multiple-choice, true-false, cloze, short answer, and essay formats. DeFina (1992) suggests that including some exams and quiz papers in a portfolio may be of some value in offering insight into students' abilities to perform in testing situations, to recall and/or apply information, and to respond to carefully crafted questions while using critical thinking skills.

Routman (1991) concedes that there are times when a test with open-ended questions can provide valuable information if students are provided with teacher expectations without being given rigid guidelines. If your teachers are simply interested in discovering what facts students know, then a fact-finding test is appropriate, but if they want to discover whether students understand what they've learned, questions that require them to use the information studied is more useful (Baskwill & Whitman, 1988). Baskwill and Whitman (1988) maintain that multiple-choice, matching, and fill-in-the-blank questions do not allow teachers to view learning processes. They suggest using questions that challenge students to think. These questions should go beyond simply providing correct answers and include questions such as the following:

• If the following facts are true, what would happen if . . .
• In light of what you know about . . . what would you do if . . .
• Based upon what you have learned, what would you do in the following situation . . .

One traditional measure frequently used in many classrooms is the cloze procedure. In traditional cloze procedure, every fifth word is deleted, for a total of fifty blanks in a passage of approximately 250 words. Correct responses are tallied, and students receive a percentage of correct responses. This format can be used to gage knowledge of a new topic, to determine appropriate readability of a passage, and to check comprehension after studying the material (Vacca & Vacca, 1993).

In a nontraditional format for cloze, teachers control how many and which words are deleted. By controlling these features, teachers can assess vocabulary knowledge, use of specific processing strategies, use of linguistic knowledge, real-world knowledge, and knowledge of story line. The main strength of using cloze in this manner is that your teachers will have detailed information about students' learning strategies (Rhodes & Shanklin, 1993; Woodward, 1994).

Before deciding whether to include teacher-made tests in portfolios, your teachers will need to determine what standards and benchmarks the tests measure and whether they provide the clearest picture of this knowledge. The key is to use a variety of measures, rather than one-time shots to determine student learning.

Text Publisher's Tests

Commercial tests include end of chapter tests, tests that accompany texts, and specific subject matter tests. Basal reader end-of-unit tests measure student mastery of the vocabulary and skills covered in the unit and are indistinguishable from workbook and skill sheets (Harman, 1992). If your teachers are using literature-based reading or basals with more authentic activities replacing workbook pages, the validity and usefulness of these tests are dubious.

Commercial tests are more obtrusive to instruction than the previous assessment tools mentioned in this chapter because they are decontextualized or created by outsiders who do not know the specific curriculum, instruction methods, activities, and student needs in your teachers' classroom. The tasks are usually not the same as those that are used for instruction, there are often time constraints, and answers are usually right or wrong. These tests can only reveal what students do in a limited setting on a test administered in a short time period and containing only the tasks that were tested (Rhodes & Shanklin, 1993).

On the other hand, commercial tests provide data that can be compared across classrooms, schools, and districts and can provide information about students' test-taking abilities and mastery of skills. The most appropriate type of portfolio for this data to placed into is the assessment or cumulative school portfolio.

Mandated Tests

Mandated tests are usually criterion-referenced, performance samples or tasks, or standardized tests. All of these measures are decontextualized because they produce scores that do not originate in the instructional context of the classroom. These tests can be mandated at the local, district, state, or provincial level (Anthony et al., 1991).

Mandated tests provide information that can be compared across classrooms, schools, and districts. These are tests that are often used to make policy decisions, indicate program strengths and weaknesses, and to make curriculum decisions. Their usefulness in day-to-day instructional decisions and those affecting individual students are often questionable. If these tests are to be placed in portfolios, their most logical placement would be in assessment or cumulative school portfolios.

Performance Samples or Tasks

Some states, provinces, and schools have mandated performance tasks. These are done primarily to provide assessment data although they resemble regular classroom activities much more than criterion-referenced or standardized tests. The essential components of performance-based assessments are that tasks to be assessed must be a learning experience and that the activity is relevant in the real world beyond the classroom (Hewitt, 1995). However, when students are removed from regular classroom settings to perform, even real-world tasks can also become obtrusive. While performance-based assessments provide data that is useful to classroom teachers and can be used for policy-making at all levels, it takes a long time to make judgements based on real student work, and it is difficult to ensure consistency of human judgement from reviewer to reviewer.

Criterion-Referenced Tests

Criterion-referenced tests are based on standards or skills that students must reach. There is usually a cutoff score for passing, and students are compared by whether they passed required portions of the test. Schools use data generated by these tests to make program and curricular decisions. Individual students can be affected when these are high-stakes tests that require passing scores to be promoted or to receive a high school diploma (Vacca & Vacca, 1993).

Criterion-referenced tests must be examined to determine the degree to which the test items match the curriculum of the school or district. Even though some types of criterion-referenced tests may have detailed coverage of specific areas, depth of coverage must not be mistaken for a closer fit to classroom instruction. When judging validity of these tests, criteria must be the same as those for the curriculum (Murphy, 1992). These criteria must match standards and benchmarks your school community has developed while building your vision.

Standardized Tests

Four of the most widely used standardized tests are the California Achievement Test, the Iowa Test of Basic Skills, the Metropolitan Achievement Test, and the Stanford Achievement Test. Common characteristics of these standardized tests include that they ask the same questions across different populations to permit comparisons, are primarily composed of multiple-choice items, and are norm-referenced (Murphy, 1992; Shultz, 1992).

By being norm-referenced, they are based on the normal curve, which means that, on a well-constructed standardized test, 50 percent of the students at a given grade level will score above a statistically derived average number of correct answers, and 50 percent will score below that number. Questions are manipulated or changed until this balance is achieved. Therefore, it is erroneous for educators, parents, legislators, the media, or the public to assume that more students should score above the fiftieth percentile. When too many districts report that more than half their students score above the fiftieth percentile, test publishers will renorm their tests to achieve the desired balance (Shultz, 1992; Rhodes & Shanklin, 1993).

There has been and continues to be a lot of debate over the usefulness of standardized tests. Test scores are treated as if they were magic numbers with school boards and districts requiring them and newspapers ranking schools and districts by their scores (Baskwill & Whitman, 1988; Shultz, 1992). Some authors of these tests believe that they have been given too much weight and power to make decisions such as determining the fate of students, teachers, principals, programs, and whole schools. They feel that parents, researchers, policymakers, and the public have become too dependent on test scores and use them to make policy decisions that the tests are not good at making. These test authors claim that the main purpose for standardized tests is to give parents, teachers, and administrators an external view of the student (Routman, 1991; Shultz, 1992).

Standardized tests have been used to assess student's knowledge of isolated facts and skills. Use of these tests has influenced teaching practices and reporting procedures. The tests have been popular because they provide numerical data for making comparisons, give quick results, are meant to be objective, and have traditionally been used to measure students' progress. As Pigdon and Woolley (1993) note, these reasons have nothing to do with learning because standardized tests cannot recognize development of thought processes, cooperative problem solving, or decision-making skills. They are just indicators of how well a student took the test on a given day, not how well that student reads or learns (Baskwill & Whitman, 1988).

Standardized tests do tell administrators, teachers, and parents how a student compares with peers, but they provide little information that is useful for daily instructional decisions and no information about the learning process over time. These tests usually operate on a deficit model of what students can't do. Often the multiple-choice question format is foreign to elementary students and does not allow students to interpret the text based on prior knowledge and experience. Right answers have been determined by the test makers and reflect their biases (Routman, 1991; Murphy, 1992; Rhodes & Shanklin, 1993).

Anthony et al. (1991) recommend that these decontextualized measures be used outside of portfolios because they are not appropriate for assessing an individual student's progress. If they must be used, these measures should provide data to be considered in program evaluation. Perrone (1992) provided several reasons for using caution with standardized test scores. These reasons included risk of loss of student self-esteem; distortion of the curriculum, teaching, and learning; and lowering of expectations. There are numerous concerns with the tests themselves. Chapter 1 provides an indepth look at standardized testing and how it compares to portfolio assessment. When you and your stakeholders are considering whether to include standardized test scores as part of student portfolios or cumulative school portfolios, we recommend answering questions such as the following:

- Do they provide information about standards that your school community has selected?

- Do the tests provide useful information about individual students?
- Are the passages short and contrived or meaningful?
- Do the tests assist students in learning?
- Do they provide useful information to make instructional decisions?
- Do they provide useful information for parents?
- Are the tests biased?

Troubleshooting: With So Many Choices, How Do I Know What to Place in Portfolios?

Often, when teachers realize the unlimited potential for items that can be placed into portfolios, they become overwhelmed and want someone else to tell them what to place in the portfolios. Many do not trust children to choose their own artifacts to include because grading or assessing has traditionally been the teacher's job, and changing roles is not easy. Others do not trust themselves in deciding which items will demonstrate student learning and attainment of standards selected by your school community. This is a time when teachers will especially need your support, guidance, and communication of trust in their abilities.

The types of assessment tools and portfolio items that your teachers choose for inclusion depend on several factors. Teachers' philosophies will play a determing factor in which tools and items they begin collecting. Chapters 4, 7, and 8 examine teachers' philosophies and provide suggestions to help you assist them in discovering what their beliefs are about teaching, learning, and assessment.

Chapter 6 deals with the nuts and bolts of managing portfolio implementation. Issues that are examined that affect the selection of items for inclusion include

- the content area(s) being taught
- the standards and benchmarks determined while the staff was getting ready to implement portfolios
- the purposes for creating the portfolio
- types of portfolios that will be used

One area that is crucial to having a true portfolio is the use of self-evaluation of learning by students, teachers, and principals. Chapter 4 provided extensive information that can help your teachers determine what types of self-assessments they will have students include in their portfolios. Suggestions and forms that will be helpful for all portfolio participants are provided.

In the end, the portfolios in each teacher's classroom will vary somewhat, even when a school community has made decisions about what artifacts should be required in them. Some teachers will only include required items, others will allow students to add additional support materials, and still others will leave out some of the required items. All of them will need your encouragement and support as they venture into the change process to continue working towards sustained portfolio implementation.

GLOSSARY

Anecdotal Records: brief, dated notes written by an observer during or after an observation of a student.

Artifact: an item that can be placed in a portfolio.

Checklist: an assessment tool that contains a list of learning traits or descriptors to observe and a system to mark the occurrence or quality of the trait during observation.

Classroom Rubric: an assessment tool used to evaluate daily classroom instruction and student work. It is a clear set of guidelines written in increasing difficulty with each level assigned a numerical value.

Conceptual Maps: a graphic organizer that is a way to represent the links or relationships between concepts in a visual form.

Criterion-Referenced Tests: commercial tests that use standards or levels of mastery to determine students' levels or proficiency. Scores are often provided in terms of having passed a certain number of competencies. These tests are often ones chosen for mandated testing at local, district, state, or provincial levels.

Decontextualized Assessments: assessments that originate outside of classroom instruction and are created by outsiders who have no direct contact with students, local curriculum, or daily instructional practices.

Descriptors: indicators or traits of observable student behavior that are clearly stated and often used in checklists and on classroom rubrics.

Dialogue Journals: a journal in which teachers and students exchange written responses with both writers choosing any topics they wish.

Indicators: descriptors or traits of observable student behavior that are clearly stated and often used in checklists and on classroom rubrics.

Interviews: an assessment tool that is conducted orally using open-ended questions.

Inventories: interviews in written form with short answer, open-ended questions, forced-choice items, Likert scale items, or any combination of these that can be used to find information about interests, attitudes, opinions, prior knowledge, self-reflection, or goal setting.

Journal Entries: loosely structured writings, with students often having the freedom to write about anything they wish in a notebook or booklet. The topics may or may not be school-related.

Learning Log: logs where students communicate how and what they have understood about a concept or theme. A vehicle for examining and describing learning processes.

Logs: more structured writings kept in a notebook or booklet with learners responding to some agreed-upon topic.

Mandated Performance Tasks: tasks where students are required to demonstrate their knowledge by producing a product. The task must be a learning experience and relevant to the real world beyond school.

Mind Maps: graphic representation of materials that uses artwork, words, and lines to connect related concepts.

Miscue Analysis: an assessment tool that examines the deviations that readers make when they read text orally. The miscues are examined to find patterns, strengths, and needs in students' use of reading strategies. Then the results are used for planning effective instruction.

Norm-Referenced Tests: tests based on the normal curve so that 50 percent of the students at a given grade level will score above a statistically derived average number of correct responses for that grade level and 50 percent will score below that number.

Peer Response Journal: a journal in which classmates serve as pen pals.

Questionnaires: interviews in written form with short answer, open-ended questions, forced-choice items, Likert scale items, or any combination of these, which are often used to elicit interests, attitudes, opinions, prior knowledge, self-reflection, or goal setting.

Reflection Logs: log in which students reflect on what they have learned, what they still have questions about, their strengths, areas needing improvement, goals for future learning, and what they want to know more about in a particular subject area or on a particular topic for a unit of study.

Retelling: an assessment that follows an oral or silent reading of narrative or expository text. The reader is asked to tell in his/her own words the information just read. Retellings can be done orally or in writing. They can be followed by guided questions by the teacher. Retellings are analyzed to determine comprehension.

Running Record: an analysis of beginning readers' oral reading to determine patterns, strengths, and needs in students' use of reading strategies. Then the results are used for planning effective instruction.

Semantic Maps: a graphic organizer that has the topic in the center, categories connected to center by lines, and details connected to each of the categories; related concepts are connected by lines.

Standardized Tests: tests with the following common characteristics: they ask the same questions across different populations to permit comparisons, are primarily composed of multiple-choice items, and are norm-referenced.

Surveys: interviews in written form with short answer, open-ended questions, forced-choice items, Likert scale items, or any combination of these and often used to elicit interests, attitudes, opinions, prior knowledge, self-reflection, or goal setting.

Transmission Model of Teaching: traditional teaching where the teacher is the expert who presents material, and the students are vessels who absorb the information provided.

Managing the Nuts and Bolts

Miss Shippee's Reflections about Her Classroom Assessment

I see our classroom as a laboratory where everyone is a teacher and all of us are learners. We are all risk takers, so it must be a safe place for us to learn from one another. My role is modeling, guiding, and encouraging.

Assessment is personal, informal, and formal. It is meant to give direction to our goals as well as serve as benchmarks for our journey. It is analyzed together in a safe, caring environment the students helped create. Children set goals, evaluate, and restructure or start with a new plan that better serves their learning needs.

Assessment tools include application of skills and performance. They may be formal, informal, self, peer, or teacher evaluations. Teacher and student sit down and talk over major evaluations. Input from the owner is the most important.

Miss Shippee's Fourth-Grade Students' Reflections about Their Portfolios

I like my portfolio because, from the beginning of the year, I get to see all the work I did from the first day of school. When it is conference time, I get to show my mom and dad all my work.

I like the portfolio because I can look back and see what I've done. I put the Vantassle farm from *The Legend of Sleepy Hollow* in it so I wouldn't lose it because I was very proud of the picture I drew.

I feel good about my portfolio because I put in my papers that I'm proud of, and I feel good about them. I have had a portfolio before, but it was only a little one. In my portfolio, there is math, social studies, geography, language arts, and science.

I feel my portfolio is a memory folder, and it holds all my favoritest papers too!

155

INTRODUCTION

IN this chapter, we discuss the logistics of portfolios or the nitty-gritty decisions about how to handle portfolios. Miss Shippee and her students had to deal with issues such as

- What were their purposes for their portfolios?
- What type of portfolio would they use?
- Who would decide what to place in their portfolios?
- What artifacts should be placed in their portfolios?
- Who will have access to them?
- What would they use as containers for their artifacts?
- Where would they store these containers?
- When and how would they access, add, and delete portfolio items?
- How will they organize their portfolio contents?
- How can peer evaluation be used to enhance their portfolios?
- Who will be the audience for these portfolios?
- Who will be the owners of these portfolios?
- How will the information gathered be used?
- How will they share their portfolios with others?
- How will their portfolios be evaluated or graded?

This chapter deals with portfolio issues of purposes, types, ownership, selection of artifacts, accessibility, containers, storage, maintenance, and organization. Issues such as types of artifacts, evaluating or grading portfolio contents, meeting various audiences' needs, stakeholders' roles, professional portfolios, decision making with portfolios, and sharing portfolio contents are examined in the remaining chapters of this book. We conclude this chapter by discussing a comment that principals frequently hear when teachers begin to consider portfolio implementation: "There's no space in my room for storage cabinets!"

WHAT ARE THE PURPOSES FOR PORTFOLIOS?

Before your teachers plunge into collecting and storing student work, they need to think about the purposes for their students' portfolios. Portfolios can serve two main functions: to improve daily instruction within the classroom or to be used beyond the classroom for schoolwide, district, state, or provincial evaluation, accountability, or curricular decision making (Anthony et al., 1991; DeFina, 1992; Hill & Ruptic, 1994). Portfolios that are used beyond the classroom will most likely be very different from those used for classroom purposes. Students are more likely to place items of personal growth and rough drafts into classroom portfolios. Some purposes that would benefit daily instruction include

- celebrating growth over time
- exhibiting a student's best work
- developing a sense of process
- reflecting risk taking and experimentation
- creating a means for self-evaluation
- determining and setting individual goals
- empowering students to develop a sense of ownership
- nurturing students
- fostering a positive self-concept
- improving instruction
- providing real-world learning opportunities
- sharing information with families and other teachers

When the main function of the portfolio is to serve schoolwide, district, state, and/or provincial needs, the purposes for portfolios are quite different (DeFina, 1992; Hill & Ruptic, 1994). For instance, if portfolios are used to evaluate a program, students will most likely include their best work because knowing portfolios will be evaluated affects the types of work students and teachers choose to include (Hill & Ruptic, 1994). Some of these broader uses of portfolio data include

- measuring school accountability
- making curricular decisions
- evaluating programs
- comparing students' portfolio results across classrooms
- observing growth in minority culture populations
- measuring student progress against standards created beyond the classroom
- facilitating faculty discussion about goals and means of reaching them
- empowering teachers
- supporting change in teaching practices and assessment

WHAT TYPES OF PORTFOLIOS ARE THERE?

Once your community of stakeholders has determined what combination of purposes your portfolios will serve, you will need to encourage teachers to consider what type or types of portfolios they will have in their classrooms. One of the problems your staff will face is the different purposes from within and beyond the classroom, which leads to surveying a variety of different types of portfolios. Current portfolio literature presents nine basic types of portfolios: class, master subject area, learning, growth, documentation, showcase, accountability, employability, and professional.

Class Portfolios

Hill and Ruptic (1994) noted that some teachers have chosen to keep a class portfolio, rather than a scrapbook, to record significant projects, units, trips, and guests. This type of portfolio would provide your teachers with another way to model how to collect, select, and reflect upon portfolio entries. What separates the class portfolio from a scrapbook is the process of selecting and reflecting on artifacts that illustrate the multitude of events that happen in the classroom. As a group, the teacher and students would decide the purpose for the portfolio, what to include in it, captions for the artifacts, reflections about each of them, and some goals for the class.

Master Subject Area Portfolios

Master portfolios contain materials from one subject area such as writing, literacy, mathematics, science, or social studies and usually remain in the classroom. Students have ongoing responsibility and ownership, with teachers offering guidance for selecting artifacts. First drafts through finished products are often included in these portfolios. They can become unwieldy quickly, because students may place any related content materials in the portfolio. Only the current year's work is included in a master subject area portfolio (Rhodes & Shanklin, 1993; Hewitt, 1995).

Learning Portfolios

Porter and Cleland (1995) recommend using portfolios as a learning strategy. Learning portfolios have also been labeled process portfolios (Valencia & Place, 1994) and working portfolios (Lamme & Hysmith, 1991a). These portfolios are also kept in the classroom and focus on valuing the learning process and self-reflection. Students often chronicle and comment on work that is part of a larger project. Items typically placed in learning portfolios include projects, writing folders, journals or logs, and other incomplete work. Teachers and students conference periodically to reflect on which artifacts were helpful in learning, which ones they enjoyed, and which ones they would do differently.

Growth Portfolio

According to Hewitt (1995), a growth portfolio is kept to demonstrate growth over time. It is imperative that entries be dated to facilitate comparisons between new work and previous efforts. Students select representative artifacts every six to nine weeks or at least twice a semester. If these selections become part of the cumulative school portfolio, students usually have the option of adding or deleting artifacts from the current year but not from previous ones.

Documentation Portfolio

Documentation portfolios can be maintained for each content area or across content areas. Both students and teachers select particular pieces of students' work to include (Rhodes & Shanklin, 1993) or include everything a student has done during a semester or school year (Hewitt, 1995). Hewitt has found that, at the high school level, this type of portfolio can serve as a way to convince some students who are tempted to drop out that they have already completed a great deal of work, are making progress, and have invested a great deal of time and effort. Valencia and Place (1994) value this type of portfolio because it provides systematic, dated evidence that is rich in description of student learning without the restrictions of clearly defined scoring criteria. These portfolios differ from learning portfolios because completed work, as well as unfinished or in progress work, is included.

Showcase Portfolio

In showcase portfolios, students have the primary responsibility for selecting their best work. These portfolios encourage student involvement, ownership, and pride in their polished products and the assessment process (Lamme & Hysmith, 1991a; Valencia & Place, 1994; Hewitt, 1995). The materials placed in showcase portfolios are meant to be shared with other students, teachers, and parents. Typical artifacts include published pieces of writing, samples from various classes, photographs of large projects, and computer disks of past work. Middle and high school showcase portfolios might also include resumes, career goals, and other samples of student work (Sanborn & Sanborn, 1994; Hewitt, 1995).

Employability Portfolio

An employability portfolio has the main purpose of demonstrating evidence of attainment of the skills needed to seek employment, college admission, or entrance into the military (Stemmer et al., 1992; Hewitt, 1995). These portfolios are usually tailored to meet the specific requirements of a job or a certain college. Michigan has passed a law that requires its eighth through twelfth graders to compile an employability portfolio that demonstrates skills in academics, personal management, and teamwork. In Michigan, a completed employability portfolio must contain these four sections: records of annual academic and nonacademic planning; academic achievement; career and job preparation; and recognition, accomplishments, and community service. While teachers give general directions and guidance in the portfolio process, the students are expected to develop their own portfolios. Rita Kirby (1993) created the checklist in Figure 6.1 to assist students in assessing their progress in each of the three required skill areas and to provide them with a guide for deciding which types of items to place in their employability portfolios.

Cumulative School Portfolio

Cumulative school portfolios satisfy schoolwide, district, or provincial requirements, follow students from grade to grade, and need to be kept in a secure location (Lamme & Hysmith, 1991a; Rhodes & Shanklin, 1993; Valencia & Place, 1994; Hewitt, 1995). These portfolios are also referred to as assessment portfolios (Hewitt, 1995), evaluation portfolios (Valencia & Place, 1994), or permanent portfolios (Rhodes & Shanklin, 1993) because they are the ones that are usually used for reporting to parents, administrators, community members, and policymakers. They must have specific, clearly defined scoring criteria. Students and teachers are selective in choosing items to include in this portfolio because it will follow students through the grades and/or be used for purposes beyond those of the classroom. Items are often selected from whatever portfolios are being kept in the classroom and are presented for outside scrutiny to assess student progress, to provide information that can be compared across classrooms, and to provide data for curricular decisions.

Professional Portfolio

A professional portfolio is one that an administrator or teacher would keep to share their learning; to demonstrate meeting job requirements; to reflect on their learning, teaching, or leadership; and to set future goals. These portfolios can be used as models, for conferencing, or to improve the owner's learning, teaching, effectiveness, or leadership capabilities.

MICHIGAN EMPLOYABILITY SKILLS PORTFOLIO
Skills Michigan employers want now and for the future

ACADEMIC SKILLS

The skills that help prepare you for future training and education. They include communicating, planning, understanding, and problem solving.

- [ ] Read and understand written materials
- [ ] Understand basic math
- [ ] Use research/library skills
- [ ] Understand charts and graphs
- [ ] Use math to solve problems
- [ ] Use tools and equipment
- [ ] Speak in the language in which business is conducted
- [ ] Write in the language in which business is conducted
- [ ] Use scientific method to solve problems
- [ ] Use specialized knowledge to get a job done

PERSONAL MANAGEMENT SKILLS

The skills that help you develop responsibility and dependability. They include setting and accomplishing goals, doing your best, making decisions, acting honestly, and exercising self control.

- [ ] Attend school/work daily and on time
- [ ] Know personal strengths and weaknesses
- [ ] Follow written instructions and directions
- [ ] Follow verbal instructions and directions
- [ ] Work without supervision
- [ ] Meet school/work deadlines
- [ ] Develop career plans
- [ ] Demonstrate self-control
- [ ] Pay attention to detail
- [ ] Learn new skills
- [ ] Identify and suggest new ways to get the job done
- [ ] Demonstrate personal values at school and work

TEAMWORK SKILLS

The skills that help develop your ability to work cooperatively with a group. They include organizing, planning, listening, sharing, flexibility, and leadership.

- [ ] Actively participate in a groups
- [ ] Listen to other group members
- [ ] Follow the group's rules and values
- [ ] Express ideas to other group members
- [ ] Be sensitive to the group members' ideas and views
- [ ] Be willing to compromise if nessary to best accomplish the goal
- [ ] Be a leader or follower to best accomplish the goal
- [ ] Work in changing settings and with different people

Source: Kirby, R. 1993. *Portfolio Information Guide.* Rita Kirby Portfolio Consultant, Mt. Pleasant, MI, p. 2. ©

Figure 6.1. Employability Skills Portfolio Checklist.

How Do You Decide Which Portfolio Type to Use?

The types of portfolios that your teachers decide to use in their classrooms will depend on the purposes for collecting the data that will be placed in them. In many schools, portfolios will need to serve more than one purpose. Often, your teachers will want to use portfolios that are geared more toward daily decision making that occurs in the classroom, but schools also need to have data to satisfy the needs of audiences beyond the classroom. There are two main solutions to this problem: keeping separate classroom portfolios and cumulative school portfolios (Lamme & Hysmith, 1991a; Wolf, 1994; Hewitt, 1995) or using combination portfolios (Valencia & Place, 1994).

Asking students to keep a showcase, documentation, growth, learning, or master subject area portfolio in their classrooms allows them to maintain responsibility and ownership of the portfolio process and assessment. When teachers, students, or both select items from these classroom portfolios for placement in a cumulative school portfolio, the requirements for accountability, comparability, program decisions, and curricular decision making can also be met.

Rather than keeping two separate portfolios, Valencia and Place (1994) used a composite portfolio that combined showcase, growth, learning, and cumulative school portfolios to address multiple purposes. This composite portfolio consisted of work selected by students, periodic self-reflections, self-evaluations of progress, several "common tools" that all students would include to allow for comparisons at particular grade levels, and materials added by the teacher or student to aid in understanding the student's drafts, working notes, and other kinds of evidence of the learning process. Your teachers may also want to combine various portfolio types to address their needs and purposes for classroom portfolios while your cumulative school portfolios would be maintained in a consistent manner throughout the grades.

HOW DO YOU SELECT ITEMS FOR INCLUSION?

The purposes, standards chosen by your school community, and type(s) of portfolios used in classrooms and the school determine what items are placed in your portfolios. Artifacts placed in a cumulative school folder will be much more restricted than those placed in a documentation portfolio, which is often open-ended.

Six aspects of a literacy curriculum in kindergarten through third grade should be included in the cumulative portfolios, with the following items being required for each area:

- language and vocabulary knowledge: samples of written responses to literature
- ownership: teacher observations and student surveys
- reading comprehension: samples of written responses to literature
- voluntary reading: teacher observation and voluntary reading logs
- word-reading strategies: running records
- writing process: samples of writing produced during writer's workshop

In their combination portfolios in a literacy portfolio project in Belevue, Washington, Sheila Valencia and Nancy Place (1994) had three purposes: to improve instruction, to improve student learning and ownership of learning, and to report to others outside of the classroom. The teachers in the project agreed to focus on four student learning objectives at all grade levels:

- interaction with text to construct meaning
- choosing to read a variety of materials
- effective communication through writing
- engagement in self-evaluation and reflection

After considerable debate and negotiation, these teachers finally reached consensus that each portfolio from kindergarten through twelfth grade would contain

- student-selected work accompanied by entry slips that explained why each piece was included in the portfolio at least three times a year
- reflections from when students reviewed their portfolio contents at least twice a year to discuss or write about their individual development in reading and writing
- common tools administered three times a year to measure the four student learning objectives: (1) interact with text—written or oral retelling; (2) reading a variety of materials—book logs kept for two-week "sweeps"; (3) communicate effectively in writing—samples of writing; and (4) self-reflection and self-evaluation—entry slips and portfolio review questionnaires
- any amount of additional work the student or teacher wishes to include to describe the student more fully

You may want to encourage your teachers to strike a balance between teacher direction and student ownership in selecting portfolio entries. Linda Rief (1990) suggests imposing external criteria such as having the students include two best pieces during a six-week period, trimester self-evaluations of process and product, and a year-end reading/writing project. Students would then determine *internal* criteria by deciding which pieces to include for their own reasons. Terri Austin (1994) also combines teacher and student control of selection of items by asking students to include certain kinds of items such as two papers from each subject area with their reasons for including them, a photocopied page from a journal, grade reflections, and a summary sheet. Her students control which items to use to satisfy these requirements.

In literacy portfolios in Manchester, New Hampshire, Jane Hansen (1994) noted that students select items that portray them as they want others to see them. Items are chosen to answer two questions: Who am I? and Who do I want to be? Students include school and nonschool items, written reflections about their items, and their goals as learners. They include a range of works to represent the whole student, with both positive and negative sides. They also include a comment sheet for classmates and parents to sign and to respond to their portfolios.

When Carol Porter and Janell Cleland (1995) asked their high school English students at Mundelein High School in Chicago, Illinois, to choose artifacts from their folders to put into their learning portfolios, they found that they needed to discuss the idea that some items in the students' folders were more meaningful than others. The students in each class generated a list of reasons for selecting items to include in their learning portfolios and displayed them in the room to use as guidelines for selection.

We suggest asking these questions when deciding what should be placed in portfolios:

- What items will satisfy the purposes for the portfolio?
- What items will indicate attainment of standards or objectives?
- Will students exclusively control the selection of the contents of the portfolio?
- Will the teacher also make selections?
- Will peer evaluations be included?
- Will parents be invited to contribute items?
- Will out-of-school items become part of the portfolio?
- Will there be required items in the portfolio?
- Will the students assist in selecting criteria for including artifacts?

WHO SHOULD HAVE ACCESS TO PORTFOLIOS?

This question should have a simple answer, but it doesn't because the issue of accessibility depends upon the purposes of and the type of portfolio being used. Of course, the owners of the portfolios must have easy access to their own work to increase opportunities for reflection (DeFina, 1992). Students need to know where their portfolios are stored and have unlimited or scheduled access to them (DeFina, 1992; Rhodes & Shanklin, 1993). You and your teachers will also need to have access to add information, evaluate student progress, or to gather data. Parents will want to have access to their child's portfolio, but students need to know how parents and others will be involved in the evaluation process. Students should also have a choice in whether parts of their portfolios will be used for peer reviews, and they need to be informed about how their portfolios will be used so that they can make judgements about any request by others to review their work (DeFina, 1992).

Students are entitled to privacy under the Family Education and Rights to Privacy Act (FERPA). Portfolios that contain material used to assess student progress, self-assessment information, and teacher comments about students are legally treated in the same way as CA60's. Confidentiality must be maintained. Often, this translates to controlled access to the portfolios.

The need for privacy conflicts with the need for easy access. For students to work on their portfolios as an ongoing part of instruction and learning, portfolios must be available in the classroom. To maintain confidentiality, portfolios must be kept in a secure area. District are dealing with this dilemma in various ways. Some store portfolios in the library where students can check out their own portfolios and work on them there. Another way to overcome this conflict is to use three types of portfolios: learning portfolios, showcase portfolios, and cumulative school portfolios (Lamme & Hysmith, 1991a).

The cumulative school portfolio is the one to store in a secure location. At the end of each marking period, teams of trained reviewers evaluate students' cumulative school portfolios that contain required entries, creative entries, self-assessments, and teacher entries. By using a team of evaluators, rather than one classroom teacher, equity and reliability are increased. These issues are explored further in Chapters 3 and 7.

In most school districts, review teams consist of teachers. Some districts have teams composed of one teacher, one community member, and one parent to evaluate portfolios. In either case, we recommend that you require a signed guardian release form permitting trained teams to evaluate the portfolio. When students reach the age of eighteen, they may sign the form themselves. Figure 6.2 is an example of a release form developed by Robert Mills, a professor at Central Michigan University. Schools who use a form such as this would meet the requirements of the Family Education and Rights of Privacy Act (FERPA).

```
PARENT RELEASE FORM *

NAME OF STUDENT_____

GRADE LEVEL_____     DATE_____


I/WE _____(parent / parents) give
my / our permission for evaluation of our son / daughter's
PORTFOLIO for assessment purposes.


I/WE understand that all materials contained in this
PORTFOLIO honestly reflect the efforts of our
son/daughter.


In addition I/WE understand that all information contained
therein has been placed voluntarily and with permission on
our son/daughter's behalf.


All persons submitting materials for this PORTFOLIO
understand that information contained therein will be
evaluated by a review team and each document or entry
assessed for student rating  purposes.


My/Our son/daughter has signed a waiver that allows for
the release of each entry in the PORTFOLIO and further
waives all rights to confidentiality for each entry under the
Family Education and Rights to Privacy Act (FERPA).


_____
PARENT'S/PARENTS' SIGNATURE/S



_____
Date of Signing

* If student attained age of majority, parents need not sign release form.
```

Figure 6.2.

HOW CAN ISSUES OF PORTFOLIO CONTAINERS AND STORAGE BE RESOLVED?

Once your teachers and stakeholders have decided what artifacts will be placed in portfolios and accessibility issues have been resolved, the next two decisions that must be made are: what will your teachers and students use as portfolio containers and where can portfolios be stored?

Portfolio Containers

Portfolios can take many forms. Which will you and your teachers choose? Will they require a uniform format or let students design their own? Bird (1992a) listed the following as common possibilities for portfolio containers:

- accordion files
- three-ring binders
- 8″ × 11″ manila folders
- specially designed, oversized, cardboard folders
- commercial portfolios
- large boot boxes

Some schools have purchased commercial portfolio containers through central office support, money provided by parent organizations, donations from businesses, or grant writing efforts of the principal or interested teachers. However, many schools have little financial resources for additional materials; therefore, student portfolio containers are often file folders made by students from classroom materials such as tagboard or posterboard or items from outside of school such as large cereal boxes, boot boxes, or large envelopes donated by local businesses. Some students and teachers prefer three-ring binders because pages can be added and removed easily while it is difficult to include audio- or videotapes, projects, and artwork.

At Lois Bird's (1992b) school, the problem of supplying containers is solved by asking each parent to send a three-ring binder at the beginning of the school year. Another wants his sophomores to develop a science resource that reflects both product and process. He holds them accountable for supplying their own three-ring binders, requires that no subject matter from other courses be included in their science portfolios, and asks them to use dividers to separate specific sections such as lab work, evaluations, learning log, and reference material. Terri Austin (1994) has each of her sixth graders collect all their work in a legal size manila folder for each six-week grading period. You and your teachers will need to decide which types of containers best serve your needs.

Storage Possibilities

One of the most common questions that principals hear from teachers is, "But where am I going to store all these portfolios?" As Hewitt (1995) notes, the answer to this question will vary widely, depending upon the purpose for the portfolio, storage space in your school, and the degree of accessibility necessary to meet your needs. In schools where funding issues have been resolved, classroom portfolios are often stored in file cabinets in the classroom, while teachers in other schools use milk crates, boxes, or trays in the back of the room, on shelves, or in closets (Austin, 1994). One teacher keeps her middle school students' learning portfolios in alphabetical order in hanging files in egg crates on her desk for easy access and files the showcase portfolios in standard file cabinets to protect them.

Using Technology to Store Portfolios

Another solution to the space problem is the use of technology for storing the portfolio on a computer disk. Hewitt (1995) warns that electronic portfolios are not a panacea either. Some problems that have occurred are that disks can be mislabeled or not labeled, can be copied over, and can contain the work of more than one student in a single file. However, schools are reporting success in using either IBM or Macintosh electronic portfolios.

Fifth-grade teachers at Bellerive Elementary School in St. Louis, Missouri, have been using commercial computerized portfolio software to scan and record writing samples, log books that students read, record samples of oral reading, maintain assessment checklists by subject areas, provide a place for students to write self-evaluation comments, and provide additional space for teacher comments. In this school, where every teacher has a Macintosh computer, microphone, and a printer, the staff found that this is not only an excellent way to store cumulative school portfolios, but it also serves as a learning tool for students to examine their own learning (Hetterscheidt et al., 1992).

At Conestoga Elementary School in rural Wyoming, portfolio assessment has been combined with laser disk technology. The school received a grant from their state department to purchase the necessary IBM hardware and technical support from IBM consultants and researchers for Project Zero at Harvard. Laser disks can store large amounts of data, add information as needed, and retrieve data as often as portfolio visitors wish, yet the laser disks are small enough to store in the student's permanent file. The system allows for permanent storage of optical data, written and drawn images, and verbal data. At the end of sixth grade, parents, student, teacher, and principal will review the disk from kindergarten through sixth grade as a rite of passage. The school's principal Jo Campbell (1992) noted an underlying belief that child development involves more than simply cognitive growth; therefore, students, parents, and staff will examine laser disk portfolio assessments to determine verbal ability, physical accomplishments, artistic achievements, and self-assurance.

At O'Farrell Community Middle School in San Diego, California, stakeholders created an "O'Farrell Standard," which is a list of performance requirements that range from community service to research projects and from demonstrated academic competence to behavior and attitudes. O'Farrell gained computer technology through grants from Apple, Panasonic, and other corporations. While most teachers use computer disks to report student progress toward specific elements of the O'Farrell Standard each quarter, two teams of teachers have taken these reports to another level of sophistication. They have created a digital portfolio for students to place and evaluate their own work by using hypercard stacks to relate each of their entries to the O'Farrell Standard and to devise a vivid electronic picture of their accomplishments. Their achievements might range from a wrap-up of their research thesis to a biographical poem, a reflection on a schoolwide "essential question" to a thoughtful analysis of their strengths, weaknesses, and goals (Cushman, 1994).

Issues to Consider about Portfolio Containers and Storage

In summary, the questions that you and your staff will need to answer about portfolio containers and storage issues include

- What will your teachers use to hold portfolio contents?
- Are there funds to provide uniform commercial containers?
- Will there be a schoolwide consensus about what type of containers will be used?
- Will individual teachers use their choice of containers for classroom portfolios?
- Will students be encouraged to personalize their classroom portfolios?
- Where will portfolios be stored?
- Where can cumulative school portfolios be stored to maintain security?
- Will your teachers be provided with file cabinets to store classroom portfolios?
- If there are no funds or space for file cabinets, will teachers make their own decisions for how portfolios will be stored or will this be a schoolwide decision?

- Are computerized portfolios of interest to the staff?
- If this is an interest, is the hardware and software currently in the building adequate for developing computer portfolios?
- If you do not have adequate technology, is funding available to acquire necessary equipment, software, and inservice?

HOW CAN PORTFOLIOS BE MANAGED?

The main concerns of managing portfolios are when and how students should review their portfolios to add and delete items. Time seems to be a recurring issue for teachers in this and other types of classroom evaluation. You will want to be sure that time for portfolio implementation is well spent and adds to your teachers' and students' knowledge. Your teachers will need to decide how much time they will provide for students to update their collections, to reflect on their work, to assist them in deciding what criteria to apply in making decisions, and to conference with the teacher and their classmates (Tierney et al., 1991; DeFina, 1992; Woodward, 1994).

The other issues that concern portfolio management deal with handling the portfolio contents. Questions that are of concern to teachers, students, and administrators include

- How much should be placed in the portfolios?
- Who should maintain them?
- How can the amount of items generated be handled?

Managing Time

Hewitt (1995) recommends having students spend an hour sorting through their portfolios every four weeks to add materials, to remove or weed out artifacts, and to choose items to place in their cumulative school folders. Students need time to write reflections to explain reasons for including each entry. You will want to encourage your teachers to take time to conference with students to formally review portfolio contents. Teachers can review students portfolios once a month, before the end of grading periods, once a semester, or at the end of the school year. Teachers can also provide small amounts of time to informally discuss why students chose to add some artifacts and remove others.

While organizing and reflecting about items in their portfolios provides students with valuable information about their learning, goal-setting opportunities, and practice in decision making, DeFina (1992) cautions that reviewing portfolios too frequently usually results in sacrificing quality evaluation, and students often become caught up in the product, rather than in the process. When evaluation occurs too often, there is little opportunity for reflection because students are too busy completing checklists or writing self-evaluation pieces. Students quickly run out of things to say because evaluating their work becomes a chore, rather than a personally satisfying task. DeFina (1992) recommends having your teachers develop a rotating schedule to evaluate only two or three students' portfolios a day so that they will be able to examine each student's portfolio at least once a month.

Linda Rief (1990) suggests having your teachers ask their students to arrange their work most effective to least effective each trimester. After they have accomplished this, they can evaluate their work by answering questions such as

- Why did you choose this item as your best work?
- How did you go about creating it?
- What were some problems that you had?
- What did you do to solve them?
- How is your best work different from your least effective one?
- What were your goals for these twelve weeks?
- What did you do to accomplish these goals?
- How successful were you in reaching them?
- What goals will you set for the next twelve weeks?

Deciding How Much Student Work to Keep

Some schools (Bird, 1992b) or classrooms (Knight, 1992; Austin, 1994) require students to collect all their work for a period of time in a classroom portfolio to provide enough data to use to reflect on themselves as learners. When no work comes home, parents will need to be provided with an explanation for this policy. Austin (1994) sends work home on Friday when her sixth graders' parents request it, but she asks that it be returned on Monday because students are often not aware of which papers are most important until they begin preparing for their conferences. Primary teachers at Lois Bird's (1992b) school informed parents that no papers would be sent home; however, they could come in and examine their children's work in their three-ring binders whenever they wished.

When Pam Knight (1992) had her high school algebra class keep all their work for a semester, she was amazed at the quantity of work they produced. Near the end of the semester, she passed out their folders and had them brainstorm answers to questions such as: What should be included in a portfolio? What would show their effort and learning in algebra? What activities had been most meaningful? She copied their suggestions and had them review their folders to collect five items that they felt represented their knowledge and effort in algebra to place in their portfolios.

In other schools and classrooms, students examine their work at the end of the week themselves and choose items to place in their portfolios. When everything is not being saved, often, teachers also choose items to include. If students are going to take materials home, teachers will need to spend time modeling what kinds of pieces would be appropriate to select for the portfolio to ensure that the artifacts chosen do reflect students' learning and meet the criteria for portfolio selections. One effective method is to have students help develop and discuss these criteria. Then post them in the classroom and provide students with a copy to place in their portfolios. If there are requirements from beyond the classroom, your teachers need to make sure that their students understand these as well. When students know the standards they are working toward, they are more likely to reach various benchmarks of good performance and can gauge their own understanding (Maeroff, 1991; Simmons, 1994).

Managing and Maintaining the Collection of Portfolio Contents

The contents of portfolios must be manageable. Hewitt (1995) maintains that the number one principle of managing portfolios is that portfolios belong to students. Because reflection is such an important part of learning, selection of artifacts should be made by the student with advice from teachers and classmates. He also suggests that even young students should be responsible for maintaining their portfolios. If they lose it, have them start a new one filled with new items. Providing student ownership and responsibility for classroom portfolios will save your teachers work and time. Teachers do not learn much from managing one or more classrooms of portfolios, while students learn a great deal from accepting this responsibility.

Hewitt (1995) suggests having your teachers supervise the portfolio, but allowing students to actually create them. If students use manila folders, they can decorate them to make their portfolios more personal and so that they will be able to identify them more easily. Some teachers color code portfolios by writing student's names in a different color for each class and then place them in alphabetical order. Numbering the folders once they are in alphabetical order further simplifies filing the entries. On the inside front cover, students can keep an evolving table of contents and a set of criteria for the artifacts that fill the portfolio. On the inside back cover, they can keep a record of student–teacher conferences to help them focus on their goals.

Management of papers can be chaotic at times. Austin (1994) found that passing papers back for students to file each day took too much class time. Next, she tried having a filing committee who worked during recess, but many papers were misfiled and students had less contact with their own work. The system that has proven to be most effective has been to record grades after her sixth graders have graded their own work and put it in a bin. On Friday, two students pass out the classroom portfolios, and five students take fifteen minutes to pass back all papers in the bin. When students receive each paper, they classify and clip it to a labeled paper for each subject area. Later they select items from these folders to place in their portfolios. In Jane Shippee's fourth-grade classroom, students had the responsibility for choosing which papers to include and which ones to take home each day.

To save space in a portfolio, Hagan (1992) suggests using a particular sample of a student's work to document several areas. Some areas that a rough draft of a story could document are current understanding of spelling, use of narrative voice, and legibility of printing. As students add new items, they are encouraged to remove others and take them home, and only a handful of samples are selected to represent progress at the end of the year.

To deal with the problem of keeping a year's worth of work for over a hundred students, Sanborn and Sanborn (1994) suggest using computer disks to keep items such as rough drafts, using photographs of posters and products that are too large to place in the portfolio, and using videotapes to document kinesthetic and visual products. Because their students accumulate a large quantity of materials, they start a new learning portfolio each quarter and store the old one alphabetically in a closet until the end of the year when students evaluate their final showcase portfolio. The students then keep or dispose of what's left from their year's work.

Summary of Management Issues

In summary, this section dealt with the decisions that need to be made about reviewing, adding items to, or removing items from portfolios. Questions that will need to be considered are the following:

- Will students review, add to, or remove items from their portfolios when they choose to do so?
- Will your teachers schedule regular times for selection and review?
- If they choose regularly scheduled times, will this be done once

a week, every two weeks, once a month, at the end of each grading period, at the end of a semester, by trimesters, or only at the end of the year?

- How will your teachers and students review portfolios, as a whole class activity, in small groups of students, or individually?
- What will happen to the portfolio at the end of the year?
- Will they be passed to next year's teacher?
- Will students take them home to keep or share with parents?
- Will portions of the classroom portfolio be included in the cumulative school portfolio?

HOW SHOULD PORTFOLIO CONTENTS BE ORGANIZED?

Once portfolio contents have been collected, the next decision that must be made is how the portfolio should be organized for the reader whether that reader is a student, a teacher, the principal, a parent, a community member, a central office administrator, or a policymaker. Once the portfolio has been organized, it is ready for review through conferences as described in Chapter 9 or through review from beyond the classroom or school as described in Chapters 3 and 7.

While contents of portfolios depend on purposes for them, types being used, criteria for including entries, and who selects artifacts, the format or organization can be developed collaboratively between students, teachers, and administrators. Part of planning should consider needs of the portfolio's readers. What will they need to know to understand the contents? To assist the reader in gaining the most information, the portfolio must be self-explanatory and selectively assembled (Maeroff, 1991).

Different classes may choose a variety of formats for organizing their portfolios. Knight (1992) and her algebra students discussed what the format for a good portfolio would be. They decided that their portfolios should be neat, typed or in ink, would be placed in a cover, must include a table of contents, and would have a personal reflection or statement for each entry that explained why this artifact was important to the learner.

Using Captions for Portfolio Artifacts

Portfolio captions help readers interpret entries in a portfolio, remind students about the reasons they chose early entries, create a monitoring device for old and new entries, and are the glue that turns a folder into a portfolio. Valencia and Place (1994) call these reflections entry slips, rather than captions, and use them to identify artifacts. Captions that are most effective serve the following functions:

- Identify the document by explaining what it is.
- Describe the context for the document.
- Explain why the artifact is included in the portfolio.
- Interpret the document.
- Explain how the artifact applies to future learning.

Reflecting on Portfolio Artifacts

Porter and Cleland (1995) note that learners must be assisted with strategies that allow them to discover why an artifact stands apart from the rest when they make choices for inclusion of items in their portfolios. Choosing which items to include may be relatively easy, but telling why the choice was made is more difficult, and explaining how the learning experience has changed one is even more difficult. They found that their high school students often needed to be reminded to include a narrative explaining why they chose each item for their portfolios and to describe what it demonstrates about their learning. It was often necessary to discuss and model qualities of an effective reflection that informs both the learner and the portfolio readers.

Craven (1992) maintains that ongoing self-assessments by students gives both learners and teachers the greatest benefit for assisting in deciding which items to place in portfolios and how to organize the material. She has her students fill out self-assessment sheets and goal-setting forms quarterly. The form in Figure 6.3 is a combination of self-assessment and goal setting for writing.

The example entry form in Figure 6.4 can be used with artifacts from any subject area. It not only requires the student to examine why the particular item was chosen, but also asks the student to reflect on what was learned from producing the work. The artifact that Michael chose to include in his seventh-grade portfolio was a picture book that was shared with students at a nearby elementary school. On the form, he shares his reflections about why he chose this entry, what he learned from creating it, and what he could have done differently.

Ways to Introduce the Reader to the Portfolio

Many portfolios include a letter of introduction for the reader. This letter serves dual purposes of sharing student learning and of interesting the reader. Porter and Cleland (1995) call this opening page an invitation to the reader. Hewitt (1995) recommends a letter format beginning with "Dear Reader." The letter includes a discussion of the contents of the portfolio, allows the student to create a context for the reader, and provides further

```
┌─────────────────────────────────────────────────────────┐
│              WRITING REFLECTION SHEET                      │
│                                                            │
│   Name_____ Date_____            │
│                                                            │
│                                                            │
│   ▪ Which piece of writing is your best for this grading   │
│     period? What makes it the best?                        │
│                                                            │
│                                                            │
│                                                            │
│                                                            │
│                                                            │
│   ▪ Which piece of writing was your least satisfactory     │
│     one? Explain why.                                      │
│                                                            │
│                                                            │
│                                                            │
│                                                            │
│                                                            │
│   ▪ What do you think good writers do when they  write?    │
│                                                            │
│                                                            │
│                                                            │
│                                                            │
│                                                            │
│   ▪ What are your goals as a writer for the next grading   │
│     period?                                                │
│                                                            │
│                                                            │
│                                                            │
│                                                            │
└─────────────────────────────────────────────────────────┘
```

Figure 6.3. Sample Entry Reflection Sheet.

REFLECTIONS ABOUT MY PORTFOLIO ENTRIES

Name __Michael Rose__   Date __April 20, 1994__

Title __The Three Hogs in the Year 2016__ Subject __English__

I created this artifact through this process:

I had to start out by writing a rough draft. I had to layout the book by deciding which illustrations I wanted to use. Then I word processed by pages. Then I formatted the book and put it together.

I was influenced to create this artifact by:

I saw a copy of The Three Little Pigs on a shelf next to me in class and thought I could write a parody of it.

These are the risks that I took when I made this artifact:

Instead of entirely coloring my pictures, I used colored pencils to make them textured.

I gained this knowledge from this experience:

I found out how books are sown together and how they are published with contracts.

This is what I learned:

I learned how to lay out a book in a presentable manner.

I chose this artifact to place in my portfolio because:

It was something I worked hard on that took me half the year to complete and it's quality work.

Figure 6.4. Sample Form for Reflections on Portfolio Entries.

evidence of the author's mechanics of writing, voice, and awareness of audience needs. Graves (1991) suggests that the letter contain the student's judgements about the importance and quality of artifacts, which provides another opportunity for self-reflection and also demonstrates the goals for the portfolio.

Organizational Formats

Once students have created a portfolio introduction and captions, entry slips, or narratives for each of their artifacts, the next decision that must be made is how to order portfolio contents. Graves (1991) noted that some portfolio authors choose to divide their work into sections for special projects, writing, and reading, while others sort their work by themes or in chronological order. Porter and Cleland (1995) noticed that their students chose to guide their readers through their portfolios by placing a divider before each item. On the divider they provided the reader with background information needed to understand the artifact that would follow. Some information they might have chosen to provide included explanation of the strategy used, purpose of the assignment, when it was completed, who worked with them, or whatever other data they felt the reader needed as an introduction to each entry. Immediately following each divider was the item that it introduced. Students also included a response that followed each artifact to explain why they chose the item and what they had learned about themselves through the experience of creating the piece.

Closing the Portfolio

Items that are used to close portfolios frequently include future learning goals, a summary that includes reflections on what students have learned about themselves, what they have learned in various subjects, changes they have noticed in their work, growth they have made in learning, and sheets for portfolio visitors' comments about their portfolios and their learning (Anthony et al., 1991; Knight, 1992; Austin, 1994; Hewitt, 1995; Porter & Cleland, 1995).

TROUBLESHOOTING: BUT THERE'S NO SPACE IN MY CLASSROOM FOR STORAGE CABINETS!

Your staff may be providing you with a variety of messages when they say that they have no space in their classrooms. Before reacting immediately to this comment, you might want to explore different concerns that your teachers may be expressing. Through observing their actions and listening to their concerns, you will be better able to gauge your staff members' readiness for beginning portfolio implementation.

If storage space is truly the issue, then brainstorming, looking at storage possibilities in the building, and alternatives to cabinets may be in order. Some teachers are saying that they don't know where to begin in managing portfolios. If this is the case, you can provide guidance using some of the suggestions provided in this chapter and through brainstorming for their ideas.

Portfolio implementation can be intimidating for many teachers who need information about what is involved in using this form of alternative assessment. These teachers will need staff development in assessment tools, self-assessment, and logistics of portfolio implementation. Information in Chapters 4, 5, and 6, along with professional readings, staff development, and conference attendance, will be helpful.

Another group of teachers may be saying that they are unsure about taking the risks involved in changing their teaching and assessment practices. The support groups and peer coaching described in Chapter 9 may be just what these teachers need along with staff development, your support, and your encouragement for taking risks in their classrooms.

Still another group may be saying that they do not want to make changes in what they are doing in their classrooms, whether it is in teaching practices or in assessing students' learning. For these teachers, saying that they have no space is a way of resisting change. Chapter 7 provides information on how to recognize resistance and ways to deal with resistance in implementing portfolios.

When you examine their concerns and actions, you can determine what your staff is really telling you when they say that they have no space in their classrooms. This is common and is part of the implementation dip which Fullan (1991) reminds us is a normal part of the change process. Remember that smooth sailing is a sure sign that significant change is not occurring.

GLOSSARY

Accessibility: the issue of who has the right to examine, add, or remove artifacts from a student's portfolio.

Captions: a brief explanation of a portfolio entry that includes the reason it was placed in the portfolio, its context, and what was learned from the artifact.

CA60's: Student permanent records that are protected under state and federal laws.

Class Portfolios: portfolios that a teacher can use to document the experiences of an entire class such as class projects, visitors, units, or trips. The main purpose for this type of portfolio is to serve as a model for how to collect, select, and reflect on entries. It can also be used to model captioning and goal setting.

Classroom Portfolios: any type of student portfolio that is stored in the classroom, with students having the major responsibility for maintaining it. Classroom portfolios can be master subject area portfolios, learning portfolios, growth portfolios, documentation portfolios, showcase portfolios, employability portfolios, or any combination of these.

Cumulative School Portfolio: portfolios that satisfy schoolwide, district, or provincial requirements; follow students from grade to grade; and need to be kept in a secure location. They are also referred to as assessment portfolios, evaluation portfolios, or permanent portfolios. These are the portfolios that are used for reporting to parents, administrators, community members, and policymakers and that have clearly defined scoring criteria.

Documentation Portfolio: classroom portfolios that can be maintained for each content area or across subjects. Both students and teachers can select the entires, or students can keep all their work for a specified period of time. These portfolios offer systematic, dated evidence that is rich in description of student learnng with having restrictions of scoring criteria.

Employability Portfolio: an employability portfolio has the main purpose of demonstrating evidence of attainment of the skills needed to seek employment, college admission, or entrance into the military.

Entry Slips: another form of captioning of portfolio artifacts.

External Criteria: criteria for which items to include in portfolios that are set by someone other than the portfolio's owner.

Family Education Rights to Privacy Act: This act, often called the Buckley Amendment, is designed to protect the privacy of students and assure fairness in the keeping and use of school records. All rights belong to parents until the child reaches eighteen years of age, after which they belong to the former child and no longer to the parents.

Growth Portfolio: a classroom portfolio that is kept to demonstrate growth over time and that dates each entry so that new work can be compared to previous efforts. If some of these entries are selected to be placed in the cumulative school portfolio, the student can only add or delete materials from the current year.

Internal Criteria: criteria established by the portfolio's owner to decide which items will meet the requirements set by others for included portfolio artifacts.

Learning Portfolios: classroom portfolios that focus on valuing the learning process and self-reflection. These portfolios usually contain work in progress such as projects, writing folders, journals or logs, and other incomplete work. Other labels for this type of portfolio are process portfolios and working portfolios.

Master Subject Matter Portfolio: a classroom portfolio that contains materials from only one subject area such as writing, literacy, mathematics, science, or social studies. Students have ongoing responsibility and ownership, with teachers offering guidance for selecting materials. They usually only contain the present year's work.

Running Records: a method of evaluating oral reading that is similar to miscue analysis, except the reader is not tape recorded, the examiner places a check above each word pronounced as the text, miscues are marked above the text, and decisions are made on the spot about the student's reading needs.

Showcase Portfolio: classroom portfolios in which students have the primary responsibility for selecting their best work. These portfolios encourage student involvement, ownership, and pride in their polished products and the assessment process. The materials placed in these portfolios are meant to be shared with others.

PART THREE

ENHANCING

Enhancing goes beyond implementation to solving problems that arise and expanding the uses of portfolio assessment. This final section will help sustain the change and build on portfolios' potential to enhance the school climate to one of a community of learners.

CHAPTER 7

Facing Special Problems

Superintendent Cousart's Support for One of His Principals

"I thought portfolio implementation was going all right at school. But, in the past week, I've received two grievances from teachers, one complaint from a paraprofessional, and one angry phone call from a parent about portfolios. After all the funding, inservice training, and planning time my teachers and staff have received to implement portfolios, why are there so many problems?" asked Jim Valdez, the principal at Central Middle School.

Superintendent Cousart thought for a few moments before he replied. "I think we have hit what Michael Fullan refers to as the implementation dip. It is common in any substantial change for things to get worse before they become better. In fact, he goes so far as to say if there are no problems, there is no significant change occurring."

"If that's the measure, we are certainly making significant changes," complained Jim. "How long will this dissention last? The differences seem to be increasing rather than shrinking. Some teachers, students, and parents are thoroughly enjoying the whole process of portfolios. They see this type of assessment as freeing them from the constraints of standardized tests. Students in their classes show what they know and what they can do. Unfortunately, it is not that way with all the staff. Teacher attitude seems to be the determining factor. A few teachers are refusing to do anything more than the requirements. For them, portfolios mean more of the same—more file folders to place more skill sheets into, more time to plan more of the same activities, and more to complain about. I've given them every form of support I can imagine. We have had a motivational speaker, visits to schools that use portfolios, teachers collaborating in teams to plan assessment activities, demonstrations of how to monitor alternative assessments, and release time to consult with one another. Nothing is working with this small group of teachers. I'm losing patience."

"It takes tremendous patience," agreed Superintendent Cousart. "This is the phase when most change initiatives fail. We erroneously believe if we do each step correctly, we will have smooth sailing. Quite the opposite is true. If we do everything correctly, we will have devisiveness, pain, and problems before we can observe improvements. Let's take each problem, examine it, and try to identify ways to overcome it."

INTRODUCTION

SHORTLY after implementation begins, most principals will feel similar to Jim. Just when you begin to think everything is coming together, the implementation dip begins. Rather than giving up, consider it a sign that significant change is happening.

In this chapter, we will discuss the common problems that surface during the implementation dip. Suggestions are made of ways we have dealt with each one. Sometimes, simply understanding why dissenters feel the way they do will help you be more patient.

HOW DO WE TAILOR PORTFOLIOS TO ACCOMMODATE PHILOSOPHICAL DIFFERENCES?

Deep inside, every educator holds a belief system about how students learn. Although the way we teach is based on these fundamental beliefs, many educators have not formally identified, examined, and revised their original theory of learning. For many, basic beliefs about learning remain powerful, subconscious sources of actions. We must consciously understand our underlying conceptions of learning and the instructional consequences of those beliefs before we can adapt portfolio assessment into our daily routines. In Chapter 4, we discussed the importance of teacher self-evaluation. Figures 4.8 and 4.11 assist teachers in assessing the congruence between what they claim to believe and what actually occurs in their classrooms. When you lead your teachers through the process of self-reflection, they can identify their beliefs about assessment practices.

Although there are numerous theories and combinations of theories of learning, three basic ones form the foundation for most educational practices. Few, if any, teachers use one pure theory. They are more likely to believe in a combination of philosophies.

Behaviorist Theory

Some educators believe children are empty vessels to be filled with information, skills, and concepts. Teachers or districts who use this philosophy decide what students will learn, when they will learn it, and how they will demonstrate that learning. Curriculum is organized around clearly defined educational objectives, and tests are used to measure the extent those objectives are obtained. Learning materials are programmed into bits of information, and students are reinforced for learning each step. Lectures, teacher-directed activities, programmed learning, and tests of basic skills are common in these classrooms. The teacher directs the flow of information, monitors student work, provides feedback with correctives, and tests for attainment of subskills (Ellis & Fouts, 1993). Mastery learning is deeply invested in this approach.

Interactive Theory

Other educators believe learning is a process of discovering meaning about the world by intellectually and socially interacting with it. Based on this set of beliefs, teachers are facilitators who arrange materials and experiences for students to discover information, solve problems, and develop higher levels of cognitive process. Appropriate social interactions, interpersonal skills, and democratic values are considered as important as academic skills. Achievement is viewed as a combination of basic skills, citizenship, participation, and decision making (Ellis & Fouts, 1993). These teachers will be more student-directed with curiosity being the main motivator. Learning centers, cooperative learning activities, thematic instruction, and performance assessments are typical in classes with this philosophy of learning.

Transformative Theory

Still other educators believe in transformational, or interpersonal, learning. Proponents of this method view learning as the construction of a personal identity that is based on a sense of meaning, purpose, and connectedness with the environment. Unconditional positive regard forms the foundation for discovering one's identity and must be felt before learning can occur. After establishing warm, human relationships, the teacher's role is to link cognitive skills with the aesthetic, emotional, and spiritual dimensions of life. Classrooms with this philosophy gives students as much control as possible over their learning.

Reconciliation Period

Ultimately, philosophical differences create a complex social problem when trying to implement portfolios. Teachers who fundamentally believe it is necessary to tell students what they need to know may have difficulty sharing decisions about portfolio entries with students. On the other hand, teachers who strive to create unconditional acceptance of students may resist applying scoring rubrics. Teachers who do not reconcile portfolio assessment with their philosophy become disillusioned about what they perceive as additional work requirements (Lamme & Hysmith, 1991a).

Expect your teachers to have widely differing beliefs about how students learn. Clearly, no one teacher or theorist has discovered the ultimate solution to resolve the diversity of learning, teaching, assessment, and evaluation (Anthony et al., 1991). The best approach is to allow teachers to construct a personal best "fit" between their beliefs and the use of portfolios. For some, their beliefs will change to accommodate portfolios. Others will adapt portfolios to their beliefs. It is not necesssary for everyone to be interpreting the convergence of portfolios and beliefs in the same way. What is necessary is for everyone to identify how portfolios can be applied within their belief of how students learn.

Changing to portfolios is a highly personal experience. We are asking teachers to reexamine how they view learning, teaching, and assessment. Each and every teacher must have the opportunity to work through this experience in a way that honors the importance of questioning the portfolio process. Teachers have to arrive at an operational meaning of portfolios before they can become comfortable with the process.

In Chapter 4, you and your teachers examined your individual beliefs to identify how portfolios will work for you. Without doing this, you cannot blend the change with your beliefs. Individuals can go through the motions of implementing portfolios, but full acceptance comes only after using portfolios and then going through the clarification process of blending portfolios with one's personal philosophy.

After using portfolios for awhile, inservice efforts should focus on ways to accommodate and support individual faculty members who are having problems understanding and accepting the basic underlying assumptions of portfolios. Giving teachers time to talk about and clarify their learning theories will help. Principals can encourage teachers to reflect about their philosophy of learning, teaching, and assessment by asking questions such as

- Explain some of the learning theories you were taught in teacher preparation.
- Now that you have more teaching experiences, how do you think students learn?
- What do you believe about your students as learners?
- Describe the social needs of your students. To what extent should these needs be met in the classroom?

We believe...

- all students and staff can learn.
- good instruction begins at the learner's developmental level.
- learning builds on the strengths of the learner.
- students learn in multiple ways.
- teachers are models of lifelong learning.
- learning is valuable during one's entire life.
- assessment is continuous.
- the goal of education is interdependence.
- teachers are facilitators and learners.
- students and teachers can make intelligent choices within the curriculum.
- sharing and demonstrating are part of learning.
- collaboration and social interaction can encourage learning.
- valuable learning occurs in all areas of our lives.

Figure 7.1.

- What are some ways individual students learn in your classes?
- Where does learning take place?
- How can we report demonstrations of learning in a way that provides concrete information compatible with parents' expectations?

You can encourage the process by articulating your beliefs about learning. Figure 7.1 is an adaptation of a list of beliefs from Reggie Routman (1991) that are congruent with a learning community.

Principals must commit to providing a school environment where teachers can take a close look at themselves. They need to feel safe enough to, privately and as a group, question their beliefs about learning, teaching, and assessment. After teachers deliberate and refine their beliefs about learning and recognize how their beliefs affect their teaching roles, they are able to tailor portfolio assessment to reflect their beliefs.

HOW CAN I PREVENT DATA OVERLOAD?

Due to the potential amount of information that can be obtained from portfolios, some districts and policymakers tend to attempt to meet several assessment needs from one format. The results are often the unbridled accumulation of items in a portfolio. Too many assessment pieces can lead to an unmanageable, unfocused jumble of information. When this happens, the potential usefulness of portfolios diminishes. A counterbalance to unrestrained inclusion is careful selection of items. A systematic framework is needed so that stakeholders receive reliable and valid data in a manageable way (Anthony et al., 1991).

Numerous and Multifaceted Data

A variety of data are needed to form a profile of student growth and achievement over time. Any single item of information in a student's portfolio is only a miniscule sample of that individual's accomplishments. The more information gathered from different days and months, the more complete is the picture of the student's growth. Each item is similar to a puzzle piece. When the pieces are put together, a whole picture of the student emerges. But how much information is enough? Some teachers keep all the work completed by their students, while others keep only the required samples. Many teachers tell us it is a challenge to differentiate important from less important information to collect. They have trouble establishing a data collection system that is simple, yet informative.

You probably will be pressured to provide your staff with a model, guide, or person to tell them exactly what to collect (Lamme & Hysmith, 1991a, b). We recommend that you and your staff develop a list of required items to lessen the stress caused by ambiguity. This will also give schoolwide uniformity for evaluating programs. At the same time, encourage teachers to add supplemental items to offer a more complete picture of each student's uniqueness. The amount of data needed depends on how the information will be used and who will receive it. As mentioned in Chapter 6, the critical key is having a clear purpose for each entry.

For the portfolio information to be useful, it must be tied to stated student learning goals that define what students should know and be able to do (Valencia et al., 1994). Without clear objectives, the overwhelming nature of the data can yield it unusable. Expect to have to keep reminding some staff members to identify the learning objective for each portfolio entry.

During the early stages of implementation, teachers tend to collect data that provide information about skills. As they become more confident, they will begin attempting to use a variety of ways to gather data. Your role will be encouraging teachers to try to collect a variety of data and recommending a variety of strategies such as those found in Chapter 4, 5, and 6 of this book.

Useful for a Variety of Stakeholders

Participation of the various stakeholders is imperative. Parents, teachers, administrators, future employers, policymakers, and politicians need to be involved in establishing the student learning goals. Student learning goals and objectives that reflect current theory and research in disciplines form the framework for portfolios. After student learning goals are developed, teachers and administrators must communicate with the stakeholders about how portfolio entries reflect progress toward attainment of student goals. When removed from the context of well-developed student objectives, portfolio assessment has little meaning. Each portfolio entry must be clearly tied to learning objectives.

Kentwood Middle School in Grand Rapids, Michigan, has as one of its student goals: "The student will be a critical and creative thinker." The learning objectives are

- A critical and creative thinker evaluates, analyzes, and applies knowledge.
- A critical and creative thinker designs, selects, and uses appropriate thinking strategies.
- A critical and creative thinker accesses and utilizes diverse resources to solve complex problems.

Demonstrating Specific Learning Objectives

Figure 7.2 illustrates their scoring rubric to determine student progress toward each objective.

Teachers observe and document the extent to which each student evaluates, analyzes, and applies knowledge; designs, selects, and uses appropriate thinking strategies; and accesses and utilizes diverse resources to solve complex problems. The same scoring rubrics can be used in all classrooms and subject areas. Physical education teachers can observe a student evaluating, analyzing, and applying knowledge of basketball rules and techniques to outsmart the defense when passing the ball. Foreign language teachers can also evaluate the extent to which a student applies proper grammar and vocabulary in a variety of conversational situations. Both teachers report to stakeholders the extent to which each student demonstrates critical and creative thinking.

Data overload is a common problem in portfolio assessment. By matching each entry with a corresponding learning objective, the number of entries can be limited to those that clearly demonstrate progress toward learning goals.

STUDENT LEARNING GOAL:
A CRITICAL AND CREATIVE THINKER

A critical and creative thinker evaluates, analyzes, and applies knowledge.

4	Uses knowledge meaningfully. Is consistently clear and accurate. Judges value of work by use of internal criteria.
3	Refines and extends beyond the task. Is usually clear and accurate. Judges value of work by use of external standards of excellence.
2	Applies knowledge to new situations. Is generally clear and accurate.
1	Demonstrates gaps in understanding. Is unclear, lacking detail. May need redirection.

A critical and creative thinker designs, selects, and uses appropriate thinking strategies.

4	Uses an efficient or sophisticated approach/procedure. Consistently uses a variety of appropriate, complex reasoning strategies.
3	Uses a workable approach/procedure. Usually uses a variety of appropriate, complex reasoning strategies.
2	Sometimes uses a workable approach/procedure. Generally uses a variety of complex reasoning strategies.
1	Results are inconsistent with procedures. Sporadically uses complex reasoning strategies.

Figure 7.2.

A critical and creative thinker accesses and utilizes diverse resources to solve complex problems.

4   Consistently gathers and processes information from a variety of sources. Solutions exhibit synthesis, generalization, or abstraction.

3   Usually gathers and processes information from a variety of sources. Solutions exhibit connections or applications.

2   Generally gathers and processes information from a variety of sources. Solutions exhibit observations.

1   Gathers and processes information from limited sources. Solutions exhibit few extensions.

Figure 7.2 (continued).

HOW DO I MANAGE RESISTANCE?

With any significant change, there will be resistance (Fullan, 1991; Friend & Cook, 1991). Once portfolio implementation begins, expect conflict and disagreement to surface. Since any group of people possesses multiple points of view, any schoolwide change will necessarily involve conflict (Fullan, 1991). Given the amount and pace of change occurring in schools, it is not surprising to find that resistance is common. Although it is uncomfortable and time consuming, principals will have to deal with resistance when teachers begin to implement portfolios.

When resistance surfaces, many principals are tempted to alleviate resistance by withdrawing portfolio implementation. If no change exists, resistance does not exist (Friend & Cook, 1991). Principals cannot be change agents without managing resistance.

Why Resistance Exists

Resistance to change typically occurs as a personal defense mechanism. When the change appears too risky for our sense of safety, most people will become resistant. Teachers are being asked to find their own approach to a relative new way of assessing students. Unless they have a high tolerance for the unknown, they will find it unnerving and unpleasant. Their need for structure, certainty, and predicatability may be too high (Covey,

1989, 1991). Do not assume that resistance is total rejection of portfolios. There are numerous reasons for resistance.

Lack of Minimal Conditions

In some situations, resistance is an appropriate response. Parents or teachers may have a legitimate reason not to participate in portfolio assessment (Friend & Cook, 1991; Fullan, 1991). Their concerns might signal lack of adequate preparation, not having the necessary resources to do them correctly, or philosophical differences within the community. In these circumstances, principals should respect the seemingly irrational, subjective side of resistance. Minimal conditions needed for teacher training, time, and/or resources might not exist.

Conflict with Values

In other situations, portfolio contents might conflict with parental values. If some parents reject the presence of the affective domain of student reflection, we recommend you omit any portfolio entries that pertain to values or emotions. Rather than discarding portfolios, it may be necessary to modify required contents to match the values and beliefs of your community.

Inadequate Explanations

The most common source of resistance comes from misperceptions of portfolios. Judgements are based on partial information or inadequate explanations of the purposes and uses of portfolios. In general, the more ambiguity there is in explanations of portfolios, the more likely it is that serious resistance will result (Friend & Cook, 1991). Even when all the steps are clearly explained, implementing portfolios involves a certain amount of uncertainty for participants. Expect your staff members to vary greatly in their understanding of portfolios, their comprehension of curriculum and assessment, and their perceptions of how the change to portfolios will affect their teaching (Clark & Clark, 1994).

Lack of Time

Frustration often occurs due to lack of time to learn new skills necessary for portfolio implementation. Whenever teachers make significant changes in activities, programs, or services, they require time to adjust to changes, become proficient, and perform differently. Time is a luxury that simply cannot be afforded in many schools. The result is that professionals often are expected to assimilate change rapidly and immediately function effectively. This unrealistic expectation leads to feelings of frustration from too many expectations being placed on educators without time to practice skills and attain an adequate level of comfort. Educators are less resistant if they have time to examine current portfolio practices, reflect on this change, and control the pace of implementation (Clark & Clark, 1994).

Loss of Autonomy

Many teachers work in isolation. They are accustomed to completing their job responsibilities with a great deal of autonomy. Generally, they rely on their own judgements and tried and true practices to carry out their roles. When portfolios are implemented, this automony is threatened. We cannot assume that autonomy is bad and collaboration is good (Fullan, 1991). Many teachers utilize isolation as a way to protect their time and energy needed for paperwork and instructional demands. Some staff members will want more social interaction, while others will have a smaller network of people from whom they seek ideas. Regardless of personal preferences for autonomy, individual teachers have a responsibility to make some contribution to the development of collaborative work cultures (Fullan, 1991).

Interpersonal Relationships

Reception to an idea is often filtered through our opinion of the person who initiates the change. Sometimes, ideas are supported or rejected based on interpersonal relationships, rather than the merits of the idea. A consistent, trusted leader is more likely to persuade the staff to try portfolios than a principal with a history of miscommunication, inconsistent follow-through, and jumping from one bandwagon to another. In some cases, resistance to portfolios may be a logical decision based on former unsatisfactory interactions with the principal or administration. Resistance becomes inappropriate when it is based on feelings about people who have left the district.

Organizational Norms

One common culprit that leads to resistance is an organizational habit of initiating each new idea that is proposed without giving staff adequate time to develop and assimilate it. Without long-range plans for institutionalizing a change, staff may become overwhelmed by change and consequently resistant (Friend & Cook, 1991). The benefits of portfolios will be overshadowed by the history of poor leadership.

Indicators of Resistance

Before you can address resistance, you will need a clear picture of how resistance is manifested. Every behavior that indicates resistance to change has alternative interpretations that appear to be rational, legitimate explanations but, when examined closely, actually function as a means of avoiding change.

Direct Resistance

The clearest and perhaps the easiest resistance to deal with is when staff members say, "No, thank you." We have heard variations expressed in the following ways:

- "Portfolio assessment sounds like a good idea, but I have 160 freshmen. I haven't time to discuss educational issues."
- "Here comes another fad. I'll wait this one out."
- "Ask someone else to pilot it. The administration hears about these things and jumps onto them."

In each example, the teacher politely declined to participate in portfolio assessment. The messages of resistance were clear.

"Yes" People

Most schools have at least one "yes" person on the staff. This is the person who agrees to any and all ideas only to avoid conflict. "Yes" people perceive that it is easier to agree overtly with your ideas and then not act upon them than it is to openly disagree with you (Friend & Cook, 1991). Only by asking for feedback and otherwise attending to a broader range of meanings for the response can you discern the incongruity between the apparent response and the actual one.

Reactive People

People who frequently use the word *they* may be refusing to take responsibility for rejecting portfolios by placing the responsiblity elsewhere such as with policy, individuals, or groups. By creating real or imagined external authority, the resistant individual attempts to present legitimate reasons to reject portfolios. The commonality of this strategy is that "they won't like or allow it." We have heard comments similar to these:

- "The parents won't go for this."
- "I heard the state is going to withdraw support for portfolios."
- "Research says this doesn't work."
- "They would have to pay me well to get my attention."

Procrastinator

Repeated procrastination in implementing a change may also be an indication of resistance. A resistant individual with a high level of skill can defer participation indefinitely (Friend & Cook, 1991). In large districts with high rates of staff transfers, individuals may be able to avoid an unwanted change completely. Not every schedule delay is due to resistance. Many events are beyond a teacher's control. However, a pattern of delays may be an indicator of resistance.

Traditionalist

Other staff members may rely on past practice as an excuse not to participate in portfolios. They want and need proof that it is not a fad. Expressions that convey reliance on tradition include

- "We've always done it this way."
- "If it ain't broke, don't fix it."
- "What's wrong with what we're doing?"

Addressing Resistance

Before you approach a resistant staff member or parent, you should first consider the other person's point of view. Keep in mind that, sometimes, concern about portfolios leads to an appropriate decision not to participate until there are modifications in the procedures, additional training, or extra resources. In all cases, it is essential to respect resistance.

Fullan (1991, p. 100) found that "the more planners are committed to a particular change, the less effective they are in getting others to implement it." Principals who assume one version of portfolios is the only way to implement them tend to be less open to modifications in the process or contents and less tolerant of delays that will inevitably occur when teachers begin implementing them. A better approach is sensitivity to the possibility that no one version of portfolios is fully correct and resistance may not be based on stubbornness or incompetence (Fullan, 1991).

Is it worth the effort? After assessing the reasons for resistance, you can decide whether to respond to the situation. In some instances, the best response may be no response at all. For example, if a teacher is planning to leave at the end of the year or retire, it may not be worth the time and energy to address this resistance. Other situations may not warrant addressing resistance, such as if administrative support is weak, resources are lacking, or personal matters are temporarily occupying the teacher's attention. You may want to postpone confronting a teacher's resistance until surrounding conditions change.

Another consideration is the degree of resistance. Individuals are more likely to participate in portfolios if they feel moderate or low-level negative feelings than if they have strong negative feelings about implementation. Persuasion won't work when negative emotions are strong. A more constructive alternative is to wait until feelings are less intense and then address the resistance (Friend & Cook, 1991; Covey, 1991; Heald-Taylor, 1989). When you do pressure them to change, allow staff members to react, to form their own opinions, to interact with other teachers who are implementing portfolios, and to obtain technical assistance (Fullan, 1991).

Persuasion

One major strategy to address resistance is your ability to convince the person to agree to try portfolios. The personal influence that you have and that others perceive you have will determine whether you can persuade others of your point of view. There are certain qualities that give personal influence its credibility. These qualities consist of goodwill and fairness, professional expertise, prestige, and charisma. Goodwill and fairness are developed by showing attention to the other person, concern for the other person, and unselfishness. Expertise comes from professional preparation, experience, qualifications, competence, and intelligence. Prestige is built on rank, power, status, and position. Charisma is derived from verbal ability, "thinking on your feet," dynamism, energy, and confidence. Each category may enhance or detract from your persuasiveness. They also are strongly related to a climate of trust that we discussed in Chapter 2.

Persuasion has several approaches. The behavioral approach uses incentives to reward teachers who implement portfolios. Providing extra paraprofessional time is frequently used as an incentive. Other rewards include sending teachers who utilize portfolios to conferences, highlighting teachers' portfolio practices in the community newspaper or school newsletter, and providing time to work on portfolios. Verbal encouragement is critical for getting through the initial difficult stages of implementation. Frequently, the principal's physical presence and quick response to requests for assistance can make the difference between continuing implementation and discarding portfolios.

Reluctant teachers can sometimes be persuaded by sending them to observe other teachers who utilize portfolios. This type of modeling works best when the teachers recognize similarities in their teaching styles, students, and subject areas. The extent to which the reluctant teacher identifies with the model corresponds with the success of modeling as a persuasive approach.

Cognitive Dissonance

When individuals receive information that is inconsistent with their ideas, they try to resolve the perceived inconsistency. Cognitive dissonance suggests that when no dissonance exists in a person, that person is unlikely to change. However, if new information is introduced that calls for modifications in already known information, the individual seeks to resolve the dilemma by making some changes. For example, teachers frequently mention a desire to improve students' responsibility for learning. Portfolios can increase students' responsibility for learning if teachers make some adjustments in the curriculum to include portfolio implementation. By linking portfolios with resolution of the discrepancy, some teachers will be persuaded to try the change.

Perceptual Approach

A perceptual approach to persuasion is based on the assumption that individuals' unique frame of references affect their receptivity to change and set parameters on their ability to tolerate change (Covey, 1991). If portfolios fall within an individual's tolerance level, then persuasion is possible. Conversely, if the change is beyond the person's tolerance level, it is unlikely to be considered, regardless of the strategies used to persuade. The principal has to determine each teacher's tolerance range and propose only incremental changes that fall into this range. For some teachers, using portfolios on a daily basis will be beyond their risk levels. However, asking them to have students work on one portfolio entry once a week might seem more manageable.

Do not expect to dispel all resistance. A realist views progress as gradually increasing the number of teachers using portfolios as a daily part of the curriculum.

HOW DO I GET TEACHERS TO WORK TOGETHER ON PORTFOLIOS?

Once implementation begins, teachers need to have access to each other to learn how to use portfolios on a daily basis. Inservices for the entire staff are necessary to develop an initial understanding of portfolios, but personal interactions are essential for any substantial change. Without an exchange of ideas, staff members are forced to learn by trial and error. When new efforts falter, teachers tend to fall back into traditional routines.

Collaboration has many benefits. When teachers plan together, a sense of community grows. Job satisfaction is increased, conflict is reduced, stress and burnout are reduced, and trust expands. Collegial relationships are fostered by talking with each other, designing instruction together, and teaching each other. This type of collaboration breaks down barriers between departments, disciplines, and grade levels. Schools where teachers share ideas about instruction have higher achievement scores than schools where teachers work in isolation. Collaboration is a strong predictor of student achievement (Clark & Clark, 1994).

The cellular organization of school prevents teachers from sharing, observing, and discussing each other's work with their colleagues (Fullan, 1991). Spending most of their time physically apart from other adults leads teachers to struggle with their problems and anxieties privately. Particularly at middle and high school levels, teachers perform their work in isolation. Facilities provide few suitable places for teachers to meet and confer while rigid schedules provide little time for teachers to exchange ideas. However, it is the school cultural norms that provide the most significant barriers to collaboration. Seeking and giving advice are often discouraged. In some schools, requests for assistance are viewed as indicators of incompetence (Clark & Clark, 1994).

It is the principal's responsibility to change the structural organization and cultural norms to break down department walls. This can be accomplished by tapping the knowledge, expertise, and talent that exists among teachers (Clark & Clark, 1994). Principals arrange time for teachers to plan ways to utilize portfolio assessment, share methodologies that are successful, and solve problems as they arise.

It is not necessary to have frequent schoolwide time to meet. A more effective method is to form small focus groups of people working on similar ways to implement portfolios. In fact, schoolwide meetings to implement portfolios may have less of an impact than multiple collaborative networks (Fullan, 1991). This is particularly true in large high schools.

Traditionally, high school and middle level teachers have met as departments to discuss curriculum and materials issues. While important, this collaboration tends to be narrow in scope. In collaborative schools, teams of teachers from different disciplines focus on common issues and problems they are experiencing with portfolios. This reflective practice empowers teachers to modify implementation to best suit the needs of their students.

Neither too much nor too little collaboration will work. Isolated, autonomous professionals need other professionals to reflect and refine their teaching. "Interactive professionalism" (Fullan, 1991, p. 142) consists of teachers and other staff members working in small groups who interact frequently in planning, testing new ideas, attempting to solve different problems, assessing effectiveness, and giving and receiving advice. Within this type of collaboration, teachers are continuous learners within a community of inquirers.

HOW DO WE ASSURE EQUITY AND DUE PROCESS?

Portfolios raise substantial legal challenges. In the previous chapter, we discussed students' right to privacy and recommended that parents sign a release form to allow teachers to evaluate portfolios. We also suggested that cumulative school portfolios be housed in a secured manner. In addition to providing for privacy rights, it is also necessary to deal with the issues of equity and due process.

Equity

When assessment is used for high-stakes purposes such as decisions about retention, placement, "no-pass–no-play," college entrance, scholarships, and district rewards and sanctions, equity questions must be addressed (Darling-Hammond, 1991). By having two portfolio sections, a standard section of required entries and a creative section of optional entries, all students have an opportunity to show their strengths. Still, the question must be raised, "Is the required evidence equitable?" Equality and equity are not the same. Equality is having everyone perform the same tasks in the same way. Equality does not lead to equity because individual differences exist and must be recognized (Gomez et al., 1991; Anthony et al., 1991). To be equitable, required evidence must given everyone an equal chance of performing at a quality level. Tasks cannot give one group of students an advantage over another group. Diversity among students must be respected in the ways students reflect their learning. Required evidence must be structured so that students with limited English proficiency, physical handicaps, and educationally disadvantaged environments can show what they know. The key is to include a variety of ways to demonstrate a learning objective and to supply tools that are needed to perform the tasks. Portfolios are not a one-size-fits-all proposition (Gomez et al., 1991).

One way to reduce inequities is to ask a committee of parents to review performance tasks. The purpose of this parent advisory committee is to broaden the tasks and ways to demonstrate achievement to allow all students to show what they know. Rather than narrowing the structure of assessment tasks, the tasks need to encourage diversity. For example, an entry to demonstrate the learning objective "a person who can clearly express his or her thoughts and feelings" can be an audiotape of a speech or debate, a painting, a computer-processed story or essay, a film, a videotape of a dance, and so on. In this definition of communication, all students have an opportunity to show their strengths. Wolf expresses it this way, "In a culture that distributes wealth and privilege unevenly, portfolios give students the opportunity to create an autobiography of themselves that is coherent, that shows growth, and that has possibility in it" (Goldberg, 1994, p. 58).

Other equity questions arise about how portfolios are evaluated. Entries must be judged in a fair, consistent, nonarbitrary, nonprejudicial way. Districts must consider if bias exists in areas of race, gender, and student behavior. Teachers' perceptions of students' behavior can significantly influence their judgements of scholastic performance. Behavior problems are especially pronounced in judgement of boys' work. Neatness of work, penmanship, and amount of work have also been found to affect teacher's judgement. The point is not to impose more formality on assessment tasks but, rather, to have clear standards and criteria that are applied consistently (Valencia, 1990; Sperling, 1994). Standards must be flexible, situational, multicultural and adapted to local needs (Lieberman, 1991).

Clear and explicit criteria with examples of typical errors for each stage of performance and careful rater training reduces scoring bias. However, when stakes are high, reducing scoring bias to even a small percent is not good enough. Because the development of incorruptible rubrics is illusive, it is essential to have two or three independent evaluators score the performance. Never allow one person to judge high-stakes performance tasks.

One other equity issue will be addressed later in this chapter, which is equity across districts. Students in districts that provide extensive staff development, support, and time for teachers to work on portfolios have an advantage over students in districts who provide little training and support for their teachers. To some degree, the quality of portfolios may be related to the quality of the teaching.

Due Process

Another legal area to consider is student due process. Parents and students have a right to know how students will be evaluated and the philosophical basis for performance-based assessment. You are required to inform students and parents about required portfolio entries with clear standards, a time line of when each completed entry is due, and the evaluation criteria. Part of the principal's job is to educate parents about the curriculum and evaluation changes. We recommend that you supplement verbal explanations at parent meetings with written explanations of the evaluation process. On the first day of school, teachers also need to explain to students how they will be assessed. It is similar to establishing the rules for a game before the game begins.

ARE PORTFOLIO ASSESSMENTS VALID TO USE FOR HIGH-STAKES DECISIONS?

Portfolios contain a wealth of information about instructional programs. Using portfolios for school and district accountability seems to be inevitable. While the potential for portfolio assessment is promising, questions remain to be resolved. Our concern is that portfolios are being required by states for large-scale assessment purposes before technical issues are solved. This premature high-stakes emphasis on portfolio assessment is filled with problems and may fail. If this happens, the concept of portfolio assessment may be discarded along with the benefits of portfolios.

Several states such as Vermont and Kentucky are using information from portfolios to make policy decisions. Kentucky has the ambitious plan to integrate information from discussions about a project, a test with a significant portion of open-ended responses, and a form of paper-and-pencil test to produce multiple indicators of student learning. Both states are experiencing numerous problems with validity, reliability, generalizability, and bias.

While the responsibility justifiably rests with teachers to devise assessment tasks and report valid information about how students are achieving, principals are responsible for ensuring that teachers gather information that is useful and understandable to policymakers (Tierney et al., 1991). The problem comes in being sure that our portfolio assessment is authentic and trustworthy and that results are communicated clearly to politicians (Lamme & Hysmith, 1991a, b). If not, efforts toward alternative assessment will fail. If principals do not provide statistically correct data and translate that information to the policy tier, alternative efforts in schools and districts may well be sabotaged by policymakers' emphases on standardized tests.

Policy Decisions

As we have become more sophisticated consumers of assessment, we have identified limitations of standardized tests. This dissatisfaction has led us to embrace alternative forms of assessment. But alternative formats alone cannot guarantee good assessment. In our rush to obtain data that show students' strengths, we must stress that it is too early to be certain about the appropriateness of alternative assessments in high-stakes decisions. Questions remain about validity, reliability, generalizability, and equity. We must apply the same scrutiny that allowed us to see the limitations, as well as the strengths, of more traditional tests.

Validity and Reliability

The accuracy of decisions based on portfolios is related to the content and nature of the assessment tasks. The extent to which the tasks are reliable and valid determines the accuracy and usefulness of portfolios for making high-stakes decisions about curriculum and programs (Valencia et al., 1994). In all cases, the process described in Chapter 3 of identifying critical goals is central to obtaining useful information. Questions of the value, relevance, and authenticity of the assessments are inextricably linked to the value, relevance, and authenticity of the student learning goals of the curriculum. If learning goals are absent, vague, or superficial, the link among assessment, curriculum, and instruction is lost, and the validity of the assessment becomes suspect (Valencia et al., 1994). One way to determine if assessments yield useful data for decision making is to ask

- What will this assessment task measure?
- What will the information tell us about students' progress toward curricular goals?
- What will the information tell us about program strengths and weaknesses?
- How will the scores help us diagnose strengths and weaknesses of the curriculum?

Generalizability

The issue of transfer and generalizability appears to be a problem area in alternative assessment (Herman et al., 1992). Herman et al. (1992) reviewed the research on writing assessment and found that writing skill does not generalize across genres. Students who write good, persuasive essays do not necessarily write good, creative stories or literary critiques. Even within a genre, students' quality of writing may vary substantially, depending on the topic (Herman et al., 1992). These findings raise questions about the generalizability of performance on tasks. If student performance is highly task-related, it becomes difficult to generalize from a limited set of assessment tasks to the broader domain of achievement. In the example of writing assessment, different decisions might be made about the English composition program of a district, depending on the type of writing used to assess students.

One solution to the issue of generalizability is to use matrix sampling. This type of assessment uses different tasks over a school or district. Each student might complete one or two tasks but a variety of genre would be sampled. Under these conditions, it is possible to get a general idea of how groups of students perform across classrooms. It solves the problem of assessing a variety of tasks that we would expect students to do within a domain (Valencia et al., 1994; Herman et al., 1992).

Equity across Districts

Earlier in this chapter, we discussed the legal issues of equity. If we are to use portfolios for making high-stakes decisions, we need to be concerned with equity across districts. The amount of extensive and continual staff development concerning portfolio assessment that teachers receive in various districts will probably result in differences in how well students are prepared to do portfolio tasks. Helping teachers and students prepare for authentic assessment requires a reexamination of instruction. This change is a process of continual work requiring constant support for teachers. Unfortunately, some districts provide less professional training and support for teachers than others. One result of unequal training is differences in student scores. To some extent, scores can be attributed to how well teachers prepare students for assessment tasks. Unless training is provided across districts by state or consortia, portfolios can promote inequities in learning experiences being assessed.

Unbiased Scores

Another critically important validity concern in school assessment is one of fairness and bias. Recent cognitive learning theory underscores the importance of background knowledge in solving problems (Herman et al., 1992). Students from different socioeconomic, cultural, and linguistic backgrounds may possess different kinds of prior knowledge and experiences. Problems of differences in background knowledge can be minimized if we are sure that all students have ample opportunity in school to acquire and apply the knowledge and skills being measured. A variety of statistical analyses can be conducted to examine potential bias. Such analyses look for differences in peformance among subgroups while controlling for other factors (Herman et al., 1992). Principals are not expected to conduct these analyses but should be aware that they are available for high-stakes decisions. If the results of a statewide portfolio assessment are used to identify school-level strengths and weaknesses, then you should request the state testing program to gather evidence that the tasks are unbiased and valid.

WHAT IS THE RELATIONSHIP BETWEEN PORTFOLIO ASSESSMENT, GRADING, AND REPORT CARDS?

Issues about grading and reporting of student learning have frustrated educators for most of this century.[1] The numerous studies and continuous debate have brought us no closer to what constitutes best practices than we had over sixty years ago (Guskey, 1994). While the movement to reform our schools and change our instructional practices progresses at an ever increasing rate, in many districts, our report card system seems to be frozen in time with students still receiving a single letter grade in each subject area (Willis, 1993).

Some feel that it is impossible to adequately and justly summarize human performance as a single point on a continuum and that letter grades should not be used at all because they do not tell the whole story (Anthony et al., 1991; K. Goodman et al., 1992). Others believe the problem is not with letter grades themselves but with "using a single grade with no clear and stable meaning to summarize all aspects of performance" (Wiggins, 1993).

As Hewitt (1995) notes in reflecting about the writing portfolios in Vermont, there is no "one-size-fits-all" answer to the question of whether and to what extent the results of portfolio assessment should be used to determine the grades on report cards. He cautions that the contents and ownership of student portfolios may be compromised by high stakes attached to the results of an assessment when they play a role in students' final grades. There is also the danger of losing valuable diagnostic information when multiple measures within a portfolio are reduced to a single score or letter grade applied at the end of a grading period (Rhodes & Shanklin, 1993; Hewitt, 1995).

As classrooms move from a testing culture with teachers being in total control, students working independently, and learning focused on studying for tests to an assessment culture with teachers and students working collaboratively, there is a blurring of learning, instruction, and assessment (Seeley, 1994). Report cards and reporting systems must reflect changes in school teaching and assessment practice.

The best way to begin thinking about grading in relation to these changes is to consider what you want to accomplish through grading (Rhodes & Shanklin, 1993). When your teachers begin devising ways to include portfolio assessment into the district's reporting system, they will need your support and assistance in creating a system that your community of students, parents, and other stakeholders can easily understand (Seeley, 1994; Rhodes & Shanklin, 1993; Wiggins, 1993). If letter grades are used, the criteria for assigning them must be clearly understood by the students, as well as the teachers and community members (Anthony et al., 1991; DeFina, 1992; Hewitt, 1995; Tierney et al., 1991).

After reviewing the literature on grading and reporting, Guskey (1994) found that teachers have a clearer grasp of what their students have learned when using a combination of the following types of learning criteria for assigning grades:

- Product criteria focus on what students know and can do at the time of the report. Grades are often assigned on the basis of culminating demonstrations of learning such as concept maps, finished thematic projects, final examination scores, and other overall assessments.
- Process criteria focus on not only final products, but also on how the student arrived at those products. Grades are usually assigned from some combination of final product evaluations, effort, work habits, quizzes, homework, participation in class or group work, projects, attendance, work samples, and other process evaluations.
- Progress criteria focus on how much students have gained or on how far they have come, rather than where they are at the end of the grading period. Grades can be derived from successive drafts, pretests and posttests, progress on homework assignments, self-evaluations, teacher observations, and other measures.

Portfolio assessment can include all three criteria. Finished projects, final exams, outlines of procedures in developing final products, and progress over time can all be reflected in a portfolio.

As an administrator, you must decide your stance on letter grades for your school and work with your teachers to resolve grading issues.[2] As your school moves toward using portfolios, questions you will need to direct to your stakeholders concerning grading include

- What/whose criteria will you use in assessing students' portfolios?
- How will you calculate traditional grades (A, B, C . . .) based on your students' portfolios, if at all?
- How will you deal with issues of subjectivity in grading?

- Will you incorporate portfolios into your usual testing routine, or will tests become part of their portfolio collections?
- Will your assessment procedures supplement or replace formal and informal tests?
- Will tests continue to play a major role in classroom placement and/or curricular objectives, or will the tests be weighed with samples of students' work for making educational decisions?
- How will using portfolios impact teachers in your students' subsequent grades or in other school districts (DeFina, 1992, p. 37)?

The procedures for problem solving in Chapter 2 and the staff development sessions in Chapter 3 provide vehicles for dealing with these questions.

HOW CAN A PORTFOLIO BE AN ALTERNATIVE TO LETTER GRADES?

Portfolios can use the most common alternatives to letter grades—narratives, checklists, continuums, and rubrics. After answering the questions listed above, your staff and stakeholders might decide not to reduce portfolios to a single letter grade. As you consider the alternatives to letter grades, you will need to be aware of the strengths and drawbacks of each alternative.

Teachers who use narratives as a reporting system are required to write how well students meet the learning standards and offer specific information for documenting progress. There are also problems and concerns associated with narrative reporting. Time for preparation of the reports is often prohibitive. Teachers' comments tend to become standardized as they complete more of them. Narrative comments can have unclear criteria and can represent idiosyncratic values. Finally, consistency from teacher to teacher may be lacking (Wiggins, 1993; Willis, 1993).

Checklists of learning objectives or a mastery approach with a list of standards can be used to indicate whether students have mastered each competence. However, this form of assessment does not indicate how well the competency was met or whether the child is progressing satisfactorily for that level. Some teachers feel uncomfortable assessing students without the ease and security of a percentage system. Also, parents often find the forms to be complicated, and they still question whether their child is doing well enough (Willis, 1993; DeFina, 1992).

Another form used for reporting is the use of a continuum, which provides a range of stages or levels of competence in various subjects. On this form, the teacher records what students can do and the focus is on learning, rather than a grade. This approach takes training for teachers to understand the concepts of the form and how to judge whether students are at one level or another. Parents sometimes find this format to be confusing when they do not understand the concepts related on the continuum (Willis, 1993).

A fourth alternative to traditional letter grades is the use of analytic and holistic rubrics described in Figure 7.2 found earlier in this chapter. One district that uses a rubric description for reporting student progress is Tucson Unified School District in Arizona. When principals and teachers felt that their report card system did not meet the new CORE curriculum and assessment procedures adopted by the state, they became part of a team of teachers, principals, and parents who studied the issue and established a new plan. The rationale they developed for using a rubric format was that teachers would provide more information to parents, and there would be increased consistency across the district so that scores could be compared across schools.

This approach also has its drawbacks. It is time-intensive to develop the rubrics because teachers and parents need to fully understand the curriculum. There would be costs to the central office to support the schools for information dissemination and training. Rhodes and Shanklin (1993) caution that, when using holistic rubrics that allow districts to examine students' abilities across schools, the standard error of measurement for any single student is so great that using individual scores is invalid. Also, a score of two at the beginning of the year and a four at the end does show significant progress, but the specific areas of improvement cannot be determined from the scores; therefore, holistic scores serve the district level better than the classroom teacher. On the other hand, analytic scoring is more beneficial for the classroom teacher but more difficult to use at the district level because of the greater risk of inconsistency in scoring.

Portfolios can include any combination of alternatives to letter grades. Multiple ways of measuring authentic tasks facilitate curricular decisions, instructional changes, goal setting, and reflection. One group of middle school mathematics teachers felt so strongly that portfolios were more powerful than letter grades that they were willing not only to send the portfolios on to the high school mathematics teachers, but also to meet with them and explain the contents (Seeley, 1994).

SHOULD PORTFOLIOS BE GRADED?

One possible way to deal with the issue of grading portfolios is to keep two portfolios (Hewitt, 1995; Tierney et al., 1991; Wolf, 1994). Hewitt

(1995) recommended keeping one portfolio for the report card that can be graded and one for the studen containing work not chosen for grading through self-selection. Tierney et al. (1991) suggested using one portfolio for the student to own and keep and another that is part of the permanent folder that contains pieces the teacher and student select from the student's personal portfolio to keep records of growth and achievement across various grade levels. Wolf (1994) recommended having the students keep a personal folio in the classroom and a portfolio for district accountability purposes. The portfolio would be more standardized in contents and could therefore be scored with holistic rubrics. The folio could either not be graded, or pieces of it could be analytically scored. The pieces for the portfolio would be selected collaboratively by the student and teacher from the personal folio to meet district or state requirements.

HOW CAN STUDENTS BE INVOLVED IN GRADING PORTFOLIOS?

As mentioned in Chapter 4, in many school systems and classrooms across North America, teachers are traditionally the only ones who participate in grading (Graves, 1991; Tierney et al., 1991; DeFina, 1992; Kohn, 1993; Rhodes & Shanklin, 1993). While none of the experts in authentic assessment are advocating that teachers relinquish total control of assessment to students, they do suggest that students be involved in the grading process (Hewitt, 1995; Porter & Cleland, 1995; Valencia et al., 1994). The suggestions listed below can provide your teachers with a starting point for beginning to involve students in grading:

- Encourage students to participate in self-evaluations.
- Allow students to choose assignments to be graded along with or in place of those the teacher selects.
- Allow students to assist in deciding which elements of a subject or project should be graded.
- Give grades on the basis of criteria that the students and teacher have developed together.
- Encourage students to give themselves a grade and to provide a rationale for that grade, and then negotiate the final grade with teacher input.
- Have students participate in peer evaluations.
- Grade a minimal amount of work that is important for students to be learning. In other words, don't put a grade on everything and find a way to grade what's important.
- Set external criteria, such as how many pieces to be graded during a marking period, and have the students select the pieces.

One fifth-grade teacher had the class decide upon the criteria to be used for reviewing portfolios. Together, they created a holistic analysis guide or rubric that was based on levels of performance on the criteria they selected. The guide was used to compare each portfolio with the descriptions in each category. The purpose of the analysis was not to rank-order students, but to examine strengths and areas needing improvement for individual students' work, rather than to compare portfolio analysis results across a group of students. In this way, the guide was used both holistically to arrive at one score and analytically to examine strengths and weaknesses through the descriptions. The guide the class developed for the teacher to use is provided in Figure 7.3. This type of guide needs to be developed and understood by the students and teachers in each classroom, rather than just adopting the one provided here. By developing their own guide or rubric, each class is guaranteed ownership and understanding of the descriptions. This class also developed the rubric in Figure 7.4 to measure their ability to resolve conflict.

Teachers and students could also be encouraged to develop a series of continua that could be used several times a year to plot individual students' achievements through their portfolio contents and to create an overall picture of student growth (Tierney et al., 1991). The continuum in Figure 7.5 is used by the Mt. Pleasant Public Schools as an end of the year evaluation form to place in third-grade students' writing portfolios that follow students through their elementary grades. Their Language Arts Task Force members created similar forms for grades one through six. When using this form, teachers are encouraged to make a holistic judgement on whether a student is average, above average, or below average in each of the three areas on the form.

Carol Porter and Janell Cleland (1995) have had their freshman English students keep portfolios. While they realized that, ideally, portfolios should not be graded, their school system still required grades and grade points four times during the year. They believed that portfolios must be a collaborative approach between students and teachers; therefore, they felt that since students had helped determine how the portfolio would support their learning, they should also be part of the process for grading.

When students were asked about grading their portfolios, they maintained that their introductions to each artifact should be evaluated for part of their grade. Their reasoning was that they had decided earlier in the year that these artifacts should each have an introduction so that the reader would know what the item is and why it is in the portfolio. Because Porter and Cleland strongly believed that students should be involved in assessment, they worked with their students to develop evaluation instruments for the portfolios.

COLLABORATION/COOPERATIVE RUBRIC

DATE_____ GROUP MEMBERS

GOAL_____ 1._____

_____ 2._____

_____ 3._____

_____ 4._____

5._____

How Did Our Group Do?	YES	NO
Made sure each person understood		
Stayed in our group		
Used quiet voices		
Praised each other's ideas		
Helped each other		
Listened to each other's ideas		
Carried out role/roles		
Finished the task		
Total		

One thing our group did very well:

_____

_____

One thing we need to do better next time:

_____

_____

Assessment Standard

E = Exceptional   E = Yes for all criteria (11 out of 11)

S = Satisfactory   S = Yes for most criteria (9 out of 11)

N = Not there yet   N = Yes for some criteria (8 or fewer out of 11)

Figure 7.3.

Conflict Resolution/Self Assessment Rubric

Name_____   Date_____

How Did I Do?	Self	
	Yes	No
1. Prevents conflicts by using appropriate words, getting away, and/or asking an adult to help		
2. Avoids using fouls so conflict doesn't get bigger (hitting, name calling, threats, bossing, making excuses, blaming, teasing, not listening, getting even, put downs)		
3. Includes the steps of conflict resolution when the Peace Table is used -Cools down		
-Demonstrates active listening		
-Uses I care words		
-Reaches a win/win solution		
-Seeks adult mediator		
Total		

Assessment
Standard

E =
Exceptional
S =
Satisfactory
N =
Not there yet

E = Yes for all
criteria
(9 out of 9)

S = Yes for
most criteria
(7 out of 9)

N = Yes for
some criteria
(6 out of 9)

4. Here is one thing I did very well.

_____

_____

5. Here is one thing I need to do better.

_____

_____

Figure 7.4.

STUDENT_____

TEACHER_____ YEAR _____

Characteristics of
THIRD GRADE END-OF-YEAR
written products

MEANING/CONTEXT		
3−	3	3+
• limited, unoriginal ideas • few or irrelevant details • limited word choices • abrupt conclusions • flat, lifeless writing	• some original ideas • some descriptive details • sentences related with "and then" • some vitality (voice) in writing	• fresh, original ideas • details, engaging topic • lively, engaging writing • creative thought • enriched vocabulary
ORGANIZATION		
3−	3	3+
• some relationship between ideas • little sentence variety • few elements of genre included • no transitions • some incomplete sentences	• sentences linked one to another and to topic • some variation in sentence structure • some elements of genre included • some transition words	• obvious overall organization • varied sentences • basic elements of genre included • some beginning paragraphing
MECHANICS		
3−	3	3+
• infrequent use of capitals or ending punctuation • numerous spelling errors • usage errors	• frequent use of capitals & end punctuation • numerous informed misspellings ("reviews" as "revuse") • infrequent usage errors	• proper nouns & I capitalized • ending punctuation accurate and varied • commas, quotation marks • some informed misspellings • few or no usage errors

Teacher comments:

Figure 7.5.

```
ENGLISH LEARNING PORTFOLIO:

QUANTITY:  12 ENTRIES =  5; 10-11 ENTRIES = 4; 8-9 ENTRIES = 3
           6-7 ENTRIES =  2;  5-6  ENTRIES = 1; 0-4 ENTRIES = 0

              1     2     3     4     5     X 2 = _____

GROWTH:  CIRCLE YES OR NO FOR EACH OF THE FOLLOWING

   1. Do freewrites show evidence of extended writing time and greater detail?
      Yes  No

   2. Do written conversations display a more genuine understanding of the
      literature?    Yes  No

   3. Are more connections being made between personal experience and
      language experiences?    Yes  No

   4. Is there evidence that the student is taking more risks?   Yes   No

   5. Is there demonstrated evidence that the student is a contributing member of
      the class community?    Yes  No

              1     2     3     4     5     X 2 = _____

REFLECTION:  CIRCLE YES OR NO FOR EACH OF THE FOLLOWING

   1. Does the learner determine which strategy best supported his/her learning?
      Yes  No

   2. Does the learner determine which strategy was least effective?  Yes   No

   3. Are students supported with specific references to the strategy displayed in
      the portfolio?    Yes  No

   4. Does the learner determine how his/her reading and writing have changed
      in the last three weeks?    Yes  No

   5. Have realistic goals been set with a plan of action?    Yes  No

              1     2     3     4     5     X 2 = _____

APPLICATION:   Each question answered with satisfactory detail and evidence
   of strategy = 5; 3 answers and strategy = 4; 2 answers and strategy = 3'
   1 answer and strategy = 1.       1   2   3   4   5   X 2 = _____

Total Possible = 50 points                    Your total is _____
       45-50 = A     40-44 = B    35- 39 = C    30-34 = D
```

Adapted from Porter, C. & Cleland, J. 1995. *The Portfolio as a Learning Strategy.* Portsmouth, NH: Heinemann, p. 133.

Figure 7.6.

PORTFOLIO GRADING SHEET		
	Student	Teacher
1. Is the portfolio neat in appearance?	Yes No	Yes No
2. Does the portfolio tell the reader about the learner you were and the learner you have become? Comments:	Yes No	Yes No
3. For each artifact in your portfolio have you explained: Where you were in your learning before you completed this work? Comments:	Yes No	Yes No
Where you are now in your learning as a result of the writing, reading, speaking, or listening of others? Comments:	Yes No	Yes No
What you learned that is represented by each artifact? Comments:	Yes No	Yes No
4. Have you drawn the reader into the portfolio by being original, creative, and/or imaginative? Comments:	Yes No	Yes No
5. Have you displayed learning in each of the following: Reading? Comments:	Yes No	Yes No
Writing? Comments:	Yes No	Yes No
Speaking? Comments:	Yes No	Yes No
Listening? Comments:	Yes No	Yes No
Grade	_____	_____

Adapted from: Porter, C. & Cleland, J. 1995. *The Portfolio as a Learning Strategy.* Portsmouth, NH: Heinemann.

Figure 7.7.

The grade sheet presented in Figure 7.6 is an adaption of one that was developed early in the school year. The goal of this evaluation was to have students make sense of what they had done so far. Once the students learned how to stay organized and to keep track of their entries, the grading sheets would reflect quality of entries more than quantity, as this first evaluation did. Although these teachers did grade the portfolios, they focused on growth and understanding to arrive at the grade and provided for student input and ownership as well.

Later in the year, as they began their first novel, the students and teachers determined seven stopping points in the novel where the students would respond to the text. After the first four responses, the students analyzed their responses and set personal goals for the last three responses. They dated these responses, included them in their portfolios in order, and wrote a reflective letter that highlighted their understanding and growth. The last piece in each portfolio was goals for reading new novels. Once again, the students helped create the grade sheet for the portfolio. In Figure 7.7, this grade sheet demonstrates the shift from quantity to quality in the analysis. Both the forms in Figures 7.6 and 7.7 are examples of holistic rubric scoring, with the capability of being used analytically as well.

TROUBLESHOOTING: WHEN DO I CALL FOR HELP?

It is virtually impossible to be a principal without encountering problems. Often, it is situations that we perceive as less important that expand into major conflicts. When we are too busy, not listening carefully to what others are saying to us, or partially answering a question, we are more likely to create unnecessary problems or fail to foresee obstacles.

In addition to the unavoidable friction that accompanies the principalship, implementing portfolios brings problems with philosophical differences of teachers and parents, data overload, staff resistance to change, breaking down department walls, legal issues, and evaluation factors. Why would anyone press for a change that will bring inevitable problems?

We need an alternative to traditional standardized assessment. Principals are accountable for providing best practices for the students. You are not expected to institutionalize a major change such as portfolio assessment without assistance. We strongly urge you to form a network with other principals who are using portfolios in their schools. Share your successes, failures, and frustrations. No one said you had to do it alone.

When do you pick up the phone and call for help? As often as you want to talk with another principal who understands what you are trying to do.

GLOSSARY

Assessment Culture: school communities where students and teachers collaborate, various audiences use grade results for a multitude of purposes, and the distinctions between instruction and assessment are blurred.

Behaviorist Theory: a belief that children are empty vessels to be filled with information, skills, and concepts.

Checklist Reporting: a reporting system that is a mastery approach in which competencies or standards are listed for students to achieve and checked off as students master them.

Cognitive Dissonance: a perceived inconsistency that occurs when individuals receive information that is inconsistent with their ideas.

Continua: an evaluation system with more than one continuum grouping used to evaluate student progress or achievement.

Continuum: a set of levels or ranges of competence with descriptions that describe characteristics of each stage or level.

Data Overload: the result of the accumulation of too many assessment pieces that lead to an unmanageable, unfocused jumble of information.

Descriptors: short phrases that describe each level of achievement on an assessment scale.

Direct Resistance: a clear decline to participate.

Due Process: the right to know how, when, and by what criteria you will be evaluated.

Equity: all people are given an equal chance of performing at their best level and are judged in a fair, consistent, nonarbitrary, nonprejudicial way.

External Criteria: criteria set by someone other than the person who is compiling the portfolio.

Interactive Professionalism: a phrase coined by Fullan (1991) that describes professionals who collaborate with other professionals to refine and improve their work.

Interactive Theory: a belief that learning is a process of discovering meaning about the world by intellectually and socially interacting with it.

Interpersonal Relationship: an opinion based on interactions with another person.

Letter Grade: symbols that represent a summary of student performance that is a mixture of a teacher's expectations and district standards.

Narrative Reporting: reports written by teachers about how students are performing in subject areas or in general. These reports usually include specifics of student strengths and weaknesses.

Organizational Norms: the existing habits within an organization.

Outside Mandates: changes that are directed by organizations external to the local district. They are usually orders from state or federal governments.

Percentage System: a grading system based on 100 points.

Perceptual Approach: an approach to persuade others based on evaluating the person's emotional receptivity to new information.

Permanent Folder: another term for a cumulative achievement folder.

Personal Folio: a collection of student work that usually is self-selected by students, can have teacher input, contains all types of artifacts, and is classroom-based.

Persuasion: a strategy to convince other people based on your personal influence that you have and that others perceive you have.

Process Criteria: learning criteria based on an end product and how the student accomplished the product. Many factors are taken into account rather than just the student's knowledge at the end of the marking period.

Procrastinator: a person who defers participation indefinitely.

Product Criteria: learning criteria based on the knowledge the learner has at the end of a grading or evaluation period. These are usually holistic in nature.

Progress Criteria: learning criteria based on the growth the student has made.

Reactive People: people who refuse to take responsibility by placing the responsibility elsewhere.

Reconciliation Period: a span of time when a staff examines their beliefs to identify how they can blend portfolios with their beliefs.

Resistance: an emotional response that is based on a rational or irrational fear to participate in changes.

Standard Error of Measurement: the extent to which assessment results would vary if repeated. The true score falls within a range, rather than on one particular point on a continuum.

Testing Culture: school communities where teachers are the authorities, students work individually, and instruction is geared to passing the test.

Traditionalist: a person who relies on past practices.

Transformative Theory: a view of learning as the construction of a personal identity that is based on a sense of meaning, purpose, and connectedness with the environment.

"Yes" People: people who agree to any and all ideas only to avoid conflict.

ENDNOTES

1. Grades often serve as external motivators where students are rewarded for good grades. Learning is better served when students are intrinsically motivated to learn because they have an interest in the topic, want to know more about it, feel that the learning has some benefit in their lives, and recognize the purpose of the learning.
2. While research studies suggest that grading and reporting is not intrinsic to instruction and student learning, reporting and grading procedures are important for the purpose of informing the stakeholders in your school community of student performance and progress towards exit standards.
3. Grading has always been idiosyncratic in nature. Teachers vary in how much weight they place on effort, process, participation, and other factors. These same factors will affect narrative reporting. Standards need to be agreed upon for teachers to follow consistently across classrooms before grades in one class are comparable to those in another.

CHAPTER 8

Going Beyond the Basics

Superintendent Macy's Reflections on Portfolio Implementation in His District

Before walking into the weekly administrative meeting, Superintendent Macy looked over the annual reports from each principal in his district. Obvious differences existed among the schools within the district that were using portfolios and those that were still in the early stages of implementation. Increased parent participation, improved student attendance, reduced teacher turnover, and larger staff development budgets were common in the schools where portfolio assessment was flourishing.

"How can I make it contagious?" he asked himself. "What makes portfolios successful in nine of my schools and not in the other five? All the administrators received the same training, have knowledgeable teachers, and similar students. In one middle school and one elementary building, teachers are still sending home weekly folders and calling them portfolios. They just can't seem to get them off the ground."

As he went into the conference room and looked around the table, he knew the answers to his questions. The difference was the principals. Schools that were successfully using portfolios had principals who were change agents. They had the knowledge, ability, and willingness to work closely with teachers through the process of change. They were the ones who nagged him the most about additional resources for their schools. He could recall their tireless persistence:

"I want to send three teachers to this conference in June."

"Wednesday, I want to take five people over to observe Whitaker School's portfolios."

"We need thirty more computers, five paraprofessionals, and subscriptions to this list of journals."

"We would like to purchase food such as spaghetti, a vegetable tray, and cookies to serve at a series of parent meetings about portfolio assessment."

"Our daily schedule needs to be changed to allow my teachers time to meet within their grade levels. Can you arrange to have the special teachers such as band, strings, art, and P.E. be at my school at the same time?''

He smiled as he recalled their enthusiasm. They were always looking for creative ways to obtain more resources for their staffs.

And, there was something else. They were vision builders. They were able to guide others to think of possibilities. Rather than accepting the status quo, they remained focused on what could be. For them, a closed door simply was a challenge to locate an alternative route to their dreams. When a staff member says, ''We can't,'' they counter with, ''If we could, how would we do it?'' By turning the question around, they were able to influence others to pool their ideas. Often, answers to their questions led to improvements in the school.

Superintendent Macy's daydreaming was interrupted by one of the principals.

''Is there any way that I can send two of my teachers to a conference on teacher portfolios? I've been reading about the benefits teachers find from developing their own portfolios. I have an idea of where we can get the money for the conference fees if you can come up with the airfare. . . .''

INTRODUCTION

IN this chapter, we will examine ways to refine and improve the use of portfolio assessment. The previous chapters dealt with preparing for portfolios, implementing the change, and resolving problems that arise. Now the full potential of portfolios can be realized. With sustained staff development, portfolios can be extended to include peer coaching, peer evaluation, and community involvement.

CYCLICAL STAFF DEVELOPMENT

Portfolio implementation is a process of growing to understand the meaning of changes within the context of school and learning. This process can be organized into three stages for a cyclical staff development program.

When implementation begins, teachers need assistance with management issues. As they try different procedures, some will work, some will not, and others will be marginal. At this early stage of implementation, staff development focuses on making progressive refinements in the processes. Mistakes are perceived as opportunities for gaining a conceptual understanding of portfolios.

Three Stages of a Cyclical Staff Development Program

• Learn the basic skills to successfully implement portfolios.
• Extend and expand the use of portfolios.
• Focus on major structural, political, and instructional issues.

Figure 8.1.

The next cyclical step is to expand and extend the use of portfolios. Staff development at this stage focuses on creating multidisciplinary assessment tasks, adding new types of entries, merging instruction and assessment into one and the same task, and becoming facilitators of learning. Over time, teachers can be encouraged to use portfolios in more complex ways and in more situations.

The final stage of staff development commences when the school culture becomes one of inquiry. Second-order changes such as described in the last section of Chapter 9 are the starting point for a transformed school culture. When this stage is reached, staff development topics are no longer about portfolios, but consist of major structural, political, and instructional issues. Figure 8.1 shows how the cyclical staff development process functions.

SUSTAINING SUPPORT

Providing sustained support is a key to successful portfolio implementation and growth in portfolio assessment in your school. Sustaining support means that principals assist in locating and securing resources necessary to continue portfolio assessment, trust their teachers to grow and change, encourage teachers to develop and attend support groups, provide conditions that support teachers in finding their individual voices in portfolio assessment, and assist teachers to develop peer coaching relationships.

At all stages, staff development approaches are effective when they combine concrete, teacher-specific training activities, ongoing sustained assistance, and regular meetings with peers and others (Fullan, 1991). In-service sessions focus on modeling successful practices and removing roadblocks. Principals identify teachers who can demonstrate successful portfolio procedures and tasks. Demonstrations by other teachers encourage risk taking and provide concrete steps to apply. Having a variety of models helps teachers understand that there are multiple ways to use portfolios, and each teacher's applications will be slightly different. To remove roadblocks, principals must also detect and prioritize problems. They must monitor how well or poorly portfolio assessment is going in classrooms and then provide additional inservice and assistance at the right time and in the right places (Fullan, 1991).

As your staff moves from one stage to the next, the types of success and problems will change. The following questions can be used to construct a list of appropriate topics for inservice sessions:

- Will you identify and demonstrate one assessment task that was particularly successful in your classroom? Briefly explain the task.
- What persistent problems are you experiencing?
- What aspects of portfolio assessment remain unclear?
- Are there important stakeholders that need additional information? If so, who are they and how do you suggest we provide this information?
- To what extent are our practices supporting our shared vision?

Problems might be identified that cannot be solved or successfully demonstrated by members of your staff. In such cases, you can find ways to resolve obstacles by contacting other principals who use portfolio assessment, reviewing earlier chapters of this book, or inviting a consultant to speak to your staff.

SUSTAINING SUPPORT BY PROVIDING RESOURCES

Securing resources to sustain support for teachers through continued conference attendance, materials, and time release needs to become a focus for principals. One potential source includes continued support from your central office. This involves maintaining the support of your superintendent and local school board through progress reports and budget requests such as the one presented in Appendix B.1. Another way to gain additional resource money is through grants. Unfortunately, many administrators are unaware of what resources are available. With your support, interested teachers can take leadership roles in writing proposals and gaining approval for grants ranging in amounts from several hundred dollars to one hundred thousand dollars. Check to discover what resources are available at county, state, and federal levels. Investigate your local library, community colleges, and universities as possible sources for obtaining information about grants. Community groups, service organizations, and private corporations can also be contacted to locate any grants that are available. You can also check to see which public and private foundations in your community, state, or province offer educational foundations (Routman, 1991).

SUSTAINING SUPPORT BY TRUSTING TEACHERS

Portfolio assessment lends itself well to assisting teachers in finding answers to their questions about instructional needs and measuring successful teaching in their own classrooms. As one principal noted, when teachers are active and self-determining participants in their own learning growth, they realize that they become change agents themselves, rather than the patients of someone else's agenda (Wells & Chang-Wells, 1992). The multiple perspectives that are collected as portfolio data can easily be analyzed using teacher inquiry processes such as triangulation, multiple lenses, and reflection. By examining data through several perspectives, including the principals, students, and parents', as well as the teacher's view, teachers ask questions, search for answers, and come to a better understanding of learning in their classrooms (Anthony et al., 1991; Wells & Chang-Wells, 1992; Hubbard & Power, 1993).

SUSTAINING SUPPORT BY ENCOURAGING PORTFOLIO SUPPORT GROUPS

One of the most effective ways to assist teachers in answering their personal questions about portfolio assessment is to encourage teachers to create and attend portfolio support groups. These groups are most effective when attendance is voluntary rather than mandated.[1] In these meetings teachers can talk frankly about issues and concerns about portfolios, instruction, and learning. Portfolio support groups also provide a way for them to begin integrating theory and practice. Many teachers find that meeting with their peers reduces anxiety, fosters collegiality, promotes professional growth, and confirms their practices. Teachers usually appreciate knowing that they are not alone and that others are struggling along with them (Routman, 1991; Matlin, 1992; Hansen, 1994).

While Johnson et al. (1990) deal with support groups for implementing cooperative learning, their recommendations apply equally well to portfolio support groups. Through frequent, continuous, and increasingly precise discussions about implementing portfolio assessment, teachers build a concrete and coherent shared language[2] that can describe the complexity of using portfolios, distinguish one assessment practice and its benefits from another, and integrate portfolios into teaching practices and strategies that they are already using. Through such discussions, teachers exchange successful procedures and materials. They also focus on solving specific problems members may be having in perfecting their use of portfolios. The following norms are adapted from Johnson et al. (1990) to assist portfolio support groups in functioning effectively:

- No one in the group has to be perfect.
- It takes time to master portfolios to a routine level of use.
- We are all here to improve our competence in using portfolios.
- We can critique each other's implementation of portfolios without anyone taking it personally.
- Each of us is secure enough to give feedback on each other's implementation of portfolios.

Rhodes and Shanklin (1993) suggest having the group focus on a particular assessment or portfolio text, assessment technique or procedure, student data that has been collected, or some combination of these, while Matlin (1992) stresses having the group members choose topics for discussion. In a typical meeting, a group can discuss ideas in a book, decide which techniques or assessments to try before the next meeting, report on what they have discovered since their last meeting, discuss new questions that have arisen during implementation, or consider possible solutions to a problem or question.

Another possibilty is to have teachers bring in samples of student portfolios or particular assessment measures for the group to share and examine for progress, signs of growth, patterns of development, or additional assessment tools to include to elicit additional information. Portfolio support groups help members support each other in implementing and improving portfolio assessment as well as sustaining interest in the effort (Johnson et al., 1990; Routman, 1991; Rhodes & Shanklin, 1993). Asking questions increases the quality of reflections and encourages members to extend their thinking to examine new possibilities and solutions to issues (Rhodes & Shanklin, 1993). Some sample questions that require reflection and encourage discussion include

- What learning behaviors can we observe and comment on easily? Not so easily? How can we deal with this in our portfolios?
- Is this assessment instrument appropriate for all students? If not, who is it appropriate or not appropriate for and why? How do we handle this issue in our portfolios?
- What does the data in our students' portfolios reveal about our instruction?

- What else do we want to know about our students? What are some ways we can find out these things?

SUSTAINING SUPPORT BY FOSTERING INDIVIDUAL VOICES

Principals must develop the ability to verbalize their own insights about portfolio assessment, their leadership practices, and their views of learning before they can facilitate change in others. Figure 4.8 in Chapter 4 may assist you and your teachers in examining your philosophy of education. Principals must not only know their own view, but must also be able to communicate their understandings in ways that are sensitive to others and that encourage teachers to find their own voices. Often, when educators are learning new theories and practices, they use the words of experts[3] but to communicate in a way that others are willing to listen to, and in a way that responds to the concerns of others, principals and teachers need to speak about their issues of concern in their own words. Rhodes and Shanklin (1993) identify the following factors that contribute to the ability to find one's own voice:

- Develop a greater understanding of the problems you are concerned about along with potential solutions to the problems.
- Gain experience in talking about issues and ideas with someone whom you perceive to be less threatening before sharing in large groups.
- Remind yourself that expressing opinions is not making waves and each person's views and ideas are valued in the group.
- Encourage others to discover the value of diverse perspectives and to discover solutions that might work best for all concerned.

Sometimes, principals become intolerant or strident when they attempt to create change in others, but unless others are willing to listen, change cannot be fostered, no matter how much you care or believe portfolios will make a difference for students. Teachers and principals need to respect the belief that everyone in the school is making the best decision for themselves and the students (Clark, 1987; Johnson et al., 1990; Matlin, 1992; Rhodes & Shanklin, 1993). Remember, there is no one correct way to implement portfolios. Talking with others in good faith[4] is making an honest effort to see differing points of view and exchanging views, rather than simply promoting your own. This stance includes being willing to listen to others with an open mind in an atmosphere that is conducive to collaboration, such as in portfolio support groups or during peer coaching (Clarke, 1987; Johnson et al., 1990; Fullan, 1991; Rhodes & Shanklin, 1993).

SUSTAINING SUPPORT BY PEER COACHING

One of the ways to provide less threatening settings for teachers to find their voices in portfolio assessment and implementation is to encourage mentoring or peer coaching. Teachers who are already using portfolios in their classrooms can have their efforts and talents recognized by giving them an opportunity to serve as mentors or peer coaches for others who are beginning to implement portfolios. Teachers need opportunities to observe and interact with other teachers. Principals can assist teachers in becoming peer coaches by providing release time for peer observation and collaboration, training for peer coaching, and time for collegial reflection during the school day. Time can be created by using specialists, para-professionals, substitute teachers, and parents to create blocks of time for planning, observing, and reflecting (Routman, 1991; Valencia & Place, 1994).

Routman (1991) maintains that coaching is a critical component for transfer of new learning. She defines coaching as "a collegial process where support, assistance, and companionship are given along with demonstrations and constructive feed-back" (p. 464). For coaching to work, both individuals must view the process as beneficial and not an evaluation of teaching competence so that there is a safe, risk-free atmosphere during the session. One way to have the process viewed as reciprocal is to encourage both teachers to serve as observers who provide feedback through "debriefing" after participation in the classroom. During debriefing, teachers share their thoughts, praise positive observations, notice behaviors, ponder questions, discuss problems, devise plans, and brainstorm solutions to try. Sometimes, having another teacher conduct interviews during instruction or taking anecdotal records on a student can give a teacher another perspective that is difficult to attain when working by oneself. Another example of using a peer for coaching might be when one teacher asks another to observe when the first is taking anecdotal records. For this to be helpful, the two teachers need to agree ahead of time on the focus of the observation and allow enough time to debrief after the observation (Johnson et al., 1990; Routman, 1991; Rhodes & Shanklin, 1993).

Appendix E.1 provides guidelines to assist portfolio support group members in dealing with one another with mutual respect when observing each other.

SUSTAINING SUPPORT BY PEER EVALUATION

In Chapter 4, we examined self-evaluation for learning and for assessment through inclusion of reflections in portfolios. Another type of evaluation that can enhance portfolio assessment is peer evaluation. Two main ways that peer evaluation can be used to expand portfolio assessments are to include peer assessments as entries along with students' self-assessments, teacher evaluations, and/or parental input and as a way to evaluate artifacts or completed portfolios. After students become comfortable using portfolios and teachers are involved in peer coaching or portfolio support groups, you can introduce them to peer evaluation.

Setting the Stage for Using Peer Evaluation

Before students can effectively evaluate one another's work, teachers will need to lay the groundwork for positive handling of constructive criticism and interactions among students. One way to do this is for teachers to model appropriate behavior for students by showing sensitivity and respect for students in their evaluations and interactions with students (DeFina, 1992). As Green (1994) noted, peer evaluation explores the nature and role of evaluation further when performed by classmates or peers. Another way to assist in laying the groundwork for peer evaluation is to review what evaluation is, why it should be done, and ways to do it. Then teachers can lead students into exploring how they can help give each other feedback about their progress.

Establishing Guidelines for Peer Evaluation

DeFina (1992) reminds us that issues of pride and privacy must be considered when establishing guidelines for peer evaluation. This involves providing students with choices in what items will be shared with peers and who will evaluate their work. Other issues that need to be explored include expectations, evaluation criteria, methods of providing meaningful feedback, and accountability of those performing the assessment.

Expectations

The teacher and class will need to decide what will be expected of those who perform evaluations. They will need to be provided with demonstrations for how to evaluate; time for reflection; opportunities to discuss results; examples of ways to interact with one another in a positive, yet constructive, manner; and most likely, reminders that the processes that learners used to reach products are important. Teachers and students will need to negotiate which activities or products are appropriate for peer evaluation in their classrooms. They will also need to decide whether they will use peer evaluation panels, whole class participation, or a combination of both. If they choose to use a panel, they might ask the following questions:

- Will there be times when the whole class will participate in peer evaluations as well as the panel?
- How will members of the panel be selected?
- Will membership be on a rotating or voluntary basis?
- How long will students serve on a peer evaluation panel?

Evaluation Criteria

Your teachers and students will need to negotiate the evaluation criteria for each type of project, activity, or product that will be assessed by peer review. Green (1994) reminds us that, when students do not have a clear set of standards for quality before beginning to evaluate themselves or others, they risk not evaluating the real learning that occurred. She recommends holding a series of discussions to develop evaluation criteria and post the results in the room for reference purposes. When the criteria are established outside of the classroom, students should also know how their work will be evaluated. In Rhode Island, students not only see the criteria that will be used to rate their work, but also use these same criteria in peer evaluations (Maeroff, 1991). When students were first asked to apply the criteria, some were reluctant to fill out the evaluation forms because they did not want to make negative comments about their peers. Teachers found that they needed to encourage students to use the evaluations to help other because they could then find out what they are doing well or needed to improve by looking through their classmates' evaluation sheets.

Methods of Providing Feedback

If peer evaluation is to benefit individual students, the feedback they receive must be meaningful to them. Green (1994) suggested the following as some possibilities for meaningful feedback: marks, rankings, grades, and comments. Teachers and students need to negotiate to determine which type of feedback best responds to learners and their products in their own classrooms. In Maxine Green's (1994) sixth-year classroom in Warrowong Primary School, her students decided to use a marking system for their reports. They used a total of fifty points possible in four categories, with twenty points possible for the text, ten points possible for conventions, ten points possible for illustrations, and ten points possible for presentation. Porter and Cleland (1995) have their high school English students include comment sheets in their portfolios to encourage peers to provide feedback for their portfolios.

Student Accountability for Peer Evaluations

When students sign their names to an evaluation for another student, they are committing to using the evaluation criteria established by the class, teacher, or others beyond their classroom; to remaining impartial or fair to everyone; to remaining on task with or without supervision; and to keeping peers' evaluations confidential unless asked to do otherwise for reporting purposes (Green, 1994).

Ways to Use Peer Evaluation

Green (1994) used a peer evaluation panel in her sixth-year class. First, she and her co-teacher, Vicki Moses, had their students become comfortable with self-evaluation. To accomplish this, they shared their beliefs about evaluation with their students. Then, they had the students brainstorm the purposes for evaluation and how they might use evaluation panels to assist with assessment. After this, the teachers and their class of fifty-seven students negotiated which tasks they would evaluate using the panel, created their evaluation criteria, and determined their feedback system. Next, the teachers and students needed to determine the qualities that a peer evaluator should exhibit. Once the class established these characteristics, students who felt they met the qualifications applied to be on the panel. The class chose five members by a secret show of hands, and this group was directly responsible to the teachers. Four of the students worked in pairs to evaluate their classmates' work. The fifth served as a co-ordinator to ensure fairness, to help reach consensus in difficult decisions, to collect and return work to be evaluated, to replace one of the members of a pair to evaluate that member's work, and to act as a liaison between the panel and the teachers. The pairs then evaluated student work and had conferences with each student to provide individual feedback. Green and Moses found this system to be quite effective for their students' ability to verbalize a greater understanding of the nature of evaluation and its relationship to the learning process.

Other teachers use peer evaluation as a whole class activity to assist in evaluating student work. In these classrooms, students may have the option to choose who will serve as a peer evaluator. They often include an opportunity for the student to self-evaluate the piece and for teachers to evaluate the work also. The form in Figure 8.2 is an example of a rubric that was used to evaluate a research report for middle school students. This form

Writing Process Rubric

Author_____ Product_____ Date_____

	Self		Peer		Teacher	
	Yes	No	Yes	No	Yes	No
Brainstorming/Prewriting						
Chooses a topic						
Gathers materials needed						
Organizes ideas						
First Draft (Sloppy Copy)						
Composes a first draft of a story or report						
Revision						
Tells enough						
Organizes to make sense						
Uses clear and exact words						
Proofreading						
C - Begins each sentence with a capital letter						
Capitalizes all proper nouns						
O - Uses straight margins						
Uses indented paragraphs						
Writes complete sentences						
P - Ends each sentence with a period, question mark, or exclamation point						
Uses commas and apostrophes where needed						
S - Checks each word by looking at it						
Sounds words out						
Uses a dictionary to help						
Final Copy						
Uses title and margins						
Publishes in a neat and legible form						
Total						

Figure 8.2. Sioux Valley Public Schools Evaluation Form.

provides space for this student's self-evaluation, peer evaluations, and the teacher's evaluation.

When students give oral book reports in Jan Eversole's fifth-grade classroom, they choose a peer to fill out the evaluation sheet shown in Figure 8.3. Mrs. Eversole also completes a second copy of the form during the report. Later, she and the student evaluator compare results on their two sheets and negotiate a final grade for the oral book report. Mrs. Eversole has found that peers' evaluations are often similar to her own evaluation of the reports.

Porter and Cleland (1995) use peer evaluations more informally as a natural outgrowth when students are selecting work to include in their portfolios. They often share what they have selected with a neighbor. As students share their choices, they find that they shape their explanations and revise their ideas as they discuss them with other learners. This is especially helpful when they are examining first drafts and published pieces for signs of growth. Their classmates are not as emotionally tied to the work and can more easily note differences between the two artifacts.

Knight (1992) found that, when she had students examine others' algebra portfolios, students took more pride in their work. Those who had put little effort into their portfolios were relieved when they had the opportunity to revise them before they were graded by their peers. She had students write comments and suggestions for improvement on grading sheets rather than on the portfolios. Once she saw the students' reactions, Knight developed a grading matrix and counted the portfolio grade as the equivalent of one-fifth of a test grade and added her comments to the peer evaluations. She felt that the benefits of having the students grade the portfolios included receiving immediate, constructive feedback from a peer and having an opportunity to read another student's work carefully to find ideas for improving their own work.

Reasons for Using Peer Evaluation

Peer evaluations can serve as a means of expanding portfolio instruction and learning in your school in the following ways:

- developing metacognitive abilities in all students
- strengthening communication skills of all students
- allowing teachers to evaluate several students at once
- encouraging students to become better critics of their own work
- increasing students' pride in their work
- having students cooperate and collaborate in the evaluation process
- having students value each other's input

ORAL BOOK REPORT
Evaluation Sheet

Name of Student _____

Title of Book _____

Evaluated by _____ Date_____

DELIVERY

	low	medium	high
Eye Contact	1	3	5
Voice Level	1	3	5
Voice Tone	1	3	5
Speed (Rate)	1	3	5

Contents

Checklist. Place a check in the box if mentioned in oral book report:

☐ Genre ☐ Author ☐ Illustrator

☐ Main Character ☐ Setting ☐ Situation

☐ Antagonist ☐ Conflict ☐ Resolution

☐ Denouement (end) ☐ Recommendation ☐ Likes/Dislikes
(optional)

Overall mark for the contents of the book report:

1	3	5
3 or more items from the checklist were missing; report was hard to understand	1 or 2 items from the checklist were missing; report was hard to understand	All of the items from the checklist were present; report was easy to understand

Figure 8.3. Sample Peer Evaluation Sheet.

- learning more about the evaluation process and its relationship to learning
- having students receive immediate, meaningful feedback
- encouraging student ownership and control of learning

INVOLVING STAKEHOLDERS

If portfolio assessment is to be sustained, there must be input and support from a wide variety of stakeholders. In this section, we explore the roles that policymakers, central office administrators, principals, teachers, students, parents, and community members play in insuring the continuation and extension of portfolio assessment.

Policymakers

Policymakers make far-reaching decisions and are concerned with the accomplishments of groups of children, rather than the achievement of individual students (Wolf, 1994). Wolf (1994) notes that, while teachers must be at the center of portfolio assessment, other stakeholders such as policymakers must be involved in its evolution and informed of its progress. Policymakers are often involved in setting standards and benchmarks that will be assessed and reported in portfolios.

Although policymakers need to be involved in portfolio assessment, their informational needs and concerns are different from those closest to the classroom. Students, teachers, and parents are interested in a broad, deep view of student performance, but policymakers' informational needs are better served by a summary of performance of groups rather than individuals (Wolf, 1994). In Chapter 9, we provide ways to produce these summaries when we examine using portfolio data to make curriculum decisions.

Central Office Administrators

Central office administrators formulate, implement, and guide broad policy in a school district. They are interested in knowing in general terms whether portfolio assessment supports present programs and curriculum or whether changes need to be made (Anthony et al., 1991).

These administrators are invaluable in developing workable long-range goals and specific goals for each year. They can help fund continued staff development, conference attendance, and needed resources such as professional literature, storage cabinets, and portfolio containers (Church, 1991).

Knowledgeable central office administrators can provide support by becoming portfolio advocates in meetings with board members, state departments of education, and legislators. To do this, many superintendents attend staff development sessions themselves, while others rely on progress reports of implementation, summaries of portfolio data to assist with curricular and program decisions, and accountability portfolios that provide evidence of school effectiveness. The section on using portfolio data to make curricular decisions, presented in Chapter 9, can help you create summaries of portfolio data to present to your superintendent. The accountability portfolios that are also presented in Chapter 9 can provide you with a means for presenting school effectiveness information to central office administrators.

Principals

As a principal, you are the crucial factor in determining whether portfolio assessment will flourish as a schoolwide venture. Appendix E.2 lists the principal's responsibilities for planning, implementing, and enhancing portfolios. For this section, we will focus on the principal's role in extending and expanding portfolio assessment. It is a multifaceted one that includes many of the following tasks:

(1) Growing in portfolio knowledge
  • reading updates about portfolio assessment
  • participating in portfolio staff development sessions
  • attending conferences
  • networking with other principals who are implementing portfolio assessment
  • keeping your own professional portfolio
  • maintaining security of cumulative school portfolios
  • investigating more efficient means of storing portfolios, such as technological support
(2) Encouraging staff and faculty to extend their use of portfolios
  • sharing portfolio assessments with parents
  • modeling self-reflection through your portfolio entries and captions
  • maintaining a climate for risk taking
  • participating in peer evaluation yourself
  • encouraging a collegial and cooperative atmosphere among staff and faculty
  • encouraging teachers to form portfolio support groups
  • encouraging teachers to find their own voices

- providing support and encouragement for peer coaching
- encouraging teachers to keep professional portfolios

(3) Collaborating with central office administrators and policymakers
- collecting portfolio data to use for curricular and program decision making
- preparing summaries of portfolio data to be used by policymakers and central office administrators
- using portfolio data to prepare school accountability reports

Teachers

The teacher in the classroom is concerned with how well each student is doing, how well the program is succeeding, and which instructional methods are meeting the students' needs. In assessing progress, teachers must establish baseline data, gather information on each student's learning, and finally, evaluate to determine whether or not progress is being made (Anthony et al., 1991; Hill & Ruptic, 1994). Appendix E.3 lists teachers' roles in planning, implementing, and enhancing portfolios. The teachers' roles in expanding portfolio assessment (Rief, 1990; Harp, 1991; Tierney et al., 1991; Bird, 1992c; Y. Goodman, 1992; Simms, 1994) include a wide variety of areas such as

(1) Continuing professional growth and personal learning
- continuing to attend conferences, staff development sessions, and support groups for portfolio assessment
- reading updates of professional literature about portfolios, assessment, and evaluation
- using their voices in portfolio assessment
- participating in peer coaching
- engaging in self-reflection of teaching and assessment practices
- setting their own professional goals to work toward
- updating their own professional portfolios
- using their professional portfolios to conference with principals

(2) Providing a safe classroom environment for students
- demonstrating a belief in their students' capabilities as learners
- valuing each student's opinions and diversity
- providing a climate that encourages risk taking
- fostering independence and self-reliance

(3) Updating classroom teaching practices
- continuing as a facilitator, rather than the expert that dispenses knowledge

- sustaining student involvement, interaction, and input in classroom portfolio activities
- continuing to provide time for decision making, drafting, reflecting, discussing, reading, and responding
- using portfolio data to make instructional decisions
- continuing to learn new instructional practices and refining others

(4) Changing assessment practices
- remaining an active kid watcher
- searching for effective ways to gather information about students' learning
- refining the process of collecting and analyzing student work samples
- finding more efficient ways to assess students' processes, efforts, progress, achievements, and products
- maintaining collaboration and negotiation with students in assessment and evaluation of learning

(5) Assessing portfolio implementation
- modeling their own professional portfolios including self-reflection, goal setting, and self-evaluation
- assisting students in managing their portfolios
- developing criteria for choosing selections with students
- providing time to conference individually with each student to further students' understanding and portfolio achievement
- assisting students in setting goals that are realistic and that can be achieved
- preparing students to lead their own parent conferences
- encouraging students' ownership of their portfolios
- celebrating students' successes
- encouraging students to participate in peer evaluation

(6) Being accountable
- keeping track of the entire group's depth of understanding
- using portfolio data to justify practices and curricular decisions within classrooms
- enforcing any criteria or portfolio requirements from beyond the classroom
- maintaining a degree of consistency across portfolios for schoolwide purposes
- using portfolio data to report to parents
- making sure appropriate items are placed in cumulative school portfolios

Students

Students are concerned with their own learning. It is important for them to have input into any evaluation of their learning because they know a lot about their own strengths and weaknesses (Bird, 1992c; Simms, 1994). Student roles in portfolio assessment include

(1) Keeping records of their own learning experiences
- engaging in self-evaluation
- engaging in peer evaluation
- collaborating with others to understand their strengths and weaknesses
- setting personal learning goals and planning how to achieve them
- collecting, selecting, analyzing, and comparing their artifacts
- accepting responsibility for their portfolios

(2) Collaborating with teachers to set criteria for portfolio entries
- writing captions, entry slips, or narratives for their portfolio artifacts
- maintaining and organizing their portfolios
- including items that meet external criteria for portfolio artifacts

(3) Preparing to present their portfolios to others
- participating in student-led conferences
- debriefing after their conferences to celebrate successes and suggest ways to improve

Parents

Parents[5] are interested in the progress and achievements of their children. Traditionally, families have been left outside the assessment process. Yet parents are a rich source of information and can contribute much to the assessment process (DeFina, 1992; Hill & Ruptic, 1994; Simms, 1994). Often, the only time that parents or guardians are involved in assessment is when teachers share information about their child's progress in school; however, in an effective assessment and evaluation program, parents are partners with the school (Anthony et al., 1991; DeFina, 1992; Rhodes & Shanklin, 1993).

When schools ask household members to reflect, respond, and contribute in the assessment process, education is acknowledged as a shared responsibility between the school and home. Some additional reasons to involve parents and family members in portfolio assessment include

- demonstrating that their perspectives are valued

- opening lines of communication about changes that are occurring in both instruction and assessment
- gaining their support for portfolio assessment
- helping students become aware that their families value school and learning
- letting students know that their families understand the learning programs and processes being used in their classrooms
- gathering information such as physical, medical, and personal matters that may affect students' learning

Having family members participate in the planning and implementation phases is essential. Now is the time for them to be involved in the assessment phase.

One of the easiest ways to gather information from parents about their children is to send a letter home requesting it; however, when your teachers do this, parents will want to know how the information will be used. Letters should also avoid educational jargon because parents who feel overwhelmed or intimidated seldom participate as partners in education through collaboration with schools. Sending several short notes that give a little information about portfolio assessment and that briefly explain in concrete terms what their children will be expected to do throughout the year is often more effective than a long newsletter that explains the whole process in great detail in one setting (Anthony et al., 1991; DeFina, 1992). Appendix E.4 is a sample of an informational letter about portfolio implementation that could be sent home at the beginning of the school year.

You can also encourage parents to attend meetings such as open houses or parent support groups for portfolio assessment. At these meetings, parents can learn about portfolios, voice their concerns about this new and different way of assessing their children, offer their suggestions for providing them with information they are interested in receiving, and see ways they can assist in the process. Having portfolio literature available for those who want more information is always another way to provide more detailed explanations of changes in assessment that are taking place in your school. Including parents in the portfolio process strengthens the educational link between school and community. Parents who are actively involved are less likely to criticize instructional and assessment practices in their children's classrooms, and they often become portfolio advocates in the larger school community (Anthony et al., 1991; DeFina, 1992; Rhodes & Shanklin, 1993).

Your teachers can also invite parents to actively participate in the formulation of their child's portfolio by having them fill out surveys or questionnaires that provide information about the child's learning outside of school (Anthony et al., 1991; DeFina, 1992). At the beginning of the school year, Sara Shriver has the parents of her Title I students fill out the parent questionnaire found in Appendix E.5. She has found that some of her students' parents are more comfortable providing information in person or over the telephone rather than in writing.

Family members can participate in the formulation of students' portfolios by giving specific responses to entries in it or by filling in forms or checklists as they observe their children at home. Any checklists or response forms that your teachers send home should include clear instructions for how to use the forms when working with their children and an expected completion date that provides enough time for busy parents to be able to become involved in the portfolio process (Anthony et al., 1991; DeFina, 1992; Hill & Ruptic, 1994). When parents, teachers, and students all reflect on the same behaviors, tasks, or work samples, triangulation of data from many sources can provide a picture of the child's learning from different perspectives. The form in Figure 8.4 is a writing rubric that has space for the student, parents, and teacher to evaluate the story and provide comments.

DeFina (1992) suggested that each assessment task that your teachers send home have a description of the nature and purpose of the assignment sent along with it so parents will understand what it is that their child is being asked to do. This also clarifies the role that the parents assume as partners in portfolio assessment and focuses their attention on instructional practices and content that is being stress in the classroom program (Anthony et al., 1991; DeFina, 1992).

Another way to have parents become involved in portfolio assessment is through participation in student-led conferences. As part of the conference, parents are often provided with the opportunity to respond to the portfolios through a checklist or a comment sheet that is part of the portfolio. Family members who read portfolios have an opportunity to see what students think and have learned through the artifacts, captions, self-reflections, and goals that are present in the portfolio. Parents can also gain a better understanding of instructional and assessment practices that may be new and confusing to them through participating in the student-led conferences and by reading portfolios (Anthony et al., 1991; DeFina, 1992; Austin, 1994; Porter & Cleland, 1995). The response form in Figure 8.5 provides an opportunity for parents to respond to portfolio items along with their child and the teacher. Other examples of parent response forms are provided in Chapter 9, where student-led conferences and parental responses to portfolios are described in more detail.

NAME:_____

DATE:_____

_____' S   STORY EVALUATION

PARENTS................. Your child is being asked to write a vacation story (see attached sheet). Please have your child explain how this form is used and complete it. These stories will be due on March 17. In writing, we are currently focusing on spelling, capitalization, punctuation, and complete sentences (including complete subjects and predicates). Please check those areas only for this assignment. I hope you enjoy sharing this activity with your child.

	Self	Parent	Teacher
Spelling Checked			
Capitalization			
End Punctuation Checked			
Complete Subjects and Predicates			

DISCUSSION QUESTIONS:

What do you like best about my writing?

What part or parts do you think need improvement?

Student Signature   _____

Parent Signature   _____

Teacher Signature   _____

Figure 8.4. Sample Parent Involvement in Assignment and Assessment.

VACATION STORY MAP

CHARACTERS	SETTING

EVENTS	PROBLEM

RISING ACTION	CLIMAX

FALLING ACTION	ENDING

Figure 8.4 (continued). Sample Parent Involvement in Assignment and Assessment.

PORTFOLIO RESPONSE SHEET

Name:_____ Date:_____

~~~~~~~~~~~~~~~~~~~~~Student Comments~~~~~~~~~~~~~~~~~~~~~~~~

I choose these artifacts because_____

_____

_____

_____

My portfolio shows my progress because_____

_____

_____

_____

~~~~~~~~~~~~~~~~~~~~~Parent Comments~~~~~~~~~~~~~~~~~~~~~~~~~

We or I think that the work in this portfolio shows_____

_____

_____

_____

~~~~~~~~~~~~~~~~~~~~~Teacher Comments~~~~~~~~~~~~~~~~~~~~~~~~

I think that the work in this portfolio shows_____

_____

_____

_____

Figure 8.5.

Community Members

Community members need to be involved in portfolio assessment from the planning stages through the dissemination of portfolio performance data. Community members must be involved in setting the standards that will be measured by portfolio contents. Through representation on committees, they assist in the development of curriculum visions, standards, and benchmarks for measuring achievement. Community members can also participate in developing a portfolio implementation plan and in determining what types of reports will provide them with the accountability information they need to be sure schools are effectively educating their children and preparing them to be productive members of their community. When community members are actively involved, they are more likely to support the efforts of the school in providing quality education for students.

Some schools have included local business representatives in reviewing employability portfolios to provide each student with realistic feedback. The employers were invited to high school to participate in mock interviews. After reviewing students' portfolios, they evaluated the content and then indicated whether the students would be qualified for jobs in their companies. The employers further assisted the students by giving them tips for improving their employability skills and ways to document them. Students also received valuable input into their areas of strengths and weaknesses from sources beyond the school (Stemmer et al., 1992). Through their involvement, community members have the opportunity to be partners with schools in educating our youth.

TROUBLESHOOTING

Currently in the United States, the average length of time school superintendents serve in a district is less than three years. Often, new superintendents come to a district with different priorities and agendas to support. This makes it more difficult for principals to sustain innovations. In many cases, teachers and principals watch while their efforts of serveral years are revised.

One technique that assures continuity of focus is community and school board support of portfolios. Over time, your efforts to include parents and community members in portfolio assessment will be worthwhile. Once they are convinced of the benefits of this type of assessment, they will not allow resources and attention to be diverted.

GLOSSARY

Change Agents: people who effect changes in their own knowledge of learning, teaching practices, and assessment through portfolio implementation and who facilitate change in others.

Conference: two or three individuals meet together to discuss the contents of portfolios, the strengths and needs of the author, and future goals for learning. Conferences can take place between students, teachers, administrators, principals, and teachers; students and teachers; parents and teachers; students, parents, and teachers; or students and parents.

Debriefing: processing information after an observation or a portfolio conference to share thoughts, praise positive observations, notice behavior, discuss parts of a conference that went well, ponder questions, discuss problems, and explore ways to improve the process.

Good Faith: acting from the belief that teachers are each doing what is best for themselves and their students and that each teacher is a professional.

Multiple Lenses: examining the student as a learner in many settings, from different points of view, within various contexts, and through various assessments.

Multiple Perspectives: examining the student's learning by using several assessments and artifacts, as well as the views of the student, teacher, and parent(s).

Parent–Teacher Portfolio Conference: a conference between the teacher and parents in which the portfolio is used to support the progress report that the teacher shares with the parents.

Peer Coaching: a collegial process where teachers support, assist, and provide companionship for one another. During peer coaching, teachers also give demonstrations and constructive feedback.

Peer Evaluation: evaluation of students' work, processes, performances, or other classroom activities by their classmates.

Peer Evaluation Panel: a panel of students who serve the function of evaluating their classmates.

Peer Review: evaluation of students' work, processes, performances, or other classroom activities by their classmates.

Portfolio Share Day: a day that is set aside for students to read and respond to other students' portfolios.

Portfolio Support Groups: voluntary meetings where teachers can share their successes, frustrations, practices, assessment strategies, implementation problems, and other topics of interest.

Teacher Voice: teachers being able to express their beliefs, opinions, knowledge, and views in their own words in language that is sensitive to others' points of view.

Triangulation: pooling information and assessment data from a variety of sources, including various measures, artifacts, and perspectives of parents, students, and teachers.

ENDNOTES

1. When attendance is mandated for support groups, they are less productive because teachers view the meetings as satisfying someone else's agenda, rather than for the purpose of providing a forum for them to explore their successes, frustrations, questions, concerns, and issues related to portfolio implementation.

2. Having a shared or common language about portfolio implementation provides a base to create a building-wide understanding of portfolio assessment. Principals, teachers, parents, and students will all know they are using the same terms to communicate with one another, and this prevents misconceptions.

3. When teachers first learn about innovations, new techniques, theories, or assessment measures such as portfolios, they often quote the experts in the field because they have not internalized the understanding of the process themselves yet. Once teachers have applied portfolios in their own classrooms and developed a personal understanding, they usually are able to discuss portfolios from their own point of view.

4. Treating teachers with good faith allows them to have their own points of view and does not mean that they are inferior or less competent because their view of learning, instruction, or assessment does not match your own. It respects teachers by modeling the belief that they are doing what is best for them and their students.

5. We recognize that many students live with relatives other than parents, and some live with friends and/or guardians. We use the term *parents* as the primary caretaker.

CHAPTER 9

Soaring: Using Portfolio Data

Mrs. Zehnder's Reflections about Her Daughter's Student-Led Portfolio Conference

When my husband and I participated in our daughter Angela's student-led conference in the third grade this spring, we were impressed with how she shared the items in her portfolio and her level of confidence. I was surprised at how much she looked forward to this conference. At home, she is often too busy to talk about what she is doing at school.

Her confidence in herself as a learner was evident as she shared her work. She knew what her work was, why it was in her portfolio, and why she had done it. Angie made decisions about what to put into the portfolio. She knew why work was good. Part of her portfolio was grading herself. She knew her own weaknesses and strengths. She also set her own goals for learning.

I learned things about Angela I didn't know before. I was surprised at the depth of what she knew. When papers came home, she did not reflect this depth because she was always in too much of a hurry to take time to share. The stories Angie chose to include showed what she was capable of. I didn't realize she could write such indepth stories until I saw her portfolio.

It was a family experience as Angie was right at the conference and shared with the family. I did not need to explain her report card to her as in the past. Her teacher was there, too. When she shared, she just supported Angela when she needed prompting.

Angela's confidence in herself as a learner gave me joy or inner warmth.

INTRODUCTION

PREVIOUS chapters focused on implementing student portfolios. In this final chapter, we will discuss using the information to make curricular, instructional, program, personnel, and leadership decisions for your school. Data contained in portfolios can provide feedback for assessing student

249

progress and educational changes, evaluating results of educational programs and their effects on students, and reporting school progress to specific stakeholders (Clark & Clark, 1994). We explain how to extract data from portfolios; develop teacher, principal, and school portfolios; and report progress by using a variety of portfolio conferences. When parents such as Angela's attend student-led conferences, the full potential of portfolio assessment is realized.

REPORTING STUDENT PROGRESS WITH PORTFOLIO CONFERENCES

Information in portfolios is meant to be shared. One way to report information gained through the data gathered in portfolios is through the use of conferencing. We will show you how to conduct portfolio conferences with a variety of stakeholders to report progress in the areas of student learning, teacher accountability, and your leadership. Information in portfolios can be useful at all levels of K–12 education. Principals can use their portfolios to present information to central office administrators, and teachers can present their portfolios to principals for evaluation and to share classroom information, but the main use of portfolios is to share information about students.

Student information in portfolios can be shared with teachers, other students, parents, administrators, and policymakers. Parent conferences for sharing portfolio data can be held by teachers, presented by teachers and students, or student-led. This section describes each of these types of portfolio conferences.

Student–Teacher Portfolio Conferences

The purposes for student–teacher portfolio conferences include arriving at student grades for a grading period; determining strengths, identifying weaknesses, and setting goals for the future; and/or providing practice for student–parent–teacher portfolio conferences or student-led portfolio conferences. The following paragraphs provide suggestions for managing student–teacher portfolio conference.

Scheduling Student–Teacher Portfolio Conferences

Teachers can schedule conferences on a revolving format to meet with individual students, small groups, and the class to review and discuss their portfolios. An alternative is for students to sign up for conferences on the chalkboard or on a large calendar when they are ready. Some convenient times to schedule individual conferences are during silent reading, individual seat work times, center activities, and peer evaluation sessions. Monthly or quarterly portfolio conferences are most beneficial for both teachers and students (DeFina, 1992; Glazer & Brown, 1993; Austin, 1994).

Reviewing Portfolio Contents

Most portfolio experts recommend that students prepare, review, and complete their portfolios before the teacher examines it (Milliken, 1991; Glazer & Brown, 1993; Austin, 1994). Glazer and Brown (1993) suggest that students be provided with a checklist for reviewing their portfolios to make sure they are ready for the conference. Figure 9.1 provides an example of a portfolio checklist that students could use.

Mark Milliken (1991) has his fifth graders complete their portfolios a week before the grading period ends. The students' portfolios are complete when the contents represent the students as learners at that point in the school year. Before he has the conference with the student, he examines the portfolio and uses a record-keeping sheet with three columns. In the left column, he records strengths, changes, improvements, questions about the contents, and any concerns that he wants to discuss with the student during the conference. Then during the conference, he lets the student handle the contents and take him through the portfolio as if he had never seen it before. He takes his information sheet with him to the conference but does not use his notes until after the student has finished presenting the portfolio contents. On the other hand, Terri Austin (1994) reviews her sixth graders' portfolios for the first time with each student. She does not examine the portfolios before her students present the contents to her during the conference.

Using the Portfolio to Determine Grades

After Austin (1994) and the student have reviewed the portfolio, the next part of the conference is when they discuss grades for the report cards. She has found that about 95 percent of the time, students give themselves grades that are very close to what she would give them. If they are in agreement, the student fills out the report card while she watches. Austin feels that this step is important because grades belong to students, and they should understand completely the reasons for each one.

If there is a discrepancy in their grades, the student and Austin discuss the problem. For the first grading period, she has found that there are usu-

SELF-EVALUATION FOR REVIEWING PORTFOLIOS

Name_____Date_____

When you can check yes for each box and have written down your list of
of artifacts, you are ready to have your teacher conference.

Have I included an introduction for my portfolio?   ☐ Yes   ☐ No

Does my introduction explain what is in my portfolio?   ☐ Yes   ☐ No

The artifacts I chose to place in my portfolio were:

Do the artifacts that I chose show my learning growth?   ☐ Yes   ☐ No

Have I explained why I chose each artifact?   ☐ Yes   ☐ No

Have I included self-evaluations that show my strengths? ☐ Yes   ☐ No

Have I included self-evaluations that show my areas that

   need improvement?   ☐ Yes   ☐ No

Have I included my goals to improve my learning?   ☐ Yes   ☐ No

Are my goals ones I can reach and that challenge me?   ☐ Yes   ☐ No

Have I included a way to respond to my portfolio?   ☐ Yes   ☐ No

Figure 9.1. Student Checklist for Reviewing Portfolios.

ally three types of students who do not arrive at accurate grades for themselves. One group consists of those who do not award themselves high enough grades. When this happens, she goes over the portfolios individually with them again, points out all their growth and achievements, has them go back through the portfolio again alone, and think about their grades. Usually, at their second conference, their grades more accurately reflect their learning.

The next group are those who think they can beat the system, but because they must have proof to support their grades, this does not happen after the first conference. We agree with Austin, who believes that teachers, as professionals, have a right to disagree with students' conclusions if the data in the portfolio do not support them. These students must also return to their seats, rethink the data in their portfolios, and rewrite their grades. After this process, the student usually has a better idea of what is acceptable.

The final group of students who have a problem with determining their grades are those who only examine part of the data to arrive at their grades. With these students, Austin takes extra time to go over the neglected elements of the portfolio to solve this problem. When there are issues that cannot be resolved between the teacher and student, Austin (1994) recommends that the student choose an arbitrator to help reach a final grade.

Using the Student–Teacher Conference for Daily Instructional Decisions

As students present their portfolios to him, Milliken (1991) asks questions about the contents, what they have learned, their strengths, their areas needing improvement, and their goals. He records their observations about their work and their responses to his questions in the right column of his portfolio conference record-keeping sheet. This evaluation is concrete because they are constantly referring to the specific work in front of them. When Milliken notices an area that needs to be strengthened that the student doesn't mention, they discuss his notes and usually create a new goal to improve this area. Often, he feels that the students set more appropriate and challenging goals than the ones he thought of when he previewed the portfolios. He places the goals he and the student agree upon in the middle column of his conferencing sheet. Figure 9.2 provides a sample of a student–teacher portfolio conference sheet that is similar to the one that Milliken used.

DeFina (1992) recommends that the student–teacher portfolio conference be used to establish trust and create a safe environment where students can engage in decision making. During these conferences, teachers

PORTFOLIO CONFERENCE SHEET

Name_____Date_____

Teacher Observations	Goals	Student Observations

Figure 9.2. Student–Teacher Portfolio Conference Sheet.

need to encourage students to discuss their own observations about their growth, compare those observations with the teacher's assessments, and together devise appropriate plans for improvement and development. DeFina suggests that these goals be written down and used as a checklist for future conferences. Teachers could use the form in Figure 9.2 for this purpose or create one of their own. DeFina also notes that teachers have many opportunities to demonstrate critical thinking and decision making during the conference, as well as assess the student's ability to reason through the complex issues of the portfolio process. To avoid overwhelming the student, he recommends setting an agenda beforehand to determine which needs will be focused upon during the conference. This is especially important for the first conference of the year.

Student–Teacher Portfolio Conferences as Practice

As Austin (1994) and DeFina (1992) note, the first student–teacher portfolio conference can be a tense situation for some students because they do not know what to expect. Austin has one of her more self-assured students become a model for the rest of the class. During this model conference, she listens carefully, asks questions that are geared to support rather than intimidate the student, and offers encouragement. Once students are comfortable with the process, they can use these teacher conferences as an opportunity to rehearse for student–parent–teacher conferences or student-led conferences. During this practice session, they can make decisions such as how to introduce the portfolio, what order they will present the artifacts, whether they will read their captions to explain why they chose those items, or whether they will discuss what the items tell about them as learners. This practice conference also gives them an opportunity to field questions from an adult and to receive feedback about the parts of the portfolio they presented well and to provide suggestions for improvement.

Student–Student Portfolio Conferences

There are three reasons to have students share their portfolios with other students: to provide an audience and feedback for the portfolio, to orient new students to portfolio and classroom procedures, and to provide an alternative way for students to practice presenting their portfolios to parents or other portfolio visitors. Each of these purposes are explored in the following paragraphs.

Porter and Cleland (1995) hold a Portfolio Share Day for their high school English students. During this time, students can celebrate their learning, learn about others, and learn from each other. When students enter the classroom, they find their portfolios displayed on large tables. The students spend several days reading and responding to their classmates' portfolios, along with those from different sections during the day. Sometimes, these teachers have students read and respond only to their classmates' portfolios, and at other times, portfolios from all eight periods are available for feedback. Students write responses that give authors feedback about not only the view of their learning that they provide, but also on how well they provided for the needs of their audience. This preparation would include their introduction to the portfolio, their organization of the artifacts it holds, their explanations for choosing each item, and a student response sheet. Figure 9.3 is a sample of a portfolio response sheet that students could use to include in their portfolios. This would provide a space for other students to record their responses to the author's work. While the students do not verbally present their portfolios to one another, Cleland and Porter feel that both authors and readers benefit because they can begin to plan for their next portfolio experience by observing the variety of formats and techniques used to assemble artifacts and written reflections on learning. Some of the learning benefits that they gain include ideas for writing topics, ways to respond to literature, strategies for reading and writing, insights for analysis in self-evaluation, and suggestions for books to read.

When new students enter the classroom, teachers are faced with the sometimes overwhelming task of explaining how their classrooms function and expanding the learning community to include these new members. Porter and Cleland (1955) recommend having a few students share their portfolios with them during a class period. Through these student–student portfolio conferences, new students can learn about the materials, strategies, teacher roles, expectations, and values of the learnng community. Authors of the portfolios can answer questions the new students may have and become responsible for introducing them to the rest of the class. It also provides the authors another opportunity to build their self-esteem and take ownership of their learning community.

When students are preparing for parent conferences, they can act as buddies for presenting their portfolios to one another. This can be done to prepare for student–teacher conferences or can occur after the student has practiced with the teacher. When students serve as buddies for the portfolio practice conferences, they ask questions that parents typically ask, provide feedback about parts of the conference that the student handled well, and make suggestions for improvement. Some teachers believe it is more beneficial when the portfolio buddies are students from other classrooms because they may not be familiar with the classroom procedures, projects, or students' work and could perhaps ask different questions that

```
┌─────────────────────────────────────────────────────────┐
│              PORTFOLIO RESPONSE SHEET                     │
│ Name_____                      │
│ Please write your reactions to my portfolio, date your response, │
│ and sign your name beneath it.                           │
│                                                           │
│                                                           │
│                                                           │
│                                                           │
│                                                           │
│                                                           │
│                                                           │
│                                                           │
│                                                           │
│                                                           │
│                                                           │
│                                                           │
│                                                           │
│                                                           │
│                                                           │
│                                                           │
│                                                           │
└─────────────────────────────────────────────────────────┘
```

Figure 9.3. Student Response Sheet for Portfolios.

would require students to reflect more about how they present their knowledge through their portfolio conferences (Anthony et al., 1991; Rhodes & Shanklin, 1993; Woodward, 1994).

Parent–Teacher Portfolio Conferences

In systems where traditional parent–teacher conferences do not include the student,[1] portfolios can be used to provide tangible evidence of a child's progress. The conference is given focus when the portfolio is used to demonstrate the student's growth. If grades are used to compare students' progress, the portfolio provides the teacher with an opportunity to show parents their student's progress in a noncompetitive context. This accomplishes a subtle shift in the parent's expectation of the conference and often defuses debates about a letter grade because the work itself demonstrates the compelling evidence of the student's achievement (Hewitt, 1995).

Portfolio conferences differ from traditional conferences in that your teachers can

- refer to the portfolio as they talk about the student's progress and show related forms that they have used to keep records of the student's strengths, needs, and goals for the student
- be sure to share and discuss the student's self-evaluations and goals with the parent(s) along with assessment of strengths, needs, and goals for the student
- finish the conference with a collaborative summary for both the parents and teacher to keep for future reference

Student–Parent–Teacher Portfolio Conferences

Most experts in portfolio assessment recommend that students be involved in their portfolio conferences. Many teachers have found three-way conferences that include the teacher, parents, and the student to be beneficial (Anthony et al., 1991; Hoyt, 1992; Rhodes & Shanklin, 1993; Woodward, 1994). When the person who is the object of the meeting is also present, information is less likely to be distorted or lost in translation. The learner is the focus, rather than the curriculum, because the student will be involved in forming plans or program adjustments to improve learning.

Anthony et al. (1991) recommend having your teachers send a brief note home with students shortly before the conference date to remind parents to bring any information to share or to bring in portfolio forms they may have completed. The reminder letter also provides an opportunity to invite the student to attend the portfolio conference. As Hoyt (1992) cautioned, successful three-way conferences require careful planning by the student, the teacher, and parents.

Rhodes and Shanklin (1993) provided an example of one teacher's use of student–parent–teacher portfolio conferences. This teacher prepared her third-grade students for three-way conferences by having them choose pieces of work or records that would help parents understand their efforts and progress. Next, she had the students examine the pieces they had chosen to complete self-evaluations of their reading and writing. During the conferences, their pieces would serve as support for their decisions. When the parents arrived for their scheduled twenty-minute conference, she had the student begin the conference by sharing the portfolio in a structured way for approximately the first five minutes of the conference while parents were encouraged to ask questions. Then the teacher clarified and expanded upon what the student shared, clearly communicated her views of the child's progress, and shared her goals for the student for the next grading period. During the final portion of the conference, she asked the parents to decide whether the child should be asked to remain or be sent out of the room. Most parents chose to have the student remain in the room unless there were family issues that needed to be discussed. Before the parent(s) left the building, the teacher asked them to complete an evaluation of the conference. She also had the students evaluate the experience the following day. This third-grade teacher found that both the parents and students appreciated the three-way conferences (Rhodes & Shanklin, 1993).

Student-Led Portfolio Conferences

Although some schools and teachers have found three-way conferences to be useful, Woodward (1994) maintains that the position of power still resides with the teacher, and the student is still on the sidelines.[2] Student-led conferences change all this. Your teachers might identify with why Terri Austin (1994) decided to give this approach a try:

My school counselor showed me a small article about two British Columbian teachers who had their students leading their own parent conferences. That same year, I had a difficult class of sixth graders. Physical violence, verbal abuse, and learning apathy were always close to the surface of any activity. I figured I had nothing to lose if I had the students give this approach a try. I told the students they would be sitting down with their parents and explaining their report card. With just that limited action, I was amazed at the difference in them. Usually the last quarter of the school year is not a good one for students. In April and May the lengthening sun-filled days entice students to stay up well past normal bedtimes and play outside later in the evenings. After the long winter months of darkness, it's hard to resist the sunshine and blue sky, and so school often becomes something that is done in between periods of being outside. Liitle homework is completed and talk centers around evening activities. But when the students realized they were the ones sharing their work and report cards to their parents, their attitude changed. They took an interest in their work and some showed more effort than they had all year. (pp. 3–4)

A student-led conference is held between a parent and student. The student is responsible for controlling and organizing the portfolio conference. When students are meaningfully involved in reporting their progress, displaying their work, and explaining the contents of their portfolios, evaluation becomes an integral part of instruction and a learning experience in its own right. The goal of this type of portfolio conference is to provide students with responsibility for their own learning and for informing their parents of their progress (Anthony et al., 1991; Austin, 1994; Woodward, 1994).

Preparing for the Conference

When a school first plans to change to student-led conferences, it is important that the parents and students are informed of the rationale for having the student take the leadership role during the conference. This can be done through newsletters and parent meetings. As the principal, you can explain the new roles of students, parents, and teachers. Without this first step, some parents may view the change to student-led conferences as simply teachers' way of shrinking responsibility for reporting student progress. Parents may need to be assured that they may still have an additional meeting time with the teacher if they request it (Anthony et al., 1991; Woodward, 1994).

Long before actual conferences, students will need suggestions for gathering samples of their work and other artifacts, filling out self-evaluations of strengths and areas needing improvement, supplying reasons for including the samples they have chosen for their portfolios, setting goals, creating a way to organize the material in the portfolio, and an introduction to the portfolio (Anthony et al., 1991; Austin, 1994; Woodward, 1994). Time will need to be allocated for this preparation.

A week before the conferences, students should write a letter inviting their parents to come to their conference. The letter could offer several possible days and times for the parent(s) to choose from, include a brief description of what the format of the conference will be, and a sample of some of the things that the parent will be able to see at the conference

(Anthony et al., 1991; Woodward, 1994). In a middle school or high school setting, the conferences could be held in the library, gym, or cafeteria. Another possibility would be to rotate to different classrooms every ten to fifteen minutes. Some middle schools have the students lead their conferences at home for the fall conferences after practicing at school and then invite the parents to come to student-led conferences at school in the spring.

The final step of preparation for the conference is providing the students with an opportunity to rehearse presenting and explaining the contents of their portfolios. Students can practice with their teachers, peers, students from other classrooms, or adults in the building who are willing to serve as substitute parents. It is also helpful to model poor and excellent conference procedures for students before they practice presenting their portfolios (Anthony et al., 1991; Austin, 1994; Woodward, 1994).

The Student's Role during the Conference

Students may begin by giving parents a tour of the room or the school for the first conference, but the main role of the student is to initiate, lead, and explain their progress through the use of their portfolios. The student takes on the role of expert in sharing the portfolio and all of its contents. Students have their materials organized and know what they want to say. In their practice sessions, the students learned that they will need to lead the discussion, and they realize that they will need to be able to answer their parents' questions. They will also ask their parents to respond to their portfolios through a checklist, evaluation sheet, or by signing a guest book with room for comments. Once parents have responded to the portfolio and conference, students usually escort them to a refreshment table in the room or in the hallway. This provides an informal atmosphere to conclude the conference (Anthony et al., 1991; Austin, 1994; Woodward, 1994).

The Parental Role during the Conference

The most important role for parents is to participate in the conference. They need to come, listen carefully to what their student is saying, ask questions to clarify the information, collaborate with the student on future goals, and praise the student's achievements. Once the conference begins and the student is sharing the artifacts in the portfolio, parents usually relax and begin asking questions about the portfolio contents, classroom procedure, or specific classroom activities. These questions give the child a chance to react naturally, rather than just delivering a prepared speech.

If a report card is part of the portfolio, it is shared near the end of the conference before the student discusses future goals for improvement. Often, the student and parents clarify and extend goals by discussing how to work on the goals both at home and at school. Before the conference is over, the student asks the parent to complete a parent reflection sheet, respond to the portfolio and conference checklist, or sign in a guest book with room for comments. The purpose of the parents' involvement in an evaluation of the conference is to provide them with the opportunity to provide feedback to their child and to the teacher. Most comments include a reflection on the entire conference and praise for their child. Figure 9.4 is an example of one format for seeking parent input after the conference.

Occasionally, parents request a time to speak alone with the teacher to verify the student's account and to get the teacher's opinion. Encourage your teachers to respect parent wishes but to schedule these meetings for a different time so that student's authority over their conference is not compromised. After participating in a well-planned, student-led conference, most parents do not request separate meetings with teachers. When parents cannot attend the conference, students can take their portfolios home to share, or the conference can be held over the phone before the portfolio is sent home (Anthony et al., 1991; Austin, 1994; Woodward, 1994).

The Teacher's Role in Student-Led Portfolio Conferences

While the conference itself is student-led and child-centered, the teacher's role behind the scenes remains important. Preparing for the organization of portfolios and daily routines are crucial. The teacher's conferences with the students that help prepare them for their parent conference are also important in establishing direction and future goals. During the actual student-led portfolio conference, the teacher's role is to remain unobtrusively in the background and to provide support for the students. One of the most difficult tasks for many of your teachers will be to simply stay quiet during conferences. Teachers need to take great care to have students remain in control of their conferences. The exception to this rule is when a student is having difficulty because parents are being overly critical. In this situation, suggest to your teachers that they might want to support the student more visibly by sitting in on the conference but remaining part of the audience and allowing the student to continue sharing the portfolio. After the conference is finished, the teacher usually leads the students in debriefing about what went well in the conferences and changes they may want to consider for the next ones (Anthony et al., 1991; Austin, 1994; Woodward, 1994).

```
┌─────────────────────────────────────────────────────────────┐
│           PARENT CONFERENCE RESPONSE SHEET                    │
│                                                               │
│   Student Name_____Date_____        │
│                                                               │
│   Please share your thoughts about my portfolio and our       │
│   conference:                                                 │
│                                                               │
│                                                               │
│                                                               │
│                                                               │
│                                                               │
│                                                               │
│                                                               │
│                                                               │
│                                                               │
│                                                               │
│                                                               │
│                                                               │
│                                                               │
│                                                               │
└─────────────────────────────────────────────────────────────┘
```

Figure 9.4. Parent Response Form.

263

The Principal's Role in Student-Led Conferences

The principal's role is also behind the scenes during the conference. Principals need to be knowledgeable about the process of conducting student-led conferences. Providing support for teachers as they prepare students to lead their own conferences with their parents is one way to ensure the success of student-led conferences. Maintaining open lines of communication with parents and the community at large is another important role for principals. Parents will want to know why teachers are not leading the conferences and how students are being assessed. Your support for the process and knowledge can reassure the school community that these conferences report information about attaining school goals. You can observe the process in action and make anecdotal notes that can be shared at a staff development session used to allow teachers to debrief soon after the conferences.

Processing Student-Led Conferences

The day after the student-led portfolio conferences, the teacher and students need to have a debriefing session while the experience of the conferences is till fresh in their minds. Your teachers will find it helpful to have students reflect on their thoughts in writing before they discuss the results of the conferences as a class. Teachers can provide students with a writing prompt or a checklist to describe their feelings and thoughts, but others use a more open format by simply asking students to reflect on the previous evenng. While the students are writing, teachers can examine the comments that the parents provided and review any anecdotal notes that teachers made during or immediately following the conferences. After everyone has finished writing, the students can share their thoughts about what went well and brainstorm ways to improve the conferences. This provides your teachers with feedback about students' perceptions, what they learned from the process, or any misconceptions that might need to be addressed. The debriefing session also provides closure for the conferences and prepares students to begin thinking about their next student-led portfolio conferences (Anthony et al., 1991; Austin, 1994).

When student-led conferences are a building-wide practice, teachers also need a debriefing session as one of their staff development sessions. At this meeting, they can discuss their perceptions, celebrate their progress in implementing portfolios, decide what changes they want to make, and share any problems they might have encountered. It is important for principals to participate and to practice active listening techniques during this debriefing session to assist teachers in identifying any parts of the procedure that might be improved.

Benefits of Student-Led Portfolio Conferences

Anthony et al. (1991) noted several benefits that come from participating in student-led portfolio conferences. These benefits include

- experiencing constructive and affirming conferences for the students
- enhancing student self-respect and efforts
- providing students with an active, meaningful role in assessing and interpreting their own learning
- asking students to focus on strengths and to give their perspective of areas they are working to improve
- offering parents opportunities to participate in rewarding and informative conferences
- increasing parent attendance at conferences
- placing emphasis on evaluation as an integral and constructive part of the learning process
- building accountability and responsibility into the self-evaluation process

MAKING DECISIONS BASED ON PORTFOLIO DATA

Portfolio assessment holds a multitude of information; however, the process of evaluating large numbers of portfolios can be the most challenging aspect of their development (Armstrong, 1994). The problem for principals is extracting and formatting the data to make it useful for making decisions.

Traditional standardized tests yield a set of numbers that we have been trained to understand. Such terms as mean, percent, range, and grade-level equivalency hold meaning for educators. To obtain this data, we administer the tests, collect them, ship them back to the testmaker, and receive a set of scores. Test makers assume sole responsibility for translating the contents of the tests to sets of numbers, charts, and graphs. The scores are then used by administrators for making decisions about changing textbooks, developing curriculum scope and sequence, implementing or discontinuing programs for student subpopulations, writing for grants, reporting to stakeholders, and making daily decisions.

Daily Instructional Decisions: Student Portfolios

When considering evaluation through portfolio implementation, it is helpful to think about what happens in the classroom as a double agenda.

The major agenda must focus on the learning that takes place through active student participation: their personal questions, the ways they use problem solving, and how they use language and thinking to learn. Your teachers must be actively involved in supporting learning; however, they must also be involved in evaluating the students as they are learning (Y. Goodman, 1992). Evaluation should not be separated from the tools of learning and the ongoing curriculum; the two must be inextricably woven together because assessment and evaluation are integral parts of education. All aspects of teaching and learning provide opportunities for learning, assessment, and evaluation. Assessment must reflect the curriculum and its goals to determine what will be assessed and how it will be assessed, while evaluation makes use of this information to make informed decisions about daily instructional activities. Teaching objectives, assessment, and evaluation cannot function effectively or purposefully without being linked together (Y. Goodman, 1992; Pigdon & Woolley, 1993; Hill & Ruptic, 1994).

Perrone (1994) cautions that the movement toward authentic assessment, performance assessment, and portfolios needs to include a serious examination of your teachers' current instructional practices and purposes that guide the curriculum within their classrooms. If simply covering the material in texts remains the goal, then performance tasks are usually too limited in scope. If small bits of information or isolated facts dominate daily activities rather than longer, integrated projects that produce more realistic pieces of work, then portfolios become nothing more than folders of unmanageable papers. Self-evaluation has limited value if students are not regularly involved in writing across a variety of topics and with various styles for diverse purposes and audiences. Finally, if the work that students complete does not include opportunities for choice and ownership, their performances lost importance.

In contrast, when teachers understand portfolio implementation, classrooms are more student-centered. Teachers trust students to learn from their mistakes as well as their strengths. Students are invited into the evaluation process through maintaining their portfolios. They are provided with advance explanation of activities along with the measurement criteria for each. Students are provided with an opportunity to question and negotiate the tasks by suggesting other viable means to reaching the desired objectives. Their students are often involved in creating the criteria for the assignment and the types of evaluation instruments that will best measure their achievement of the desired objectives or benchmarks. These teachers realize that students who are suggesting other ways to handle a task are thinking about it, developing ownership for learning from it, and more likely to take responsibility for completing it (DeFina, 1992).

Curriculum Decisions: Student Portfolios

Portfolio assessment provides descriptive, extensive information. However, for schoolwide decisions, the scores need to be converted into numerical summaries. You can present summary scores in a variety of formats such as plotting raw scores, charting average scores, or showing the percent of students reaching some absolute standard (Herman et al., 1992). The method you select depends on the kinds of comparisons you want to make.

Range

The range of student performance is one way to illustrate the distribution of scores on one dimension. A graph of the scores gives a picture of class performance showing how each student scored. The graphs can reflect raw scores or categories of scores such as "not yet," "developing," and "achieving." When working with a large number of portfolios, combining scores into categories makes the format easier to read. Graphs of the scores, such as in Figure 9.5, will tell you how well students succeed from year to year. By comparing several years of data, this format can be used to identify trends in student performance.

Averages

Average scores show how the bulk of students are doing. You could have average scores for individual classes, grade levels, or subject areas. This format can be used to compare classes or groups of students. For example, you could compare Mrs. Jones's fourth-hour American history class that is piloting a new textbook with her second- and fifth-hour classes who use an older textbook. The four-hour class might score 3.8 using four categories of scale scores, while the other means are 2.5 and 2.3. Figure 9.6 is a bar graph showing the three sections of American history classes. The class average scores will be one factor in the decision to adopt the new textbook.

Percent Reaching Standard

Schools using mastery learning typically set a standard of 80 percent mastery of skills and knowledge. However, some use a two-tiered standard such as "not yet achieved" and "achieved," while others use a three-tiered standard such as "not yet adequate," "adequate," and "exemplary." You would then report on the percent of scores in each category. For example, "83 percent of the students scored at or above the 80 percent level." Using

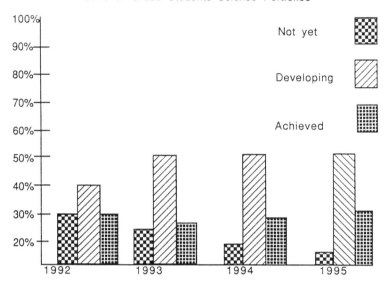

Seventh Grade Students Science Portfolios

Figure 9.5. Range of Scores.

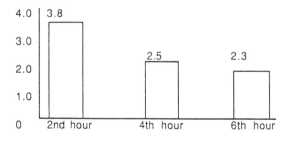

American History Class Scores

Figure 9.6. Average Scores of Classes.

a three-tier standard, they might say, "17 percent of the students have not yet achieved the knowledge, 60 percent have mastered the task adequately, and 23 percent scored in the exemplary range." Figure 9.7 illustrates a pie chart of a two-tier and a three-tier standard. This method of reporting scores gives a visual description of the current status of achievement.

Balancing Numerical Data with Samples of Student Work

Portfolio assessments provide a wealth of information about classroom instruction and school programs. Although it would be overwhelming to use all the data in student portfolios to evaluate instruction and programs, we don't want to lose valuable information by simply reducing the scores to a few numbers. Reducing portfolios to a series of numbers ends up looking very similar to standardized testing (Armstrong, 1994). Numbers alone don't tell us enough information. Yet looking at several hundred individual portfolios in depth tells us too much. One solution to the dilemma of too much versus too little information is to present samples of student work to help illustrate the results (Herman et al., 1992). An example of the best, the average, and the poorest levels of student work will allow you to combine rich information with descriptive scores. If you keep a file of examples over several years, you can watch how the general level of performance for each particular group progresses. Does the exemplary lab report of five years ago seem average now? Or does the average American history portfolio of five years ago seem better than the exemplary one from this year? A combination of samples and summary scores will yield far more information than only summary scores.

Multiple measures of the same learning goal provide alternative views of performance to create a more complete picture of student and school achievement. In most situations, never make an important decision based on only one score. But creating and scoring performance assessments ef-

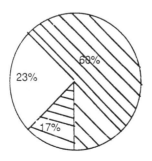

Figure 9.7. *Percent Reaching Standard.*

fectively can be complicated. Expect to begin with only a few schoolwide, on-demand assessment tasks and add one or two more each year. Reevaluate the tasks, refine sections, and record results over time. Within a few years, you will have a foundation of rich, valid, reliable information about student achievement, instructional practices, and program effectiveness.

As Perrone (1994) reminds us, powerful ideas, challenging curriculum, and different modes of assessment are linked ideas that necessitate a growing discourse about curriculum purposes, student understandings, and ways teachers can foster student learning. The next section of this chapter examines the role portfolios can play in making personnel decisions. Teachers' portfolios are introduced as a tool for professional growth and accountability decisions.

Personnel Decisions: Teacher Portfolio

Teachers across the country are beginning to keep their own portfolios because they recognize the need to assess their own learning and professional progress. In a community of learners, the teacher's portfolio models the process by letting the students see how to do it, rather than simply following instructions. Your teachers can also use their professional portfolios as an opportunity to explore their philosophy of teaching, to validate and question their practices, to provide evidence of their own professional growth, to reflect on curricular decisions for their students, to document interactions with parents, and to create their goals for future teaching and professional growth (Graves, 1991; Hansen, 1994; Hill & Ruptic, 1994).

In some districts, such as Todd County, South Dakota, the professional teacher's portfolio replaces the more traditional means of teacher evaluation. During a teacher–principal conference, goals are established for the portfolio, which are built around the district's vision, mission, and exit outcomes. The teacher then collects evidence of progress towards attainment of the goals and writes a reflective journal notation that explains how the artifact connects directly to a goal. Peer review teams consisting of the principal and three teachers meet monthly to discuss, share, review, and critique one another's portfolios. In the spring, each teacher writes a reflective narrative assessing his or her portfolio. This summative assessment includes a thorough analysis of each goal and how well it was met. The principal and another member of the peer review team also independently write assessments of the portfolio. The teacher's original goals, written assessment of the goals, rubric assessment, and the principal's final assessment of the portfolio are kept on file in the same manner that a traditional evaluation is kept on file. If necessary, the teacher may write revised goals, or the teacher may be placed on a plan of assistance.

Teachers usually choose to focus on

- one subject area portfolio such as writing, literacy, or mathematics, which reflects the areas they teach
- an area in which they are changing in their classroom practices such as portfolio implementation, whole-language practices, literature-based reading, math manipulatives, thematic teaching, integrated learning, or others
- an overall teaching performance portfolio that examines teaching effectiveness, student achievement, assessment practices, and professional activity

Types of Entries

Teacher's portfolios often contain personal information, achievements, professional activities, classroom samples, pictures of their students, and reflections about their teaching and professional growth. Some teachers also include samples of their writing, logs of books they are reading, and letters from parents (Hill & Ruptic, 1994). Some items that might be included in teachers' portfolios are

- a resume
- audio or videos of actual lessons taught
- feedback received from others
- names of workshops or inservice classes attended
- memberships in professional organizations
- awards received
- parent or student evaluations
- district committees on which they serve
- personal narratives
- samples of student work
- self-reflections on professional growth
- teaching philosophy and teaching practices that reflect their philosophy
- artifacts that represent instructional strategies tried
- reflections on the effectiveness of strategies attempted
- documentation of a positive learning environment
- goals for future growth in instruction and assessment

Methods That Teachers Use to Organize Their Portfolios

Teachers choose many different ways of organizing their portfolios. Some teachers begin with their goals, and each of their artifacts relate to how they are striving to reach those goals. This type of organization is common in districts that are substituting portfolio assessment for traditional teacher evaluation procedures.

Other teachers may use portfolios for job interviews. These portfolios are usually colorful and focus on teaching philosophy, teaching techniques, teaching effectiveness, and samples of student work.

A few teachers are more comfortable with a portfolio that is filled with papers, favorite books, items that hold special memories, and student work samples. This less formal portfolio still has some form of organization that links the entries to the whole portfolio.

Others prefer to organize portfolios into sections such as personal information, professional growth, classroom strategies, and so on. Each portfolio is unique and will represent the personal and professional aspects of your teachers (Hill & Ruptic, 1994).

Using Self-Reflection of Portfolio Entries

Unless portfolio entries are supported by reflective narratives, the portfolio is simply a collection of random pieces or a scrapbook. When teachers go through the process of reflection on their portfolios and the artifacts they contain, they can gain valuable insights (Hill & Ruptic, 1994; Porter & Cleland, 1995). As Graves (1991) noted, until one participates in the process of maintaining a portfolio, it appears to be a simple task without deep thinking or strong emotional involvement.

Teachers in Todd County District found that, when they began to examine their learning and teaching, they became quite frustrated because the list of possibilities for what to include in their portfolios seemed endless. At this point, they realized that the concerns students had voiced about having a difficult time deciding what to include in their portfolios represented valid struggles. The problem came in narrowing an unwieldy collection down into something that was manageable. They finally decided to focus on the district's vision, mission, and exit outcomes. Then each artifact that was chosen had to reflect at least one of these goals. Through this reflection, choosing from the possible entries became manageable.

Setting Personal and Professional Goals

When your teachers reflect on the contents of their portfolios, they can examine their instructional decisions, discover gaps in their learning, determine which strategies were successful in the classroom, and view their changes and professional development over time. Through this process, they can celebrate risk taking, engage in inquiry, and set future goals that can guide their next portfolios. These goals are usually the final reflection that closes the current portfolio and is often the starting point for the next one (Porter & Cleland, 1995).

Benefits of Having Teachers Create Professional Portfolios

When teachers create their own portfolios, their views change on the connection between learning and evaluation. By documenting their role as learners, they can begin to strive to connect evaluation and learning through constantly searching for opportunities to reflect on the teaching and learning that occurs in their classrooms. Through attempts to gather evidence from many sources, your teachers can come to value reactions and questions from students and parents, observations from peers, and time to write and reflect on their own work. Portfolios can support professional growth, self-awareness, and change in your teachers. Going through the process themselves can inform their teaching decisions, curriculum plans, and community building. Portfolios evaluate performance within a framework of narration and evidence through self-reflection and goal setting for improvement in future teaching practices (Kieffer, 1994, Zubizarreta, 1994).

Principal–Teacher Conferences

Principals and teachers can both benefit from portfolio conferences. Through teachers' presentations of their portfolios, principals can gain valuable information about teachers' beliefs, instructional practices, portfolio implementation, professional growth, and personal goals. However, just as principals are sometimes reluctant to share their self-reflections and frustrations with their superintendent, teachers may not yet have developed enough trust to risk sharing their personal voices with principals.

When principals communicate to teachers their support and acceptance of whatever level of development each teacher has reached in creating a teaching portfolio, teachers often become more willing to take risks in sharing their failures, as well as showcasing their teaching accomplishments. Because teachers can perceive principal–teacher portfolio conferences to be a threatening or stressful event, it may be wise to hold the conferences on a voluntary basis and invite teachers to participate, rather than requiring the conferences as part of portfolio implementation. One way to encourage your teachers to see benefits of a portfolio conference with you and to help gain their trust is by sharing your portfolio with them, describing how you used it at your principal–central office conference, telling your teachers about some of the risks that you took in your conference, and explaining how it helped you in learning more about yourself as a principal and a learner.

The focus of the teachers' portfolios should be their choice. They may wish to share their literacy portfolio, one for a specific content area, their implementation of portfolios, a general teaching portfolio, or another type of portfolio they have created. Their portfolios will usually consist of an introduction to provide a focus, a table of contents for easy reference of sections, their beliefs or philosophy, supporting artifacts with accompanying captions or narratives that explain the significance of each piece, and their goals. When teachers feel comfortable with their portfolios and the conference procedures, they will usually include their self-evaluations and reflections. Many teachers also include their professional growth and areas in which they feel a need to receive further training, additional support, or professional development.

Teachers benefit from the principal–teacher portfolio conferences in several ways:

- They experience the same process that their students do when they present their portfolios.
- They can use the process to serve as a model for students by sharing their portfolios with the students and telling how the portfolio was used in the conference. They can also share their feelings about any risks they took and about what they learned from the process.
- They have an opportunity to showcase their strengths as a teacher.
- They can share their beliefs about teaching and instructinal methods that work well for them.
- They can discuss their progress toward portfolio implementation.
- It provides them with an opportunity to receive feedback.
- It provides them with a reason to organize their thinking and to reflect upon their teaching practices.
- It assists them in setting goals for their own learning and professional development.
- They can share their frustrations and ask for support in meeting their needs.

Perhaps one of the greatest reasons to encourage teachers to participate in principal–teacher portfolio conferences is that they provide an excellent vehicle for improving communication, building trust, encouraging risk taking, sustaining portfolio implementation, enhancing teacher voice, creating collegiality, and promoting teacher inquiry into their teaching practices and student learning.

Leadership Decisions: The Principal's Portfolio

We believe it is also important for principals to compile a portfolio. In addition to the obvious benefits that come through modeling, principals' portfolios encourage reflection, self-evaluation, and professional growth. They can be a particularly effective tool for improving your leadership practices.

Types of Entries

Numerous types of entires will give you a rich source of information to study your practices. We recommend that principals make their first entry a statement of beliefs or a list of beliefs about schools and learning. Until going through this process, many principals tell us they have never formally articulated their beliefs and that writing them for their portfolios created a personal awareness of the basis for many of their decisions. One principal confided that, while going through this written process, he realized a large discrepancy existed between his practices and what he believed. The next year, he changed districts.

Additional types of entires can be selected based on what you want to know about yourself as a leader. Others might include

- student, staff, and parent opinion surveys
- annual reports
- discipline records that indicate why students were referred, intervention strategies, and followup
- facility usage after regular school hours by staff, students, and community
- formal and informal staff development programs illustrating the variety, length, number of participating staff, and results
- examples of efforts to support teacher leadership by organizing task forces, ad hoc decision making, and collegial support groups
- examples of program and/or instructinal changes such as reductions in tracking, development of interdisciplinary units, and increased time special education students are included in regular classrooms
- examples of reaching out to the community through attendance at service clubs, weeky newsletters to parents, attendance at special events, and newspaper articles about your school
- a log of your efforts in a particular area such as portfolio implementation that traces the development over time, what worked, what didn't, and what needed adjustments

- proposals for funding that were successful and unsuccessful and efforts to attain additional resources
- photographs of school awards, school events, and people who made special contributions

Methods for Organizing Principals' Portfolios

We have found that principals who keep a portfolio usually use one of two methods of organizing them. Portfolios can provide information on a specific process of change, or they can be designed to provide information on your leadership skills in general. Some record progress in the activities for which they are directly responsible such as school improvement initiatives, vision building, instructional development, facility maintenance, community relations, allocation of resources, personal development, and staff evaluation. The categories may vary, depending on the district. Others use portfolios to monitor and improve in one area such as implementing portfolios to monitor and improve in one area such as implementing portfolios into the school, utilizing time more productively, changing the school climate, or other complex tasks. Both methods provide insights into your leadership style, any discrepancies between your beliefs and actions, and your strengths and weaknesses. Either method is an extremely profitable use of time.

Data placed in your portfolio should be formative in nature and provide information that you can use to monitor growth over time. Each entry needs a caption that explains its significance within the context of your professional goals. Captions answer the question, "Why am I placing this in my portfolio?" They also must contain reflection in the form of self-evaluation that addresses, "How am I doing and how can I alter my behavior to improve my professional practices?" Without captions and self-evaluation, it is no more than a scrapbook.

Questions That Can Guide the Purposes of Principals' Portfolios

While portfolios serve numerous purposes, the main one is to provide information and feedback to improve your effectiveness. Portfolios can assist you to focus on the goals valued by the school community, facilitate learning and teaching, identify unintended effects of decisions, apply policies in an unbiased way, and maximize the use of your time (Clark & Clark, 1994).

Several questions can guide you in the development of your portfolio:

- What do I want to know about myself as the school leader?
- How am I going to use the information when I obtain it?

- What types of portfolio entries will give me this information?
- How and when will I obtain the information?

Goldring and Rallis (1993, pp. 99–103) offer more specific questions for teams to evaluate principals and schools. The following reworded questions can be used by the principal for self-evaluation:

- Do all groups of stakeholders understand the mission of our school? How do I communicate our school mission to each group?
- Is teacher leadership emerging? How can I encourage teachers to take more responsibility?
- Are decision-making bodies being used to their fullest? What decisions have they made? Are they asked to make decisions about substantive issues or superficial ones?
- What opportunities for professional growth have been established and utilized by the staff and myself?
- What inroads have I made with the different constituencies?
- What kind of changes are occurring in the school? How do they affect the school climate?
- How are students progressing toward our learning goals? Are some goals being attained and other not? How can we improve progress?
- Have I tapped all possible resources? How are resources allocated?
- What tasks am I currently doing that could be delegated either to an individual or to a committee?

Using Reflections on Portfolio Entries to Identify Trends

As principals review and reflect on their entries, trends begin to emerge. Portfolio entries can offer a picture of how your activities and behaviors directly affect school processes and school learning. Many actions can be identified as directly supporting the school's mission, while other actions reduce the school's effectiveness. Some principals are surprised how much time they spend on discipline problems with the same 3 percent of the students, while they allocate little time for the other 97 percent. Others report discovering critical areas that they have overlooked, such as establishing task forces to empower teachers. Many realize there are a number of tasks they are currently doing that could be delegated to the school secretary and parent volunteers.

As a principal, you may also wish to receive feedback from your staff about your role in implementing portfolios. The checklist in Figure 9.8 could be used to compare your self-evaluation with those of your staff

PRINCIPAL'S PORTFOLIO IMPLEMENTATION EFFECTIVENESS

Date_____

	☐ SELF		
1 = Ineffective 3 = Effective	☐ STAFF		
2 = Somewhat Effective 4 = Very Effective	1	2	3	4

	1	2	3	4
INVOLVING STAKEHOLDERS:				
Obtaining central office support, endorsement, and commitment				
Disseminating information to parents and community members				
Collaborating in planning for portfolio implementation				
Providing inservice for parents or family members				
Encouraging stakeholders to actively participate in implementation				
PROVIDING LEADERSHIP:				
In creating the school's vision				
In establishing curriculum standards and benchmarks				
In establishing a problem-solving procedure				
PROVIDING AN ATMOSPHERE THAT PROMOTES CHANGE:				
Encouraging risktaking in trying new ways to assess learning				
Encouraging collegiality and cooperation among staff members				
Encouraging teachers to find their voices in assessment practices				
Encouraging self-reflection in teaching, assessment, and evaluation				
PROVIDING PORTFOLIO AWARENESS OPPORTUNITIES:				
Supplying professional reading and multi-media materials				
Arranging portfolio workshops and demonstrations				
Encouraging teachers to attend portfolio conferences				
Visiting other schools or districts who are implementing portfolios				
Allowing time for staff to learn about portfolio implementation				
ASSISTING IN PORTFOLIO IMPLEMENTATION:				
Collaborating to develop a school-based implementation process				
Continuing staff development for evaluating and refining the plan				
Encouraging support groups for portfolio implementation				
Supporting peer coaching				
Supporting the use of portfolio data for daily instruction				
Using portfolio data for curricular decisions				
Maintaining confidentiality of cumulatiave school portfolios				

Comments:

Figure 9.8. Principal's Portfolio Implementation Effectiveness Form.

members. This comparison can assist you in checking your effectiveness in leading portfolio implementation at your school. Discovering whether your perceptions correlate with those of your faculty can provide you with valuable information in deciding which areas might need to be addressed in future staff development sessions and for adjusting your interactions with staff.

Benefits of Professional Portfolios for Principals

Todd County School District in South Dakota has based portfolio assessment for their administrators on the following premise:

> Most of all, the portfolio evaluation process is a form of self-evaluation; it honors diversity; helps administrators identify strengths and weaknesses; causes an administrator to reflect on his or her own work, and causes an administrator to take responsibility for improving. Portfolio assessment also encourages administrators to be increasingly reflective, encourages them to integrate what they know, and encourages professional dialogue. (1994, p. 1)

Professional portfolios hold a rich source of evidence about your practice and its impact on the school. As the formal leader of the school, you are ultimately accountable and responsible for attainment of school goals. Portfolios can assist you in making progress toward those goals.

Principal-Central Office Conferences

Some of the information gathered for your own self-assessment can be utilized at principal–central office conferences. Entries illustrating your professional growth, school improvement, vision building, instructional leadership, facility maintenance, community relations, allocation of resources, and professional development can be evidence of your leadership abilities. Depending on your relationship with the superintendent, you may or may not want to include your reflections, self-evaluation, or peer/staff evaluations. Many principals have taken their complete portfolios into conferences with their superintendent and have reported receiving acceptance of their weaknesses and frustrations, assistance to attain their improvement goals, and an increase in camaraderie. Others have not developed a sufficient level of trust with the superintendent to disclose their frustrations and perceived shortcomings. Still, data in your portfolio form a basis for evaluation of growth over time.

When you attend a central office conference to review your effectiveness, we recommend having an agenda that focuses on the school goals. Begin with reviewing each goal and showing evidence from your portfolio of progress toward attaining the goals. Expect some goals to be more illusive than others such as changes in school climate. Also, remember that the implementation dip will account for lack of progress in some areas (Fullan, 1991).

Portfolio entries can be organized into categories of your activities and behaviors that directly affect school goals. Additional information may also be useful. Documentation of student achievement, systematic observations of planned events, budget reports, projections for future needs, and unresolved or recurring problems beyond your control such as a leaking roof can add to the meeting's productivity.

After discussing progress toward school goals, the agenda should move to your professional development and goals for your growth. Areas for concentration will emerge from your portfolio entries. Perhaps you will want to shift the way you spend your time, enroll in a course at a nearby university, or attend a conference. In any event, by having two or three goals in mind prior to the conferences, you are showing initiative and self-direction, two important leadership skills.

We have worked with some principals who have been cautious about using portfolios in conferences with the superintendent. After a great deal of encouragement on our part, they usually try it. Frequently, we receive enthusiastic phone calls saying it was extremely helpful.

Program Decisions: School Portfolios

School portfolios supply a wealth of information about the extent to which a school is progressing toward its goals. Assuming the mission of your school is more than doing well on standardized tests, school portfolios can be designed to document the complexities of the school's accomplishments. Formative and summative data can be gathered to reflect the total school context (Goldring & Rallis, 1993). Portfolios can be organized to provide information on the processes and products of a school (Clark & Clark, 1994). When well-designed, they can provide

- insights into how well programs are operating
- the degree to which programs are serving their students
- strengths and weaknesses of the school
- cost-effectiveness of programs

The information is then used to make decisions and adjustments in programs, practices, and allocation of funds. It offers a more complete evaluation of the school than traditional annual reports.

School portfolios begin and end with the school's goals. Formative evaluation consists of gathering information about practices and programs with the purpose of making adjustments and facilitating improvement. It is considered constructive in nature. Information obtained is used to improve and monitor programs and services for students. Data collection procedures usually include surveys, interviews, discussions, and observations (Clark & Clark, 1994). Some examples of formative questions are

- What are the most common problems teachers are having with portfolios?
- What changes can be made in the schedule to provide time for interdisciplinary teams to meet?
- How can I convince Mrs. Jones to try portfolios in her classroom?
- Are parents satisfied with the portfolio process?

Summative evaluation is more result-oriented. Rather than focusing on processes at work in the school, it is designed to judge the school's products. It is used by administrators and school board members who will make the final decision about program continuation (Goldring & Rallis, 1993). Summative evaluation data are measures of the final results of our efforts. They are then compared with information from previous years to identify trends. Examples of questions that reveal summative data are

- To what extent do portfolio contents reflect the school's learning goals? What goals are being measured? Are any goals omitted from the portfolios?
- In what ways have standardized test scores changed since implementing portfolios? Have SAT, ACT, California Achievement Test, or Stanford Achievement Test scores improved in some subsections? Have they gone down in some subsections?
- Has the school climate improved? One indicator might be teacher and student absentee rates. Another is participation in after-school activities.

Goldring and Rallis (1993) recommend using a school-based team to coordinate the evaluation activities. The team's responsibility is to provide evidence of accountability to the school's constituents who are involved in program development, implementation, and use. This consists of the principal, teachers, staff, parents, and students. Its task is to develop a nontraditional type of accountability designed to support a well-informed constituency, a community of learners, visionary leadershp, and action research, which are factors described at the end of this chapter as crucial to changing the school climate into one of inquiry. For school portfolios to work, an environment of trust, collegiality, communication, and community must exist (Wortman, 1992; Clark & Clark, 1994). It requires the principal to challenge traditionally held beliefs of school management and to replace former beliefs with shared accountability as well as shared decision making.

School portfolios open the school doors for community scrutiny. When parents, teachers, and other community members are asked to collect and analyze data in regards to student success and school programs, it requires a great deal of confidence in your leadership and in the members of the task force. It is more than listening to, responding to, and acting on ideas and suggestions of others (Clark & Clark, 1994). School portfolios transform shared leadership to a community of learners.

The team's work is comprehensive. It compares the school's programs and processes in relation to the school's goals and complies the information in the form of a portfolio. Data, reflection, and suggestions coexist. The portfolio is then used by the stakeholders to make improvements in the practices, services, and programs and to make recommendations to the administration. This type of assessment recognizes everyone's responsibility for success and provides opportunity for reflection (Goldring & Rallis, 1993).

When selecting members for the task force, structure it in a way that participants have a clear sense of purpose; are committed to compiling evidence on specific school goals; recognize the limitations placed on their delegated authority; have expertise in collaboration; are knowledgeable of school programs, services, and processes; and represent the various stakeholder groups. The team should consist of two to three teachers, one or two staff members, four to five parents, one or two community representatives, two or three students, and one principal. Avoid having more than twelve to fifteen members.

A successful task force requires training by the principal in collaboration techniques, school operations, and evaluative procedures. Adults in our society typically do not have small-group and interpersonal skill training to work together productively (Johnson & Johnson, 1989). You will need to review the cooperative skills found earlier in this book.

Members also need directions to organize the portfolio and a process to obtain the entries. Clark and Clark (1994, p. 271) recommend using the following components to organize the evaluation:

- Identify and select ways to obtain the information.
- Identify funding, personnel, and time to obtain the information.
- Collect the entries. Use time lines and distribute the responsibilities.
- Analyze the entries. Write why each entry is included, write captions for each entry, and reflect on trends.

- Write appropriate reports for differing constituencies. Deliver the reports to the principal to distribute.

It is best not to begin school portfolios until student portfolios are an integral part of your school's curriculum and assessment. School portfolios support a school culture of inquiry. Save them for this soaring stage of implementation.

WHERE DO WE GO FROM HERE?

You have escorted a promising idea through a comprehensive process of change to become an integral part of your school's curriculum and assessment. With continued staff development, visionary leadership, and community involvement, portfolio assessment will improve. This will not happen without diligence and planning on the part of the principal.

Clark and Clark (1994, p. 292) identify five factors that are crucial in maintaining a change. They emphasize that all stakeholders must be involved in the following factors:

- understanding that portfolio assessment is a neverending process
- encouraging visionary leadership
- keeping a well-informed constituency
- creating a community of learners
- facilitating action research

Viewing Portfolios as a Cyclical Process

Portfolio assessment is a continuous process of challenging the status quo through goal setting, problem solving, trying alternative approaches, expanding portfolio uses, and evaluating results. School curriculum and structure can always be improved. Portfolios are one of several ways to do this.

Throughout this book, we have emphasized the importance of viewing portfolios as a process in which all teachers, students, and community members have to discover for themselves what portfolios mean to them. An understanding of portfolios becomes the starting point for the next level of understanding. It is cyclical.

Each teacher progresses at a different rate and in slightly different ways. Some might have students write about what they have learned. Others use projects to demonstrate learning. A few rely on checklists and forms. All are applying portfolios in a way that fits their teaching styles, philosophy of teaching, and comfort levels. There are no prepackaged answers on how to use portfolio assessment. If some kits appear on the market, they will limit the possibilities of portfolios. Teachers must go through the continual process of discovering their own way to use portfolios.

Students and parents must also go through the process of becoming familiar and comfortable with nontraditional assessment and student–teacher, student–teacher–parent, and student-led conferences. Portfolio assessment demands that students be active participants in goal setting, reflection, and self-evaluation.

How does the principal keep the process going? Peer coaching, sustained support, school accountability reports, and evaluative conferences force us to continually ask ourselves, "What are we doing; it is working; how else could we do this; and why are we doing things this way?" By implementing peer coaching, providing support for teachers, using portfolios in school reports, and participating in evaluative conferences, principals can lead the school to continually improve.

Encouraging Visionary Leadership

Principals are not only expected to be visionary leaders, they are also expected to encourage staff members, students, and community members to assume various important responsibilities in setting the school's direction. Portfolio assessment sets the stage for others to grow in leadership roles. We refer you to Chapter 2 for more information on enabling and facilitating shared decision making. When given the autonomy to make decisions about portfolios, teachers and students empower themselves to press for improvement and growth.

As stakeholders become more comfortable with shared leadershp, the types of issues they take on change. In the early stages of portfolio implementation, teachers and students tend to focus on management issues. Eventually, such things as finding time to work on portfolios, planning student–teacher conferences, and deciding what pieces of work to keep become routine. Later, the focus is on developing assessment tasks, identifying rubrics, and explaining them to parents. The next problem many staffs, students, and parents raise is the need to change student report cards to match the scoring rubrics for portfolios. Each issue is more complex. As each problem is resolved, the school becomes closer to its shared vision. The role of the principal, then, is to build a culture within which members define and pursue ways to attain school goals (Goldring & Rallis, 1993).

Keeping an Informed Constituency

Teachers, students, administrators, parents, and community members must be well informed in order to make good decisions about their school (Clark & Clark, 1994). It is the responsibility of the principal to provide current information to stakeholders about new insights and procedures for portfolio assessment. The principal must keep current by reading professional journals and books, attending conferences, listening to other educators, and being aware of political changes. Then, pertinent information and trends can be gathered and interpreted to your constituency to expand their knowledge base.

Portfolios offer additional information about students, programs, and policies that is not available through traditional assessments. Principals can compile, graph, and apply information from portfolios to convey trends and examples of learning to all stakeholders.

As portfolio assessment becomes an integral basis for decision making, some community members will still be uncomfortable with its place in the school. Teachers prefer portfolios over traditional standardized tests. Some of the public does not (Erickson, 1995). Data from both forms of assessment can offer more information than either form alone. It takes several years for principals to satisfy the questions and concerns of the public about the validity and reliability of portfolio assessment. Expect and welcome questions as an opportunity to express the merits of portfolios.

Creating a Community of Learners

Portfolios play a crucial role in creating learning environments in which everyone is involved in learning. When teachers reflect on the practice of teaching, solve problems in collegial support groups, set goals for their own professional improvement, and experiment with new approaches, they are learners (Clark & Clark, 1994). In collaborative cultures, staff members continuously examine how they conduct their practice and why, make changes based on their shared vision of schooling, confront the naysayers with explanations, and continue to grow themselves (Henderson & Hawthorne, 1995). The culture of the school shifts to an atmosphere of cooperative inquiry, which facilitates a constant search for better ways to learn and teach. In schools such as this, everyone is a learner.

As the principal, you have a proactive role in creating an environment in your school that supports a community of learners. Leaders of learners can be recognized by what they do. How do you do this? You model, experience, display, and celebrate what is expected of a learner. Principals in these schools actively engage in discussions with teachers, parents, and community members about the knowledge base; publicly inquire and reflect about programs and practice; and continuously articulate and clarify learning goals (Wortman, 1992; Clark & Clark, 1994). Leaders can sustain, revise, and refine a community of learners.

Encouraging Action Research

Action research is inquiry about a school within the context of collegial support (Hubbard & Power, 1993; Clark & Clark, 1994). It is a way for teachers and principals to investigate instructional practices with the purpose of enhancing their professional development. Staff and community members identify concerns, gather and analyze data, engage in problem solving, develop action plans, and assess the meaning of the results (Henderson & Hawthorne, 1995). It links staff members with vital sources of knowledge, provides opportunities for intellectual growth outside the school, supports continual teacher and principal learning, and encourages teachers and principals to investigate the organizational aspects of their schools.

Action research provides a way for those closest to school issues to find answers that generate continual quality improvement. Portfolios provide a structure to answer specific programmatic and instructional questions about current school practices and policies. They are a powerful tool for maintaining and improving supportive, collaborative climates. Schools that utilize action research frequently find that, when given the opportunity to study teaching practices and policies in a supportive environment, teachers began to pursue teaching and learning practices not previously in their repertoire (Henderson & Hawthorne, 1995; Wells & Chang-Wells, 1992; Hubbard & Power, 1993).

As school culture changes, conversations move beyond discussing what to place into portfolios and into the complexities of working with diverse human beings toward a shared vision. The focus turns to incongruencies between school practices and beliefs and to acceptance of finding ways to align actions and beliefs. The closer school communities come to congruence between beliefs and actions, the more the culture is transformed to one that fosters growth of all participants. Portfolios are a catalyst to assist you in accomplishing these goals.

GLOSSARY

Average Scores: a type of descriptive statistic using the mean to describe a set of raw scores. The average is obtained by summing all the scores in a set and dividing by the number of scores.

Conferencing: two or three individuals meet together to discuss the contents of portfolios, the strengths and needs of the author, and future goals for learning. Conferencing can take place between students, teachers, administrators, principals, and teachers; students and teachers; parents and teachers; students, parents, and teachers; or students and parents.

Debriefing: processing information after an observation or a portfolio conference to share thoughts, praise positive observations, notice behavior, discuss parts of a conference that went well, ponder questions, discuss problems, and to explore ways to improve the process.

Descriptive Scales: a ranking system used in rubrics that uses words such as *not yet, developing,* or *achieving* to explain students' performance.

Evaluation Scales: a ranking system used in rubrics to judge students' performance based on an underlying standard of excellence and that uses terms such as *excellent, good, minimal,* or *no attempt.*

Parent–Teacher Portfolio Conference: a conference between the teacher and parents in which the portfolio is used to support the progress report that the teacher shares with the parents.

Percent Reaching Standard: a type of descriptive statistic. You decide what score point represents each category and then calculate the percent of students who achieved each category.

Portfolio Share Day: a day that is set aside for students to read and respond to other students' portfolios.

Professional Portfolio: a portfolio that an administrator or teacher keeps to share their learning; to demonstrate meeting job requirements; to reflect on their learning, teaching, or leadership; and to set future goals.

Range: the difference between the lowest score and the highest score. When using a graph to visually show the differences between scores, each raw score is plotted to illustrate how the scores are distributed.

Student-Led Portfolio Conference: a conference between a student and parents in which the child shares his or her portfolio contents, including artifacts, assessments, self-evaluations, strengths, needs, and goals.

Student–Parent–Teacher Portfolio Conference: a conference in which the student and teacher share the information in the student's portfolio with the parents who may also be involved in sharing information about the student's learning at home.

Student–Student Portfolio Conference: a conference between two or more students to provide feedback on the contents of a portfolio, to introduce new students to the classroom, or to rehearse for portfolio conferences with parents.

Student–Teacher Portfolio Conference: a conference between a teacher and student about the contents of the student's portfolio.

Summary Scores: grouping raw scores into categories for ease in working with large numbers of scores. Average scores, range of scores, and percent reaching standard are several ways to summarize data.

Three-Way Conference: a conference in which the teacher, student, and parents all share information about the students progress.

ENDNOTES

1. While many schools still conduct traditional parent–teacher conferences that do not include having students present at the conference, the benefits of portfolios are not being utilized to the greatest benefit because students learn from presenting their portfolios to their parents, and the parents learn more about the capabilities of their children.
2. Student-led conferences take the most preparation of any of the three types of parent conferences with portfolios, but they provide the most benefits for students, parents, and teachers.

APPENDIX A.1: Parent/Guardian Survey

As a member of the school community, I have the following views about what my child is learning.			
	Very Much	Some	Not at All
1. I am familiar with the learning goals in this school. Comments:			
2. I am familiar with the learning goals in each subject. Comments:			
3. I am familiar with the way learning is measured in this school, i.e., tests, conferences, reports. Comments:			
4. I understand the measures used to evaluate my child. Comments:			

As a member of the school community, I have the following views about what my child is learning.			
	Very Much	Some	Not at All
5. I know what tests the school uses to measure my child's learning. Comments:			
6. I understand why tests are used and what they tell me. Comments:			
7. The evaluations or reports issued by the school tell me what knowledge my child has learned in each subject. Comments:			
8. I am satisfied with the current evaluation system in the school. Comments:			
9. I am satisfied with the way information about my child's learning is reported to me. Comments:			

As a member of the school community, I have the following views about what my child is learning.			
	Very Much	Some	Not at All
10. I would like to see reports and evaluations that tell me more about what my child has learned. Comments:			
11. I would like to become more involved in how my child is evaluated. Comments:			
12. I would like to participate in making decisions about assessment and evaluation in my child's school. Comments: Additional Comments:			

APPENDIX A.2: Teacher Questionnaire

What are your opinions about assessment in our school?

1. Have you attended any workshop or conference sessions that have focused on aligning curriculum goals with assessment? If yes, what was the focus of the sessions?

_____

_____

2. Do you serve on any curriculum committees? If yes, which ones?

_____

_____

3. Are you interested in working on aligning curriculum goals with assessment? If yes, when would you be available to meet?

_____

_____

4. What assessment tools do you currently use? Do you feel there are any gaps in the information that they provide for you?

_____

_____

5. Are you satisified with the assessment tools that are used in our schools?

_____

_____

6. Do you feel that the assessment tools available to you measure the goals and outcomes for our curriculum?

_____

_____

7. Do you feel our current assessment tools are sufficient to inform parents about what their child has learned?

_____

_____

8. Are there elements of our current assessments that you feel should not be altered? If yes, which ones? If yes, why should these remain the same?

_____

_____

9. Do you feel our current manner of reporting student learning to parents could be improved? If yes, which areas would you like to see changed? Why?

_____

_____

10. Have you attended any workshop or conference sessions about alternative assessment such as portfolios? If yes, do you have any handouts that you could share at a staff meeting?

_____

_____

11. Have you read any articles or books about alternative assessment? If yes, which ones were interesting or helpful to you?

_____

_____

12. Are you interested in learning more about alternative assessments, such as portfolios?

_____

_____

13. Who do you think might be interested in using a wider variety of assessment tools in our school?

_____

_____

14. What are some ways you evaluate your students other than traditional tests?

_____

_____

15. Are you using any type of portfolios in your classroom? If yes, what are you doing? Are you willing to share what you are doing with others?

_____

_____

16. Do you know any teachers who are using portfolios in their classrooms?

_____

_____

17. Additional comments about assessment.

_____

_____

APPENDIX A.3: Principal's Checklist for Readiness
to Implement Portfolios

As a principal. I rate myself as high. medium. or low on these key factors of readiness for implementation of portfolios:

	High	Medium	Low
1. I am flexible. risk taking. proactive. honest. sincere. and fair.			
2. I have training in implementation processes.			
3. I have ample knowledge of the district's curriculum. effective instruction. strengths of my teaching staff. and program issues.			
4. I manage time well and develop a facilitation. building operation. student behavior balance among instructional leadership routine administration. community relations. and school improvement.			
5. I am aware of community concerns about assessment and school goals.			
6. I believe in. establish. and sustain long-range goals and have a high tolerance for diversity of goals.			
7. I am an encourager of growth and an effective strategist.			
8. I create a climate of collegiality. trust. interaction. ongoing learning. and risk taking.			
9. I establish strong communication and relationships with and among teachers. consultants. board members. administrators. and community.			
10. I use collaborative. collegial decision making and delegate authority.			

	High	Medium	Low

11. I create an atmosphere that supports experimentation and allows failure.

12. I make myself available as a sounding board for teacher problems and ideas.

13. I develop strategies to clarify and classify problems, prioritize problems, and prevent problems.

14. I assist in developing clear problem-solving procedures and solve problems collaboratively to reflect others' problem-solving styles and to promote ownership of portfolio implementation.

15. I promote teacher mentoring.

16. I am involved in professional reading about portfolios.

17. I am prepared to get actively involved in matching portfolio implementation to curriculum standards.

18. I arrange for staff development that relates to school goals and portfolio assessment.

19. I am exploring consultant and material resources.

20. I am committed to attending all inservice related to portfolios.

APPENDIX B.1: Example of a Proposal to a School Board

Lincoln Public Schools

To: Lincoln Board of Education
From: Joanne Lewis, Principal
Subject: Portfolio Assessment

The staff at Harris Middle School is concerned about the limitations of traditional standardized tests. We recognize a need for alternative ways to assess student learning. We are not proposing elimination of standardized tests. Rather, we would like to consider additional methods to attain a more complete view of what our students are learning. One method of assessment that is consistent with current research is portfolio assessment.

We are requesting approval to learn more about this promising practice. The information presented below briefly describes the benefits of portfolio assessment, legal implications, a budget, and a projected time line of one, two, and three years. Currently, we are requesting support for six months of staff development to lay the groundwork for implementation. Next January, we will provide you with an update of our progress and a specific implementation plan.

Need for Alternative Assessment

- Traditional multiple choice tests measure factual knowledge.
- Norm-referenced and criterion-referenced tests tell us how well our schools and district are doing in comparison to others.
- As society has changed, the workforce requires higher-level thinking and decision making.
- Standardized tests are not intended to be used for decisions about daily instruction.
- Multiple sources of information provide a clearer view of learning.

Definition of a Portfolio

A portfolio is a purposeful, systematic collection of student work over time that includes

- student participation in selection of content
- evidence of student self-reflection
- criteria for selection
- criteria for judging merit

Benefits of Portfolio Assessment

- empowers students to accept responsibility for their learning
- empowers teachers to select and create measures of student's talents
- requires communication among administrators, teachers, students, noncertified staff, parents, and community members
- is consistent with current research in teaching and learning
- provides a clearer connection between what is taught, what is learned, and what is assessed
- makes schools accountable for students acquiring the skills and abilities needed in today's world

Legal Implications

- Confidentiality will be maintained.
- Students own their portfolios.

Budget for First Year

• guest speaker/consultant, 3 half-days	$1500.00
• materials:	
resource books	200.00
• school improvement/inservice expenses	
conferences for teachers to attend, 5 @ 500	2500.00
travel to other schools, 100 miles @ .25	250.00
substitutes for teachers to attend conferences and visit schools	
5 teachers for 3 days @ 50	750.00
15 days for 30 teachers 1/2 day	750.00

Budget Projections for Second Year

• guest speaker/consultants, 3 half-days	$1500.00
• materials	
expandable folders/student, 1100 @ 8.00	8800.00
35-mm film and processing, 45 @ 4.25	127.50
VCR film, 60 @ 2.00	120.00
audiotapes, 90 @ 1.00	90.00
filing cabinets, 45 @ 209	9405.00
• school improvements/inservice expenses	
conferences for teachers to attend	$2500.00
substitutes for teachers to attend conferences and inservice	1500.00

Time Line

(*1*) June and July: planning for change
  • Order resource books.
  • Gather background information.
  • Schedule consultant.
  • Schedule visits to other schools in the fall.
  • Four teachers and principal attend conference.
(*2*) September and October: developing awareness
  • Four teachers share information from the conference.
  • Put a report about the conference in school newsletter.
  • Put a display in the lounge about portfolios.
(*3*) November and December: obtain commitments
(*4*) January through May: staff development
  • Examine the possibilities.
  • Identify the Focus.
  • Choose evidence to evaluate.
  • Create performance standards.
(*5*) September: implementation

APPENDIX B.2: Performance Standards for Effective Communication (Criteria for Assessing Learning Goals)

Effective Communication

A. Expresses ideas clearly
   4 Clearly and effectively communicates the main idea or theme and provides support that contains rich, vivid, and powerful detail.
   3 Clearly communicates the main idea or theme and provides suitable support and detail.
   2 Communicates important information but not a clear theme or overall structure.
   1 Communicates information as isolated pieces in a random fashion.

B. Effectively communicates with diverse audiences
   4 Presents information in a style and tone that effectively capitalize on the audience's level of interest and level of knowledge or understanding.
   3 Presents information in a style and tone consistent with the audience's level of interest and level of knowledge or understanding.
   2 Presents information in a style and tone inappropriate for the audience's level of interest or the audience's level of knowledge.
   1 Presents information in a style and tone inappropriate for both the audience's level of interest and level of knowledge.

C. Effectively communicates in a variety of ways
   4 Uses multiple methods of communication, applying the conventions and rules of those methods in highly creative and imaginative ways.
   3 Uses two different methods of communication, applying the conventions and rules of those methods in customary ways.
   2 Attempts to use two methods of communication but does not apply the conventions and rules or those methods.
   1 Uses only one method of communication when more than one method is clearly needed or requested and does not correctly apply the conventions and rules of that method.

D. Effectively communicates for a variety of purposes
   4 Clearly communicates a purpose in a highly creative and insightful manner.
   3 Uses effective techniques to communicate a clear purpose.
   2 Demonstrates an attempt to communicate for a specific purpose but makes significant errors or omissions.
   1 Demonstrates no central purpose in the communication or makes no attempt to articulate a purpose.

E. Creates quality products
    4 Creates a product that exceeds conventional standards.
    3 Creates a product that clearly meets conventional standards.
    2 Creates a product that does not meet one or a few important standards.
    1 Creates a product that does not address the majority of the conventional standards.

Student Self-Assessment Form

Effective Communication Standards

A. I communicate ideas clearly.
    4 I communicate ideas by making sure I have a strong main idea or topic and carefully organized details that explain or support the idea or topic. I make sure the details help make the bigger ideas useful and interesting.
    3 I communicate ideas by making sure I have a clear main idea or topic and enough details to explain or support the idea or topic.
    2 I communicate some important information, but I do not organize it well around a main idea or topic.
    1 I communicate information in unorganized pieces.

B. I communicate well with different audiences.
    4 I present information to various audiences in a way that makes the most of their specific knowledge and interests.
    3 I present information to various audiences in a way that suits their specific knowledge and interests.
    2 I present information to various audiences in a way that does not completely suit their knowledge and interests.
    1 I present information to various audiences in a way that conflicts with their knowledge and interests.

C. I communicate well using a variety of media.
    4 I use many methods of communication and I follow the correct processes and use the accepted standards of those mediums. I also use the mediums in new and different ways.
    3 I communicate using two mediums and follow the correct process and use the accepted standards for both of those mediums.
    2 I try to communicate using two mediums, but I make errors in the processes and misunderstand the accepted standards of the mediums I am using.
    1 I do not even try to communicate in more than one medium.

D. I communicate well for different purposes.

4 I clearly explain the purpose of my communication by selecting and using very effective and original methods. My explanation goes beyond just stating the purpose; it adds meaning to the information I am communicating.

3 I clearly explain the purpose of my communication by selecting and using effective methods.

2 I try to explain the purpose of my communication, but I make errors in the explanation or leave out information that would make it clear.

1 I do not try to explain the purpose of my communication, or I don't really have a clear purpose.

E. I create quality products.

4 I create products that exceed conventional standards.

3 I create products that clearly meet conventional standards.

2 I create products that do not meet one or a few important standards.

1 I create products that do not address the majority of the conventional standards.

APPENDIX C.1: Using Learning Strategies for Content Area Reading

Student: _____ Date: _____

Topic: _____

Strategies I used to learn about this topic *before* I read the material included

_____ Writing what I already know about it in my journal
_____ Creating a semantic map of what I know about the topic
_____ Previewing the reading material
_____ Skimming the material before reading it
_____ Looking at any bold words and headings

Strategies I used to learn more about this topic *while* I read the materials included

_____ Using context clues to figure out unknown words
_____ Using the dictionary
_____ Rereading materials to clarify any confusing information
_____ Relating the new information to what I already knew
_____ Adding a new information to my semantic map
_____ Finding answers to my own questions
_____ Asking new questions as I read more
_____ Taking notes
_____ Creating a graphic organizer
_____ Creating an outline
_____ Making note cards

Strategies I used to help me remember the information *after* I read included

_____ Writing what I learned in my journal
_____ Reorganizing information on my semantic map
_____ Answering my questions
_____ Summarizing the material
_____ Discussing the information with classmates
_____ Drawing pictures or diagrams
_____ Making a data retrieval chart of the information
_____ Explaining the information to someone else
_____ Using the information to solve a problem or create a project

APPENDIX C.2: Primary Self-Evaluation of Learning Attitudes

Student: _____   Date: _____

Circle how you feel about each one:

1. I like to find things out for myself.	yes	not sure	no
2. I think learning is important.	yes	not sure	no
3. I like to share my ideas by writing.	yes	not sure	no
4. I like to share my ideas by talking.	yes	not sure	no
5. I like to share my ideas by drawing.	yes	not sure	no
6. I like to read stories.	yes	not sure	no
7. I like to find out things by reading.	yes	not sure	no
8. I like to work with numbers.	yes	not sure	no
9. I like to figure things out.	yes	not sure	no
10. I like to learn about people and places.	yes	not sure	no
11. I like to do experiments.	yes	not sure	no
12. I like to learn about plants and animals.	yes	not sure	no
13. I can learn even if the work is hard.	yes	not sure	no
14. I feel mistakes can help me learn.	yes	not sure	no

Please answer these questions:

1. I would like to learn more about:

2. If I could change something at school, it would be:

3. What I like best at school is:

APPENDIX C.3: Self-Evaluation Form for Assignments or Projects

Student: _____   Date: _____

Type of Work: _____ Assignment   _____ Project   _____ Other

Title of Work: _____

1. This assignment or project will help me to:

2. I learned more about how to:

3. I had trouble with or was not sure about:

4. I feel I did a good job on this part:

5. I could improve this work by:

6. The items that I check below show what I think about this work:

_____ I tried my hardest   _____ I had trouble
_____ I had to think carefully _____ I felt successful
_____ I had to ask for help   _____ I worked carefully
_____ I had to rush to finish   _____ I worked quickly
_____ I felt this was easy   _____ I liked this work
_____ I had to reread   _____ I knew a lot about this

APPENDIX C.4

Agreement Contract

Contract Parties: Date: 2/2/94

1. Author/Illustrator: *Michael Rose*

2. Publisher: *Mrs. J. Huffman*

It is Mutually Agreed that the Author/Illustrator will write an original book of super quality and prepare appropriate illustrations for said book within a period of time not to exceed 33 working days. Within the allotted time frame, the Author/Illustrator will assemble said book, design a book jacket, and bind all material with the express purpose of an outstanding piece of writing for many audiences.

Proposed Book Title: *The Three Little Hogs in the Year 2016*

Brief Synopsis of Story: *The three little hogs go and steal materials so they can build houses and live the life of robbers but while they're stealing furnishings for their houses the police sent out the ultimate law enforcement device, Robowolf, who will try to apprehend the hogs.*

Number of Pages: __16__ Media for Illustrations: ____colored pencil____

Author/Illustrator hereby agrees to explore and expand his or her creative potentials; to pay attention to all instructions; and to be appreciative of the creations of other authors and illustrators henceforth.

Publisher agrees to recognize and value the creative efforts of the Author/Illustrator; to promote the development of professional attitudes and discipline; to encourage the growth and advancement of imagination and writing skills; and to express both respect and enjoyment in the elements within and the results of Author/Illustrator's said book.

Michael L. Rose

Author/Illustrator

Mrs. J. Huffman

Publisher

APPENDIX C.5: Literature Evaluation Form

Name: _____ Date: _____

Title: _____ Author: _____

My response activities:

What I have learned:

Areas I need to work on:

Areas I have improved in:

My future goals are:

APPENDIX C.6: Goal Setting

Goal Setting for: _____ Date: _____

The skill I plan to develop during this marking period is: _____

_____

Here are some techniques I can use to develop this skill:

1) _____

2) _____

3) _____

Some evidence of this skill development that I can include in my portfolio is:

_____

_____

_____

Source: Rita Kirby. 1994. *Portfolio Development Materials*. Handout of blackline masters. Mt. Pleasant, MI: Rita Kirby. Portfolio Consultant.

APPENDIX C.7: Primary Reading and Writing Survey

Name: _____ Date: _____

1. Here is what I think about myself as a reader:

2. I enjoy these kinds of books:
   because:

3. These kinds of books are hard for me:
   because:

4. When I am reading, I have trouble with:

5. I need more help with:

6. I use some of these strategies when I read:
   _____ guess about what may happen in a story
   _____ look at pictures for clues about the story
   _____ fix it when I make a mistake
   _____ sound out new words
   _____ use other words to help me find the meaning of a word

7. This is how I think about myself as a writer:

8. Here are a list of things that help make writing easy for me:

9. This is what makes writing hard for me:

10. This is what I do when I am writing and I don't know how to write a word:

11. These are some things that I like to write about:

12. This is how I have improved as a writer:

APPENDIX C.8: Evaluation for Mobile

Characters from *The Lion, the Witch and the Wardrobe*

Name: _____ Date: _____

☆	7 Characters Neatly drawn Brightly colored Written in cursive, or neatly done manuscript (or computer)
✚	5 Characters Neatly drawn Colored
✓	3 or 4 Characters Some areas not colored Sloppy work
▬	1 or 2 Characters No coloring Sloppy work

APPENDIX C.9: Self-Evaluation

Nine-Week Self-Evaluation for: _____ Date: _____

Skill Areas for Review

1 = Excellent   2 = Average   3 = Needs Improvement

_____ Attendance/Punctuality (Did you attend school daily, on time?)

Explanation (example) _____

_____ Meeting Deadlines (Did you meet school deadlines?)

Explanation (example) _____

_____ Demonstrating a Positive Attitude (Did you convey a positive attitude about learning?)

Explanation (example) _____

_____ Knowing Personal Strengths and Weaknesses (Did you use your strengths and try to improve your weaknesses?)

Explanation (example) _____

_____ Demonstrating Self-Control (Was your behavior appropriate to different situations?)

Explanation (example) _____

_____ Demonstrating Positive Personal Behavior (Did you show politeness, honesty, etc.?)

Explanation (example) _____

_____ Working Cooperatively with Peers (Did you cooperate in group situations?)

Explanation (example) _____

Source: Rita Kirby. 1994. *Portfolio Development Materials.* Handout of blackline masters. Mt. Pleasant, MI: Rita Kirby, Portfolio Consultant.

APPENDIX C.10: Self-Assessment Sheet for Weather Maps

Name: _____ Date: _____

Topic: Weather Map

1. What was your job (role) during the project? List all jobs you were involved in, including presentations.

2. What grade would you give yourself for your work? Explain why you deserve this grade.

3. How did your group work together cooperatively? What did you like? What would you change?

4. What grade would you give yourself on cooperative effort (how much you co-operated with others)?

5. How much did you enjoy this project?

Student grade estimate: _____ Teacher final grade: _____

APPENDIX D.1: Anecdotal Comments Sheet

Name: _____ _____	Date: _____	Grade: _____

Reading:

Writing:

Mathematics:

Social Studies:

Science:

APPENDIX D.2: Anecdotal Notes

Focus: _____ Social Behavior _____ Cooperative Group Work _____ Reading _____ Writing _____ Mathematics _____ Social Studies _____ Science _____ Other		
Date	Child	Comment

APPENDIX D.3: Anecdotal Record Sheet

Focus: _____ Whole Class _____ Individual Topic and/or Student Name: _____			

APPENDIX D.4: Observation Form for Student Ownership

S = Student Initiated
T = Teacher Initiated

Date/Name	Evidence Where Students Are Making Decisions about Activity or Learning	Evidence of Student Choices	Evidence of Self-Evaluation	Comments

Date/Name   Comments

APPENDIX D.5: Writing Checklist

Checklist Items	+ ✓ − 0	Comments
1. Using approximate spelling of unknown words		
2. Experimenting with punctuation		
3. Experimenting with writing styles		
4. Writing in a variety of styles		
5. Borrowing and adapting writing techniques learned from reading experiences		
6. Expressing opinions and thoughts about the day's events in a journal		
7. Offering arguments on paper		
8. Providing support for critical appraisal of one's own writing		
9. Providing support for critical appraisal of one's own progress in writing over time.		

Name: _____ Date: _____

Focus: _____

Context: _____

Adapted from: Rhodes, L. K., and Shanklin, N. 1993. *Windows into Literacy: Assessing Learners K–8*. Portsmouth, NH: Heinemann. p. 240.

APPENDIX D.6: Sample Checklist of Group Observations

Checklist of Group Discussions

Date: _____   Context: _____

Checklist Items	Student's Name									
Willingness to participate in public events that require spontaneous reactions										
Offering novel solutions to problems										
Offering multiple solutions to problems										
Sharing personal concerns or fears										
Volunteering to undertake responsibilities										
Willingness to undertake responsibilities										
Willingness to adopt an unpopular role or position										
Offering original interpretations of texts										
Willingness to speak in a large group										
Willingness to argue with the teacher										

	Student's Name									
Willingness to modify an expressed position in the light of new information or superior reasoning										
Ability to detect a logical fault in one's own argument										
Ability to draw inferences										
Commenting on the effect of one's own contributions to a discussion										
Asking others how they arrived at conclusions										
Notes:										

Adapted from: Rhodes, L. K. and Shanklin, N. *Windows into Literacy: Assessing Learners K–8,* p. 241.

APPENDIX D.7: Student Attitude Inventory

Name: _____ Date: _____

1. What do you like to do when you are not at school?

2. What would you like to learn this year?

3. What school subjects do you like the best? Why?

4. What school subjects are your least favorite? Why?

5. What do you want to do when you are finished with school?

6. What are you best at doing in school? Out of school?

7. What is something you would like to do better at school? Out of school?

8. What would your best friend say about you?

9. What would you like the class and me to know about you?

APPENDIX D.8: Reading Think Aloud Inventory

Name: _____ Date: _____

Story Read: _____

1. These are the predictions I made when I read the story:

2. I asked myself these questions while I read:

3. The story made me think about when I . . .

4. These are some words I got stuck on and this is what I did to figure them out:

5. I already knew this before I read the story:

6. I used these fix-up strategies to understand parts that didn't make sense to me:

7. The story reminds me of this book or movie because:

APPENDIX D.9: Elementary Reading/Writing Inventory

Name: _____ Date: _____

Directions: Check the answer that best tells what you do at home.

1. Someone reads to me:
   - Every Day
   - Often
   - Once in Awhile
   - Almost Never

2. I read out of school:
   - Every Day
   - Often
   - Once in Awhile
   - Almost Never

3. I write out of school:
   - Every Day
   - Often
   - Once in Awhile
   - Almost Never

4. I like to read:
   (check all you like)
   - Stories/Novels
   - Poems
   - Newspapers
   - Magazines
   - Information Books
   - Others _____

5. Some things I read this week at home: (make a list for each type)

For School

For Me

_____   _____

_____   _____

6. I like to write:
   (check all you like)
   - A. B. C's
   - Letters
   - Journal/Diary
   - Stories
   - Poems
   - Pictures – Drawing
   - Others: _____

7. At home I like to:
   (check the one you like most)
   - Read Alone
   - Read to Others
   - Be Read to

8. Other things you want to share about your reading and writing at home:

APPENDIX D.10: Writing Strategies I Use Sheet

Writing Strategies I Use

Name: _____

Strategies: Date:

1. _____

2. _____

3. _____

4. _____

5. _____

6. _____

7. _____

8. _____

9. _____

10. _____

11. _____

12. _____

APPENDIX D.11: Prompts for Learning Logs

Learning Styles

- I work best when the lights are . . .
- I work best when I can . . .
- I do best on activities that . . .
- I like to work with others when . . .

Learning Strategies

- When I don't understand something I . . .
- Before I start to work on a project, I . . .
- When I need to study, I . . .
- When I want to remember something, I . . .

Preferences

- The thing I liked best about this lesson was . . . because . . .
- The most interesting part of our day was . . .
- I would like to learn more about . . .
- My favorite class this week was . . . because . . .

Strengths

- Today I learned that I could . . .
- I am good at . . .
- I have learned how to . . .
- I can help others with . . .

Areas to Improve

- I wish that I could get better at . . .
- I need to work on . . .
- The hardest thing for me to do is . . .
- I need help with . . .

Goals

- This week I want to work on . . .
- I want to learn how to . . .
- I plan to get help with . . .
- I am going to take responsibility for . . .

APPENDIX D.12: Problem-Solving Mathematics Rubric

4 Rating = Exemplary Response

- Chooses appropriate strategy (Problem Solving)
- Finds all possible solutions (Problem Solving)
- Provides clear, coherent explanation (Communication)
- Includes clear diagrams, drawing, model if appropriate (Communication)
- Computes correctly (Computation)

3 Rating = Satisfactory Response

- Chooses appropriate strategy (Problem Solving)
- Finds most solutions (Problem Solving)
- Provides reasonably clear explanation (Communication)
- Includes diagrams, drawings, even though they may be unclear or incomplete (Communication)
- Generally uses appropriate mathematical terms (Communication)
- Computes correctly (Computation)

2 Rating = Minimal Response

- Chooses an inappropriate strategy (Problem Solving)
- Finds one possible solution (Problem Solving)
- Explanation is somewhat unclear (Communication)
- Diagrams, drawings are somewhat unclear (Communication)
- Misuses or confuses mathematical terms (Communication)
- Computation has mirror errors (Computation)

1 Rating = Inadequate Response

- Chooses an inappropriate strategy (Problem Solving)
- Finds one or no solution (Problem Solving)
- Explanation is unclear or missing (Problem Solving)
- Diagram, drawings are unclear, missing, or inappropriate (Communication)
- Fails to use mathematical terms (Communication)
- There are serious computation errors (Computation)

0 Rating = No Attempt

APPENDIX D.13: Sample of a Teamwork Skills Form

Students Name _____ Sport _____

Athletic Evaluation by Coach

_____ Actively participates/is productive on team (completed season)
_____ Follows team rules and values
_____ Attends practice regularly, on time
_____ Works with peers in a team effort
_____ Follows directions
_____ (Other) _____
_____ (Other) _____

Comments _____

_____

_____

_____

Coach's signature _____ Date _____

1 = Excellent
2 = Average
3 = Needs improvement

Source: Rita Kirby. 1994. *Portfolio Development Masters*. Handout of blackline masters. Mt. Pleasant, MI: Rita Kirby, Portfolio Consultant.

APPENDIX E.1: Guidelines for Participating in a Portfolio Support Group

- Each member of the group has something the others can learn regardless of experience with portfolios or personal characteristics.
- Observation and feedback must be reciprocal.
- The focus for the observation should be discussed before the actual observation. Teachers may be interested in having specific students observed, watching a conference, administering a specific assessment tool, or some other aspect of portfolio implementation.
- Feedback and comments should focus on what has taken place not on personal competence.
- Members' personal worth should not be confused with their current level of competence in portfolio implementation.
- Discussions about how effective members are in using portfolio assessment should be concrete and practical.
- Each member has professional strengths, and respect for each other's overall teaching competence should be communicated.

APPENDIX E.2: Principals' Roles in Planning, Implementing, and Enhancing Portfolio Assessment

(*1*) Growing in portfolio knowledge
- reading professional material about portfolio implementation
- participating in portfolio staff development sessions
- attending conferences
- visiting schools that have implemented portfolios
- establishing networks with other principals who are implementing portfolio assessment
- beginning your own professional portfolio

(*2*) Collaborating with central office administrators and policymakers
- obtaining support for portfolio implementation
- preparing and sharing reports of progress in portfolio implementation
- collecting portfolio data to use for curricular and program decision making
- preparing summaries of portfolio data to be used by policymakers and central office administrators
- using portfolio data to prepare school accountability reports or portfolios

(*3*) Providing leadership in preliminary planning for portfolio implementation
- initiating and participating in the creation of the school's vision
- making sure all stakeholders are involved in the planning process
- taking the lead as stakeholders establish curriculum standards and benchmarks for achievement
- assisting in establishing a problem-solving procedure
- collaborating with stakeholders to devise a school-based portfolio implementation process

(*4*) Setting the stage for implementing portfolio assessment
- exploring various sources for funding possibilities
- providing resources such as professional reading materials and multimedia presentations about portfolios
- providing professional development opportunities for faculty to become acquainted with portfolios
- finding ways to provide time for teachers to learn about portfolio implementation

(*5*) Encouraging staff and faculty to implement portfolios
- modeling self-reflection through your portfolio entries and captions
- creating a climate for risk taking
- encouraging a collegial and cooperative atmosphere among staff and faculty
- encouraging teachers to form portfolio support groups
- encouraging teachers to find their own voices
- providing support and encouragement for peer coaching
- encouraging teachers to keep professional portfolios
- encouraging teachers to participate in a school climate of inquiry

(6) Maintaining portfolio implementation
- providing ongoing cyclical staff development
- maintaining security of cumulative school portfolios
- disseminating portfolio information to the public and parents
- investigating more efficient means of storing portfolio such as technological support
- encouraging faculty to continue to refine portfolio implementation
- encouraging parents and community members to become involved in continued support for portfolio implementation

APPENDIX E.3: Teachers' Roles in Planning, Implementing, and Enhancing Portfolio Assessment

(*1*) Continuing professional growth and personal learning
- attending conferences, staff development sessions, and support groups for portfolio assessment
- reading professional literature about portfolios, assessment, and evaluation
- visiting schools that are implementing portfolios
- developing their own voices in portfolio assessment
- participating in peer coaching and portfolio support groups
- engaging in self-reflection of teaching and assessment practices
- setting their own professional goals to work towards
- beginning to keep their own professional portfolios
- using their professional portfolios to conference with principals

(*2*) Providing a safe classroom environment for students
- demonstrating a belief in their students' capabilities as learners
- valuing each student's opinions and diversity
- providing a climate that encourages risk taking
- fostering independence and self-reliance

(*3*) Updating classroom teaching practices
- becoming a facilitator, rather than the expert that dispenses knowledge
- planning for student involvement, interaction, and input in classroom portfolio activities
- providing time for decision making, drafting, reflecting, discussing, reading, and responding
- using portfolio data to make instructional decisions

(*4*) Changing assessment practices
- becoming a kid watcher
- using a variety of ways to gather information about students' learning
- collecting and analyzing student work samples
- assessing students' processes, efforts, progress, achievements, and products
- collaborating and negotiating with students in assessment and evaluation of learning

(5) Assessing portfolio implementation
- modeling their own professional portfolios, including self-reflection, goal setting, and self-evaluation
- assisting students in managing their portfolios
  - developing criteria for choosing selections with students
  - providing time to conference individually with each student to further students' understanding and portfolio achievement
  - assisting students in setting goals that are realistic and that can be achieved
  - preparing students to lead their own parent conferences
  - encouraging students' ownership of their portfolios
  - celebrating students' successes

(6) Being accountable
- keeping track of the entire group's depth of understanding
- using portfolio data to justify practices and curricular decisions within classrooms
- enforcing any criteria or portfolio requirements from beyond the classroom
- maintaining a degree of consistency across portfolios for schoolwide purposes
- using portfolio data to report to parents
- making sure appropriate items are placed in cumulative school portfolios

APPENDIX E.4: Sample Portfolio Letter for Family Members

Date: _____August 29, 1996_____

Dear: ___Mr. & Mrs. Smith_____

    This year your child will be participating in keeping a classroom portfolio to assess and evaluate progress, learning, and achievement. ___Rachel___ will be collecting samples of work to show what has been learned, to discover areas of strengths and weaknesses, and to set future learning goals. I will examine the portfolio to help me plan appropriate instruction for ___Rachel___. I will also add my evaluations and comments to the information collected.

    At times during the year, I will ask you for information to add to the portfolio, to collect observations about your child's learning, and to review the work in the portfolio through conferences. Through working together as a team, I hope that you, ___Rachel___, and I can guide growth in learning and school achievement throughout the year.

    If you have any questions about the portfolio that we will be using this year, or if you would like to come to school to talk about what we will be doing, please feel free to call me at school. I am looking forward to working closely with you and ___Rachel___ this year.

                                              Sincerely,

                                            Evonne Black

                                            Mrs. Evonne Black

APPENDIX E.5: Sample Parent Questionnaire

Parent Questionnaire
Title I

Parent: _____ Date: _____

Child: _____

Information	Yes/No	Comments
I read to my child 2–3 times a week.	_____	_____
My child reads to me 2–3 times a week.	_____	_____
I feel comfortable helping my child learn to read and write at home.	_____	_____
We have a special place in our home for reading and writing together.	_____	_____
We have materials and books at home for child use when reading and writing.	_____	_____
My child has a good attitude about reading and writing.	_____	_____

Strengths that I see my child has are: _____

_____

Areas in which I feel my child needs help are: _____

_____

Ahlgren, A. & Rutherford, F. J. 1993. "Where is Project 2061 today?" *Educational Leadership,* 19–22.

Alexander, W.M. 1988. "Schools in the middle: Rhetoric and reality." *Social Education,* 52(2), 107–109.

Anderson, D., Kressler, A., & Strong, M. 1993. "Introducing portfolio assessment to the word processing curriculum." In *Alternative Assessment: Emerging Theories and Practices at Holt High School,* Bruce Kutney, ed. Holt, MI: Holt Public Schools, pp. 41–49.

Anthony, R.J., Johnson, T.D., Mickelson, N.I., & Preece, A. 1991. *Evaluating Literacy: A Perspective for Change.* Portsmouth, NH: Heinemann Educational Books, Inc.

Armstrong, T. 1994. *Multiple Intelligences in the Classroom.* Alexandria, VA: Association for Supervision and Curriculum Development.

Arter, Judith A. 1990. *Understanding the Meaning and Importance of Quality Classroom Assessment.* Portland, Oregon: Northwest Regional Educational Laboratory.

Atwell, N. 1987. *In the Middle.* Portsmouth, NH: Heinemann Educational Books, Inc.

Atwell, N. 1989. *Coming to Know: Writing to Learn in the Intermediate Grades.* Portsmouth, NH: Heinemann Educational Books, Inc.

Austin, T. 1994. *Changing the View: Student-Led Parent Conferences,* Portsmouth, NH: Heinemann.

Baker, P., Curtis, D., & Benenson, W. 1991. *Collaborative Opportunities to Build Better Schools.* Chicago, IL: Illinois Association for Supervision and Curriculum Development.

Ballard, L. 1992. "Portfolios and self-assessment." *English Journal,* 81:46–48.

Baskwill, J. & Whitman, P. 1988. *Evaluation: Whole Language, Whole Child.* New York: Scholastic.

Bent, E. 1990. "Who should have control?" In J. M. Newman, ed. *Finding Our Own Way: Teachers Exploring Their Assumptions.* Portsmouth, NH: Heinemann Educational Books, Inc. pp. 57–61.

Bertrand, J.E. 1991. "Student assessment and evaluation." In *Assessment and Evaluation in Whole Language Programs.* 2nd ed. B. Harp, ed. Norwood, MA: Christopher-Gordan Publishers, Inc. pp. 17–33.

Bird, L.B. 1992a. "Getting started with portfolios." In *The Whole Language Catalog: Supplement on Authentic Assessment*, Kenneth S. Goodman, Lois B. Bird, and Yetta Goodman, eds. Blacklick, OH: SRA, p. 128.

Bird, L.B. 1992b. "Learning to use portfolios: An interview with Pam Anderson." In *The Whole Language Catalog: Supplement on Authentic Assessment*, Kenneth S. Goodman, Lois B. Bird, and Yetta Goodman, eds. Blacklick, OH: SRA, pp. 126–127.

Black, S. 1993. "Portfolio assessment." *Executive Educator,* 15(1):28–31.

Caine, R.M. & Caine, G. 1991. *Making Connections: Teaching and the Human Brain.* Alexandria, VA: Association for Supervision and Curriculum Development.

California Department of Education. 1989. *Caught in the Middle — Educational Reform for Young Adolescents in California Public Schools.* Sacramento, CA: California Department of Education.

Cambourne, B. & Turbil, J. eds. 1994. *Responsive Evaluation: Making Valid Judgments about Student Literacy.* Portsmouth, NH: Heinemann, p. 21.

Campbell, J. 1992. "Laser disk portfolio: Total child assessment." *Educational Leadership,* 49(8):69–70.

Campbell, P., Edgar, S., & Halsted, A.L. 1994. "Students as evaluators: A model for program evaluation." *Phi Delta Kappa,* 76:160–165.

Carnegie Council on Adolescent Development. 1989. *Turning Points — Preparing American Youth for the 21st Century.* New York: Carnegie Corporation.

Charters, W. & Jones, J. 1973. On the neglect of the independent variable in program evaluation (occasional paper). Eugene, OR: University of Oregon.

Ching, J.P. & Slaughter, H.B. 1992. "Holistic evaluation: Teachers, students, peers, and parents contribute. In *The Whole Language Catalogue Supplement on Authentic Assessment.* Kenneth S. Goodman, Lois B. Bird, and Yetta M. Goodman, eds. Santa Rosa, CA: American School Publishers, pp. 130–131.

Church, C.J. 1991. "Record keeping in whole language classrooms." In *Assessment and Evaluation in Whole Language Programs.* 2nd ed. B. Harp, ed. Norwood, MA: Christopher-Gordon Publishers, Inc. pp. 177–200.

Clark, M.A. 1987. "Don't blame the system: Constraints on 'whole language' reform." *Language Arts.* 64(4):384–396.

Clark, S.N. & D.C. Clark. 1994. *Restructuring the Middle Level School.* Albany, NY: State University of New York Press.

Clingman, C. 1992. "The classroom assessment specialist: Collector, collaborator, and communicator." In *Perspectives on Assessment.* R. Smith and D. Birdyshaw, eds. Grand Rapids, MI: Michigan Reading Associations.

Cockrum, W. & Castillo, M. 1991. "Whole language assessment and evaluation strategies." In *Assessment and Evaluation in Whole Language Programs,* Bill Harp, ed. Second edition. Norwood, MA: Christopher-Gordon Publishers, Inc. pp. 73–86.

Cooledge, N.J. 1992. "Rescuing your rookie teachers." *Principal,* 72(2):28–29.

Cooper, W. & Brown, B.J. 1992. "Using portfolios to empower student writers." *English Journal,* 81:40–45.

Covey, S.R. 1989. *The 7 Habits of Highly Effective People.* New York. Simon & Schuster.

Covey, S.R. 1991. *Principle-Centered Leadership.* New York. Simon & Schuster.

Craven, B.A. 1992. "Portfolios as tools for assessment." In *The Whole Language Catalog: Suppplement on Authentic Assessment* by Kenneth S. Goodman, Lois B. Bird, and Yetta M. Goodman, eds. Blacklick, OH: SRA, p. 125.

Cross, C.T. 1991. "Round table committed to systemic reform." *Associated School Boards of South Dakota Bulletin*, Vol. 18, No. 20.

Cushman, K. ed. 1994. "In this case, teaching to the test is good: Another way to evaluate schoolwide progress," *Changing Minds*, 9:3–6.

Darling-Hammond, Linda. 1991. "The implications of testing policy for quality and equality." *Phi Delta Kappan*, Vol. (3): pp. 220–225.

David, J. 1989. "Synthesis of research on school-based management." *Educational Leadership*, 46(8):45–52.

Davis, B.J. 1993. "Student assessment overview." Handout presented at a staff development meeting for the Gratiot-Isabella Regional Educational Service District at Mt. Pleasant, MI.

DeFina, A.A. 1992. *Portfolio Assessment.* Jefferson City, MO: Scholastic Professional Books.

Dewitz, P., Carr, C.M., Palm, K.N., & Spencer, M. 1992. "The validity and utility of portfolio assessment." In *Literacy Research, Theory, and Practice: Views from Many Perspectives.* Forty-first Yearbook, C. K. Kinzer and D. J. Leu, eds. Chicago, IL: The National Reading Conference.

DiSalvo, D. 1989. "Educational leadership into the 1990s: Role of the superintendent." In S. Freedman and R. Zerchykov (Eds.), *School-Based Improvement: Implications for Superintendents' Leadership*, p. 3 (Documentation of a two-day working conference, Massachusetts Department of Education, Quincy, MA, March 22, 1989 and May 3, 1989).

Donahoe, T. 1993. "Finding the way: Structure, time and culture in school improvement." *Phi Delta Kappan*, 74(7):534–539.

Doyle, D.P. & S. Pimentel. 1993. "A study in change: Transforming the Charlotte-Mecklenburg Schools," *Phi Delta Kappan*, 74(7):534–539.

Dudley-Marling, C. 1995. "Complicating ownership." In *Who Owns Learning? Questions of Autonomy, Choice, and Control*, Curt Dudley-Marling and Dennis Searle, eds. Portsmouth, NH: Heinemann, pp. 1–15.

Dudley-Marling, C. and Searle, D. eds. 1995. *Who Owns Learning? Questions of Autonomy, Choice, and Control.* Portsmouth, NH: Heinemann.

Edmonds, R. 1981. *Improving the Effectiveness of New York City Public Schools* (ERIC Document Reproduction Service No. 243 980).

Educational Department. 1991. *Literacy Assessment in Practice: R-7.* South Australia: Education Department of South Australia.

Eichhorn, D. 1966. *The Middle School.* New York: Center for Applied Research in Education.

Eisner, Elliot W. 1991. "What really counts in schools." *Educational Leadership*, 48(5):10–17.

Ellis, A.K. & J.T. Fouts. 1993. *Research on Educational Innovations.* Princeton Junction, NJ: Eye on Education.

Erickson, H.L. 1995. *Stirring the Head, Heart, and Soul: Redefining Curriculum and Instruction.* Thousand Oaks, CA: Corwin Press, Inc.

Five, C.L. 1995. "Ownership for the special needs child: Individual and educational dilemmas." In *Who Owns Learning? Questions of Autonomy, Choice, and Control,* Curt Dudley-Marling and Dennis Searle, eds. Portsmouth, NH: Heinemann, pp. 113–127.

Friend, M. & Cook, L. 1991. *Interactions: Collaboration Skills for School Professionals.* Toronto, Ont: Copp Clark Pitman.

Froese, V., ed. 1991. *Whole Language: Practice and Theory.* Boston, MA: Allyn & Bacon.

Fu, D. 1991. "One bilingual child talks about his portfolio." In *Portfolio Portraits,* Donald H. Graves and Bonnie S. Sunstein, eds. Portsmouth, NH: Heinemann Educational Books, pp. 171–183.

Fullan, M.G. 1987. "Implementing educational change: 'What we know.' " Paper prepared for the World Bank, Washington, D.C.

Fullan, M.G. 1991. *Understanding Teacher Development.* Hargreaves and Fullan, editors. New York: Teachers College Press.

Fullan, M.G. 1993. *Change Forces: Probing the Depths of Educational Reform.* Bristol, PA: Falmer Press.

Gardner, H. & Boix-Mansilla, V. February, 1994. "Teaching for understanding within and across the disciplines," *Educational Leadership,* 14–18.

George, P.S., Stevenson, C., Thomason, J., & Beane, J.A. 1992. *The Middle School—And Beyond.* Alexandria, VA: Association for Supervision and Curriculum Development.

Glazer, S.M. & Brown, C.S. 1993. *Portfolios and Beyond: Collaborative Assessment in Reading and Writing.* Norwood, MA: Christopher-Gordon Publishers, Inc.

Glickman, C. 1991. "Pretending not to know what we know," *Educational Leadership,* 4–10.

Goldberg, M. 1994. "A portrait of Dennie Palmer Wolf," *Educational Leadership,* 56–58.

Goldring, E.B. & S.F. Rallis. 1993. *Principals of Dynamic Schools: Taking Charge of Change.* Newbury Park, CA: Corwin Press, Inc.

Gomez, M.L., M.E. Graue & M.N. Bloch. 1991. "Reassessing portfolio assessment: Rhetoric and reality," *Language Arts,* 68(8):620–628.

Goodman, D. 1992. "Evaluating for and with parents." In *The Whole Language Catalog Supplement on Authentic Assessment* in Kenneth S. Goodman, Lois B. Bridges, and Yetta M. Goodman, eds. Blacklick, OH: SRA, p. 132.

Goodman, K.S. 1986. *What's Whole in Whole Language?* Portsmouth, NH: Heinemann Educational Books, Inc.

Goodman, K.S., Bird, L.M., & Goodman, Y.M. 1992. *The Whole Language Catalog: Supplement on Authentic Assessment.* Santa Rosa, CA: America School Publishers.

Goodman, K.S., Goodman, Y.M., & Hood, W.J., eds. 1989. *The Whole Language Evaluation Book.* Portsmouth, NH: Heinemann Educational Books, Inc.

Goodman, Y.M. 1978. Kid watching: An alternative to testing. *Journal of National Elementary Principals.* 57(4), 41–45.

Goodman, Y.M. 1992. "Teachers' professional sense." In *The Whole Language Catalog*

Supplement of Authentic Assessment, Kenneth S. Goodman, Lois B. Bird, and Yetta M. Goodman, eds. Blacklick, OH: SRA, p. 43.

Gordon, G. 1992. *One Teacher's Classroom: Strategies for Successful Teaching and Learning.* Armadale, Australia: Eleanor Curtain Publishing.

Graves, D. 1984. *Writing: Teachers and Children at Work.* Portsmouth, NH: Heinemann Educational Books, Inc.

Graves, D.H. 1991. "Portfolios: Keep a good idea growing." In *Portfolio Portraits,* Second edition. Norwood, MA: Christopher-Gordon Publishers, Inc.

Graves, D.H. 1991. "Portfolios: Keep a good idea growing." In *Portfolio Portraits* by Donald H. Graves and Bonnie S. Sunstein, eds. Portsmouth, NH: Heinemann, pp. 1–14.

Graves, D.H. & Sunstein, B.S. (Eds). 1992. "Introduction." In *Portfolio Portraits.* Portsmouth, NH: Heinemann Educational Books, Inc.

Green, M. 1994. "Children as evaluators: Understanding evaluation from the inside." In *Responsive Evaluation* by Brian Cambourne and Jan Turbil, eds. Portsmouth, NH: Heinemann, pp. 83–103.

Guskey, T.R. 1994. *High Stakes Performance Assessment: Perspectives on Kentucky's Educational Reform.* Thousand Oaks, CA: Corwin Press, Inc.

Gustafson, C. 1994. "A letter from Stacey." *Educational Leadership.* 52(2):22–23.

Hagan, M. 1992. "A large step for a school, a small step for a profession." In *The Whole Language Catalog: Supplement on Authentic Assessment* by Kenneth S. Goodman, Lois B. Bird, and Yetta M. Goodman, eds. Blacklick, OH: SRA, pp. 48–49.

Hansen, J. 1994. "Literacy portfolios: Windows on potential." In *Authentic Reading Assessment: Practices and Possibilities* by Sheila W. Valencia, Elreida H. Hiebert, and Peter P. Afflerbach. Newark, DE: International Reading Association, pp. 26–40.

Harman, S. 1992. "The basal 'conspiracy.' " In *The Whole Language Catalog Supplement on Authentic Assessment* in Kenneth S. Goodman, Lois B. Bridges, and Yetta M. Goodman, eds. Blacklick, OH: SRA, p. 35.

Harp, B. ed. 1991. *Assessment and Evaluation in Whole Language Catalog: Supplement on Authentic Assessment,* 2nd ed. Norwood, MA: Christopher-Gordon Publishers.

Harp, B. 1993. *Bringing Children to Literacy: Classrooms at Work.* Norwood, MA: Christopher-Gordon Publishers, Inc.

Harrington-Lueker, D. 1990. "The engine of reform gathers steam: Kentucky starts from scratch." *American School Board Journal,* Vol. 177, No. 9:17–21.

Harrison, C., Killion, J., & Mitchell, J. 1989. "Site-based management: The realities of implementation." *Educational Leadership,* 46(8), 55–58.

Hart, D. 1994. *Authentic Assessment.* New York: Addison-Wesley.

Heald-Taylor, G. 1989. *The Administrator's Guide to Whole Language.* Katonah, NY: Richard C. Owen Publishers, Inc.

Henderson, J.G. & R.D. Hawthorne. 1995. *Transformative Curriculum Leadership.* Englewood Cliffs, NJ: Prentice Hall.

Herman, L.J., Aschbacher, P.R., & Winters, L. 1992. *A Practical Guide to Alternative Assessment.* Alexandria, VA: Association for Supervision and Curriculum Development.

Herter, R.J. 1992. "Writing portfolios: Alternatives to testing." *English Journal,* 80(1):90–91.

Hetterscheidt, J., Pott, L., Russell, K., & Tchang, J. 1992. "Using the computer as a reading portfolio." *Educational Leadership,* 49:73.

Hewitt, G. 1995. *A Portfolio Primer: Teacher, Collecting, and Assessing: Putting the Pieces Together.* Portsmouth, NH: Heinemann.

Hiebert, E.H. 1994. "Definitions and perspectives." In *Authentic Reading Assessment: Practices and Possibilities* by Sheila W. Valencia, Elreida H. Hiebert, and Peter P. Afflerbach, eds. Newark, DE: International Reading Association, pp. 6–12.

Hill, B.C. & Ruptic, C. 1994. *Practical Aspects of Authentic Assessment: Putting the Pieces Together.* Norwood, MA: Christopher-Gordon Publishers, Inc.

Hill, P. & Bonan, J. 1991. "Site-based management: Decentralization and accountability." *The Education Digest,* 57(1):23–25.

Holland, M. 1993. "Documentations of a kidwatcher." In *Windows into Literacy: Assessing Learners K–8,* Lynn K. Rhodes and Nancy Shanklin. Portsmouth, NH: Heinemann. pp. 37–41.

Holmes Group. 1990. *Tomorrow's Schools: Principles for the Design of Professional Developments.* East Lansing, MI: A Report of the Holmes Group.

Hopkins, D. 1990. "Integrating teacher development and school improvement: A study in teacher personality and school climate." In B. Joyece (Ed.), *Changing School Culture through Staff Development* (pp. 41–67). Alexandria, VA: Association for Supervision and Curriculum Development.

Howell, G.L. & Woodley, J.W. 1992. "Self-evaluation in the whole language classroom: Lesson from values clarification." In K.S. Goodman, L.B. Bird, and Y.M. Goodman (eds.). *The Whole Language Supplement of Authentic Assessment.* Santa Rosa, CA: American School Publishers, p. 87.

Hoyt, L. 1992. "Involving students in parent-teacher conferences." In *The Whole Language Catalog: Supplement on Authentic Assessment,* Kenneth S. Goodman, Lois B. Bird, and Yetta M. Goodman, eds. Blacklick, OH: SRA. p. 136.

Hubbard, R.S. & Power, B.M. 1993. *The Art of Classroom Inquiry: A Handbook for Teacher Researchers.* Portsmouth, NH: Heinemann.

Huberman, M. 1988. "Teacher careers and school improvement." *Journal of Curriculum Studies,* 20(2):119–32.

Huddle, G. 1984. "How complex is the principal's job? What actions can principals take to be more effective?" *NASSP Bulletin,* 68(476):62–67.

Hutchinson, R. 1991. "Reporting progress to students, parents, and administrators." In *Assessment and Evaluation in Whole Language Programs,* 2nd ed., B. Harp, ed. Norwood, MA: Christopher-Gordon Publishers, Inc.

Jaeger, Richard M. 1991. "Legislative perspectives on statewide testing: Goals, hopes, and desires." *Phi Delta Kappan,* Vol. 3. pp. 239–242.

Johnson, D.W. & Johnson, R.T. 1989. *Leading the Cooperative School.* Ednina, MN: Interaction Book Company.

Johnson, D.W., Johnson, R.T. & Holubec, E.J. 1990. *Circles of Learning: Cooperation in the Classroom,* 3rd Ed. Ednina, MN: Interaction Book Company.

Kaufman, R. & J. Herman. 1991. "Strategic planning for a better society," *Educational Leadership,* 48(7):4–8.

Kieffer, R.D. 1994. "Portfolio process and teacher change." *NRRC News: A Newsletter of the National Reading Research Center.* Anthens, GA: National Reading Research Center, December, p. 8.

Killion, J.P. & Todnem, G.R. 1991. "A process for personal theory building." *Educational Leadership,* 48(6):14–17.

Kirby, P.C., Paradise, L.V., & King, M.I. 1992. "Extraordinary leaders in education: Understanding transformational leadership." *Journal of Educational Research,* 85(5):303–311.

Kirby, R. 1993. *Portfolio Information Guide.* Rita Kirby Portfolio Consultant, Mt. Pleasant, MI, p. 2.

Kirby, R. 1994. *Portfolio Development Masters.* Handout of blackline masters. Mt. Pleasant, MI: Rita Kirby Portfolio Consultant.

Kitagawa, M.M. 1992. "Self-observation/teacher observation surveys in the language arts." In *The Whole Language Catalogue Supplement on Authentic Assessment,* Kenneth S. Goodman, Lois B. Bird, and Yetta M. Goodman, eds. Santa Rosa, CA: American School Publishers, p. 93.

Knight, P. 1992. "How I use portfolios in mathematics." *Educational Leadership,* 49(8):71–72.

Kohn, A. 1993. "Choices for children: Why and how to let students decide." *Phi Delta Kappan,* Vol. 75(1):9–19.

Kressler, P. 1993. "Learning journals in the history classroom." In *Alternative Assessment: Emerging Theories and Practices at Holt High School,* Bruce Kutney, ed. Holt, MI: Holt Public Schools, pp. 50–57.

Kutney, B. 1993. "Practical strategies for assessing student revisions." In *Alternative Assessment: Emerging Theories and Practices at Holt High School,* Bruce Kutney, ed. Holt, MI: Holt Public Schools, pp. 58–65.

Lamme, L.L. & C. Hysmith. 1991a. "One school's adventure into portfolio assessment," *Language Arts,* 68(8):629–640.

Lamme, L.L. & C. Hysmith. 1991b. "One school's adventure into portfolio assessment," *The Whole Language Catalog: Supplement on Authentic Assessment,* Kenneth S. Goodman, Lois B. Bird, and Yetta M. Goodman, eds. Blacklick, OH: SRA. pp. 122–123.

Leithwood, K. & Jantzi, D. 1990. Transformational leadership: How principals can help reform school culture. Paper presented at American Education Research Association Annual Meeting.

Leithwood, K. & Montgomery, D. 1986. *The Principal Profile.* Toronto, Ontario: OISE Press.

Leithwood, K. & Steinbach, R. 1989. A comparison of processes used by principals in solving problems individually and in groups. Paper presented at Canadian Association for the Study of Educational Administration Annual Meeting.

Leithwood, K. & Steinbach, R. 1990. Improving the problem-solving expertise of school administrators: Theory and practice. Paper presented at the Canadian Society for Studies in Education Annual Meeting.

Levy, T. 1988. "Making a difference in the middle." *Social Education,* 52(2):104–106.

Lewis, A. 1990. *Making It in the Middle.* New York: The Edna McConnell Clark Foundation.

Lieberman, A. 1991. "Accountability as a reform strategy," *Phi Delta Kappan*, 1(3):219–220.

Lipham, J. 1981. *Effective Principal, Effective School*. Reston, VA: National Association of Secondary School Principals.

Little, J.W. 1981. The power of organizational setting (Paper adapted from final report, School success and staff development). Washington, D.C.: National Institute of Education.

Little, J.W. 1982. "Norms of collegiality and experimentation: Workplace conditions of school success." *American Educational Research Journal*, 19, 325–40.

Little, J.W. 1990. "The 'mentor' phenomenon and the social organization of teaching." In C. Cazen (Ed.), *Review of Research in Education* (Vol. 16, pp. 297–351). Washington: American Educational Research Association.

Louis, K. & Miles, M.B. 1990. *Improving the Urban High School: What Works and Why*. New York, NY: Teachers College Press.

Madaus, George F. 1991. "The effects of important tests on students: Implications for a national examination system." *Phi Delta Kappan*, Vol. (3):226–231.

Maeroff, G.I. 1991. "Assessing alternative assessment." *Phi Delta Kappan*, 73(4): 272–282.

Marburger, C.L. 1989. *One School at a Time*. Columbia, MD: The National Committee for Citizens in Education.

Marzano, R.J. 1994. "Commentary on literacy portfolios: Windows on potential." In *Authentic Reading Assessment: Practices and Possibilities* by Sheila W. Valencia, Elfrieda H. Hiebert, and Peter P. Afflerbach, eds. Newark, DE: International Reading Association, pp. 41–45.

Marzano, R., Pickering, D., & McTighe, J. 1993. *Assessing Student Outcomes: Performance Assessment Using the Dimensions of Learning Model*. Alexander, VA: ASCD.

Matlin, M.L. 1992a. "Principals speak out: Teacher evaluation." In *The Whole Language Catalog: Supplement on Authentic Assessment*, K.D. Goodman, L.M. Bird, and Y.M. Goodman, eds. Santa Rosa, CA: American School Publishers. p. 83.

Matlin, M.L. 1992b. "Teacher evaluation." *The Whole Language Catalog: Supplement on Authentic Assessment* by Kenneth S. Goodman, Lois B. Bird, and Yetta M. Goodman, eds. Blacklick, OH: SRA. pp. 122–123.

Matthews, C. 1992. "An alternative portfolio: Gathering of one child's literacies." In *Portfolio Portraits*, Donald H. Graves and Bonnie S. Sunstein, eds. Portsmouth, NH: Heinemann, pp. 158–170.

Mayher, J.S. 1990. "Foreword." In *Finding Our Own Way: Teachers Exploring Their Assumptions*. J.M. Newman, ed. Portsmouth, NH: Heinemann Educational Books. pp. xii–xvi.

McEvoy, B. 1987. "Everyday acts: How principals influence development of their staffs," *Educational Leadership*, 44(5):73–77.

McHenry, E. 1990. *What Research Says about School Reform, School Management, and Teacher Involvement* (ERIC Document Reproduction Service No. ED 322 579).

McKibbin, M. & Joyce, B. 1980. An analysis of staff development and its effect on classroom practice. Paper presented at American Educational Research Annual Meeting.

McNeil, J. 1995. *Curriculum: The Teacher's Initiative.* Englewood Cliffs, NJ: Merril.

Midland Public Schools. 1994. *Kindergarten.* Midland, MI: Author.

Milliken, M. 1991. "A fifth-grade class uses portfolios." In *Portfolio Portraits* by Donald H. Graves and Bonnie S. Sunstein, eds. Portsmouth, NH: Heinemann.

Ministry of Education, Victoria. 1988. *School Curriculum and Organisation Framework.* Melbourne, Australia: Ministry of Education, Victoria.

Morrow, L.M. & Smith, J.K. 1990. *Assessment for Instruction in Early Literacy.* Englewood Cliffs, NJ: Prentice-Hall.

Murphy, S. 1992. "Tests: fancies and fallacies." In *The Whole Language Catalog Supplement on Authentic Assessment* in Kenneth S. Goodman, Lois B. Bridges, and Yetta M. Goodman, eds. Blacklick, OH: SRA, p. 26.

Mutchler, S.E. & P.C. Duttweiler. 1989. *Implementing Shared Decision Making in School-Based Management: Barriers to Changing Traditional Behavior.* Austin, TX: Southwest Educational Development Laboratory.

Nathan, R. 1995. "Parents, projects, and portfolios: 'Round and about community building in room 14." *Language Arts.* 72(2):82–87.

Newman, J.M. ed. 1990. *Finding Our Own Way: Teachers Exploring Their Assumptions.* Portsmouth, NH: Heinemann Educational Books.

Norton, D.E. 1992. *The Impact of Literature-Based Reading.* New York, NY: Longman.

Office of Educational Leadership. 1990. *Transforming Education: The Minnesota Plan.* St. Paul, MN: Minnesota Department of Education, Office of Educational Leadership.

Office of Research, Evaluation, and Assessment. 1990. *Toward School-Based Management/Decision-Making: A Research Perspective.* Brooklyn, NY: Office of Research, Evaluation, and Assessment, New York City Board of Education.

O'Neil, J. 1994. "Making assessment meaningful: 'Rubrics' clarify expectations, yield better feedback." *ASCD Update* 36(6):1, 4–5.

Pappas, C.C., Kiefer, B.Z., & Levstik, L.S. 1990. *An Integrated Perspective in the Elementary School: Theory into Action.* New York: Longman.

Patterson, J.L. 1993. *Leadership for Tomorrow's Schools.* Association for Supervision and Curriculum Development.

Paulson, F.L., Paulson, P.R., & Meyer, C.A. 1991. "What makes a portfolio." *Educational Leadership,* 48(5):60–63.

Pearson, P.D. 1994. "Commentary on California's new English-language arts assessment." In *Authentic Reading Assessment: Practices and Possibilities* by Sheila W. Valencia, Elreida H. Hiebert, and Peter P. Afflerbach, eds. Newark, DE: International Reading Association, pp. 218–227.

Perrone, V. 1992. "On standardized testing." In *The Whole Language Catalog Supplement on Authentic Assessment* in Kenneth S. Goodman, Lois B. Bridges, and Yetta M. Goodman, eds. Blacklick, OH: SRA, pp. 32–33.

Perrone, V. 1994. "How to engage students in learning." *Educational Leadership,* 51(5):11–13.

Pigdon, K. and Woolley M. 1993. *The Big Picture: Integrating Children's Learning.* Portsmouth, NH: Heinemann Educational Books, Inc.

Porter, C. & Cleland, J. 1995. *The Portfolio as a Learning Strategy.* Portsmouth, NH: Heinemann.

Purkey, C.S., & Smith, M.S. 1982. "Too soon to cheer? Synthesis of research on effective schools." *Educational Leadership,* 49:64–69.

Radger, L., Dilena, M., Peters, J., Webster, C., & Weeks, B. 1991. *Literacy Assessment in Practice: R-7 Language Arts.* Adelaid, South Australia: Education Department of South Australia.

Reardon, S.J. 1991. "A collage of assessment and evaluation from primary classrooms." In *Assessment and Evaluation in Whole Language Programs,* Bill Harp, ed. Second edition. Norwood, MA: Christopher-Gordon Publishers, Inc., pp. 87–108.

Rhodes, L.K. ed. 1993. *Literacy Assessment: A Handbook of Instruments.* Portsmouth, NH: Heinemann.

Rhodes, L.K. & Natherson-Mejia, S. 1992. "Anecdotal records: A powerful tool for ongoing literacy assessment." *The Reading Teacher.* 45(7):502–509.

Rhodes, L.K. & Shanklin, N. 1993. *Windows into Literacy: Assessing Learners K–8.* Portsmouth, NH: Heinemann.

Rief, L. 1990. "Finding the value in evaluation: Self-assessment a middle-school classroom." *Educational Leadership,* 47(6):24–29.

Rosenholtz, S. 1989. *Teachers' Workplace: The Social Organization of Schools.* New York, NY: Longman.

Routman, R. 1988. *Transitions: From Literature to Literacy.* Portsmouth, NH: Heinemann Educational Books, Inc.

Routman, R. 1991. *Invitations: Changing as Teachers and Learners K–12.* Portsmouth, NH: Heinemann Educational Books, Inc.

Salvio, P.M. 1994. "Ninja warriors and vulcan logic: Using the cultural literacy portfolio as a curriculum script." *Language Arts,* 71(6):419–424.

Sanborn, J. & Sanborn, E. 1994. "A conversation on portfolios," *Middle School Journal,* 26(1):26–29.

Seeley, M.M. 1994. "The mismatch between assessment and grading." *Educational Leadership,* 52(2):4–6.

Sergiovanni, T.J. 1992. *Moral Leadership: Getting to the Heart of School Improvement.* San Francisco, CA: Jossey-Bass.

Shepard, Lorrie A. 1991. "Will national tests improve student learning?" *Phi Delta Kappan,* 3:232–238.

Short, K. & Kauffman, G. 1992. "Hearing students' voices: The role of reflection in learning." *Teachers Networking—The Whole Language Newsletter,* Katonah, NY: Richard C. Owen Publishers, Inc., 11:3.

Shultz, E. 1992. "Enemy of innovation." *Teacher Magazine,* 57:28–31.

Simmons, R. 1994. "The horse before the cart: Assessing for understanding." *Educational Leadership,* 51(5):22–23.

Simms, N. 1994. "Organising the classroom for responsive evaluation: Pushing ahead in years 3–6." In *Responsive Evaluation: Making Valid Judgements about Student Literacy,* Brian Cambourne and Jan Turbill, eds. Portsmouth, NH: Heinemann. pp. 60–82.

Sirotnik, K. & Clark, R. 1988. "School-centered decision-making and renewal." *Phi Delta Kappan,* 69:660–664.

Slotnik, W.J. 1993. "Core concepts of reform." *The Executive Educator,* Dec. 32–34.

Smith, R.L. & Birdyshaw, D. (Eds.) 1992. *Perspectives on Assessment, Vol. I.* Grand Rapids, MI: Michigan Reading Association.

Smith, W.F. & Andrews, R.L. 1989. *Instructional Leadership: How Principals Make a Difference.* Alexandria, VA: Association for Supervision and Curriculum Development.

Sparks-Langer, G.M. & Colton, A.B. 1991. "Synthesis of research on teachers' reflective thinking." *Educational Leadership,* 48(6):37–44.

Sperling, D.H. 1994. "Assessment and reporting: A natural pair." *Educational Leadership,* 52(2):10–13.

Stake, Robert E. 1991. "The teacher, standardized testing, and prospects of revolution." *Phi Delta Kappan,* Vol. (3). pp. 243–247.

Stemmer, P., Brown, B., & Smith, C. 1992. "The employability skills portfolio." *Educational Leadership,* 49(6):32–35.

Sunstein, B.S. 1991. "Staying the course: One superintendent." In *Portfolio Portraits.* Donald H. Graves and Bonnie S. Sunstein, eds. Portsmouth, NH: Heinemann, pp. 129–145.

Tierney, R.J., Carter, M.A., & Desai, L.E. 1991. *Portfolio Assessment in the Reading-Writing Classroom.* Noorwood, MA: Christopher-Gordon Publishers.

Todd County School District. 1994. Todd County School District portfolio assessment for teachers and counselors. Todd County, SD.

Unia, S. 1990. *Finding Our Own Way: Teachers Exploring Their Own Assumptions.* J.M. Newman, ed. Portsmouth, NH: Heinemann Educational Books.

Vacca, R.T. & Vacca, J.L. 1993. *Content Area Reading,* 4th ed. New York, NY: Harper Collins Publishers.

Valencia, S.W. 1990. "Alternative assessment: Seperating the wheat from the chaff." *The Reading Teacher,* 44, pp. 60–61.

Valencia, S.W. 1991. "New assessment books." *The Reading Teacher,* 45, pp. 244–245.

Valencia, S.W., Hiebert, E.H., & Afflebach, P.P. (eds.) 1994. *Authentic Reading Assessment: Practices and Possibilities.* Newark, DE: International Reading Association.

Valencia, S.W. & Place, N.A. 1994. "Literacy portfolios for teaching, learning, and accountability: The Bellevue literacy assessment project." *Authentic Reading Assessment: Practices and Possibilities.* Valencia, S.W., Hiebert, E.H., and Afflebach, P.P. (eds.). Newark, DE: International Reading Association.

Van Meter, E. 1991. "The Kentucky mandate: School-based decision making." *NASSP Bulletin,* 75, 52–62.

Walberg, Herbert J. 1990. "Productive teaching and instruction: Assessing the knowledge base." *Phi Delta Kappan,* Vol. 71(6):470–478.

Watson, D. & Henson, J. 1991. "Reading evaluation: Miscue analysis." In *Assessment and Evaluation in Whole Language Programs,* second edition by Bill Harp, ed. Norwood, MA: Chistopher-Gordon Publishers, Inc., pp. 51–72.

Weaver, C. 1990. *Understanding Whole Language from Principles to Practice.* Portsmouth, NH: Heinemann Educational Books, Inc.

Weaver, C. 1994. *Reading Process and Practice from Socio-Psycholinguistics to Whole Language.* Second edition. Portsmouth, NH: Heinemann Educational Books.

Wells, G. & Chang-Wells, G.L. 1992. *Constructing Knowledge Together: Classrooms as Centers of Inquiry and Literacy.* Portsmouth, NH: Heinemann Educational Books.

Whitaker, T. & Valentine, J. 1993. "How effective school leaders involve staff members." *Schools in the Middle,* Nov.:21–24.

Wibel, W.H. 1991. "Reflection through writing." *Educational Leadership,* 48(6):45.

Wiggins, G. 1992. "Creating tests worth taking." *Educational Leadership,* 49(8):26–34.

Wiggins, Grant. 1993. "Assessment: Authenticity, context, and validity." *Phi Delta Kappan.* Vol. 75(3):200–214.

Wilcox, C. 1993. "On running and reading." In *Windows into Literacy: Assessing Learners K–8,* Lynn K. Rhodes and Nancy Shanklin. Portsmouth, NH: Heinemann. pp. 138–142.

Wiles, J. & Bondi, J. 1986. *The Essential Middle School.* Tampa, FL: Wiles, Bondi, and Associates, Inc.

Williamson, R.D. & Johnston, J.H. 1991. *Planning for Success: Successful Implementation of Middle Level Reorganization.* Reston, VA: NASSP.

Willis, D. 1993. "Learning and assessment: Exposing the inconsistencies of theory and practice." *Oxford Review of Education.* 19(3):383–402.

Wilson, B. & Corcoran, T. 1988. *Successful Secondary Schools: Visions of Excellence in American Public Education.* Philadelphia, PA: Falmer Press.

Wilson, J. 1993. "Assessment and evaluation." In *The BIG Picture: Integrating Children's Learning,* Keith Pigdon and Marilyn Woolley, eds. Portsmouth, NH: Heinemann.

Wilson, L. 1992. "Children as evaluators." *Teaching Pre K–8,* 23:64–67.

Winograd, P., Paris, S., & Bridge, C. 1991. "Improving the assessment of literacy." *The Reading Teacher,* 45:108–117.

Wolf, Kenneth. 1988. "The schoolteacher's portfolio: Issues in design, implementation, and evaluation." *Phi Delta Kappan,* 73(2):129–136.

Wolf, K. P. 1994. "Commentary on literacy portfolios for teaching, learning, and accountability: The Bellevue literacy assessment project." In *Authentic Reading Assessment: Practices and Possibilities.* S.W. Valencia, E.H. Hiebert, and P.P. Afflebach, eds. Newark, DE: International Reading Association, pp. 157–166.

Woodward, H. 1994. *Negotiated Evaluation: Involving Children and Parents in the Process.* Portsmouth, NH: Heinemann.

Wortman, R.C. 1992. "Principals speak out: Formative evaluation of teachers from a whole language perspective." In *The Whole Language Catalog: Supplement on Authentic Assessment.* K.S. Goodman, L.M. Bird and Y.M. Goodman, eds. Santa Rosa, CA: American School Publishers, pp. 84–85.

Zubizarreta, J. 1994. "Teaching portfolios and the beginning teacher." *Phi Delta Kappan.* 76(4):323–326.

INDEX

LEONIE M. ROSE is associate professor of reading education in teacher education and professional development at Central Michigan University. She teaches graduate and undergraduate courses in reading and language arts and is director of the CMU Summer Reading Clinic. She is building coordinator of Mary McGuire Professional Development School in the Mt. Pleasant Public School District. She has been an elementary teacher and reading specialist in Indiana. She received an M.S. in education with an emphasis in K–12 reading and a Ph.D. in curriculum, language arts, and reading at Indiana State University. Professor Rose's current research interests include work on portfolios at the building level, student ownership of learning, integrating curriculum, alternative assessment in university reading and language arts courses, international reading programs, and creating miscue analysis software. She has published articles on reading in a variety of educational journals. She currently serves on the editorial review boards for *Journal of Reading Education* and *The Michigan Reading Journal*. She enjoys traveling, tennis, collecting antiques, needlework, and spending time with her husband and son.

NANCY J. JOHNSON received her Ph.D. from Arizona State University, where she was director of external affairs, overseeing university–school district programs and public relations for the College of Education. She left ASU to open a new elementary school, hire a staff of forty-five, and be the principal for over 600 kindergarten through sixth-grade students. After several years as principal, she became director of instruction for the K–12 district, which had approximately 11,000 students.

In 1991, Nancy joined the faculty in educational administration and community leadership at Central Michigan University where she was responsible for preparing elementary principals. While in Michigan, she and Dr. Rose began writing *Portfolios: Clarifying, Constructing, and Enhancing.*

Shortly before the book was completed, she moved to South Dakota to marry Michael Johnson, a professor at South Dakota State University. She is now an associate professor at the University of Sioux Falls.